# SUPERMAN ADVENTURES

## THE MAN OF STEEL

Collection Cover Art by Bruce Timm

SUPERMAN Created by
JERRY SIEGEL and JOE SHUSTER.
By Special Arrangement
with the Jerry Siegel Family.

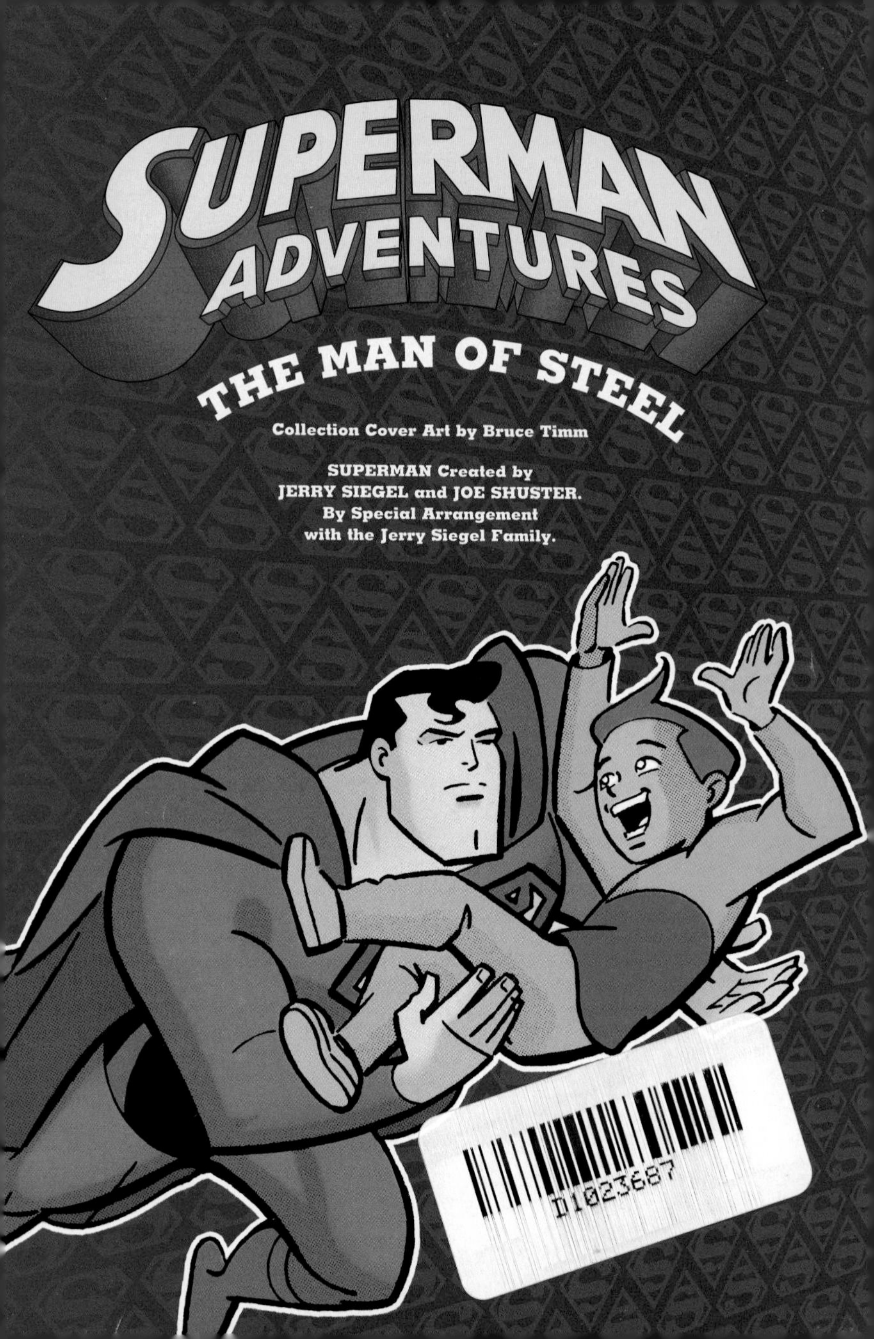

Joey Cavalieri Rachel Gluckstern
Charles Kochman Mike McAvennie
Editors – Original Series
Maureen McTigue Assistant Editor – Original Series
Rachel Pinnelas Editor
Robbin Brosterman Design Director – Books
Louis Prandi Publication Design

Bob Harras Senior VP – Editor-in-Chief, DC Comics

Diane Nelson President
Dan DiDio and Jim Lee Co-Publishers
Geoff Johns Chief Creative Officer
John Rood Executive VP – Sales, Marketing & Business Development
Amy Genkins Senior VP – Business & Legal Affairs
Nairi Gardiner Senior VP – Finance
Jeff Boison VP – Publishing Planning
Mark Chiarello VP – Art Direction & Design
John Cunningham VP – Marketing
Terri Cunningham VP – Editorial Administration
Alison Gill Senior VP – Manufacturing & Operations
Hank Kanalz Senior VP – Vertigo & Integrated Publishing
Jay Kogan VP – Business & Legal Affairs, Publishing
Jack Mahan VP – Business Affairs, Talent
Nick Napolitano VP – Manufacturing Administration
Sue Pohja VP – Book Sales
Courtney Simmons Senior VP – Publicity
Bob Wayne Senior VP – Sales

SUPERMAN ADVENTURES: THE MAN OF STEEL

DC Comics, 1700 Broadway, New York, NY 10019
A Warner Bros. Entertainment Company.
Printed by RR Donnelley, Salem, VA. 9/27/13.
ISBN: 978-1-4012-4706-5

Library of Congress Cataloging-in-Publication Data

Millar, Mark.
Superman Adventures : the Man of Steel / Mark Millar, Dan Slott, Roger Stern.
pages cm
"Originally published in single magazine form as JUSTICE LEAGUE UNLIMITED 34, SUPERMAN ADVENTURES 17-18, 40-41, SUPERMAN & BATMAN MAGAZINE 1, 3, 5, 7."
ISBN 978-1-4012-4706-5
1. Graphic novels. I. Slott, Dan. II. Stern, Roger. III. Title.
PN6728.S9M563 2013
741.5'973—dc23

SUSTAINABLE FORESTRY INITIATIVE
Certified Chain of Custody
At Least 20% Certified Forest Content
www.sfiprogram.org
SFI-01042
APPLIES TO TEXT STOCK ONLY

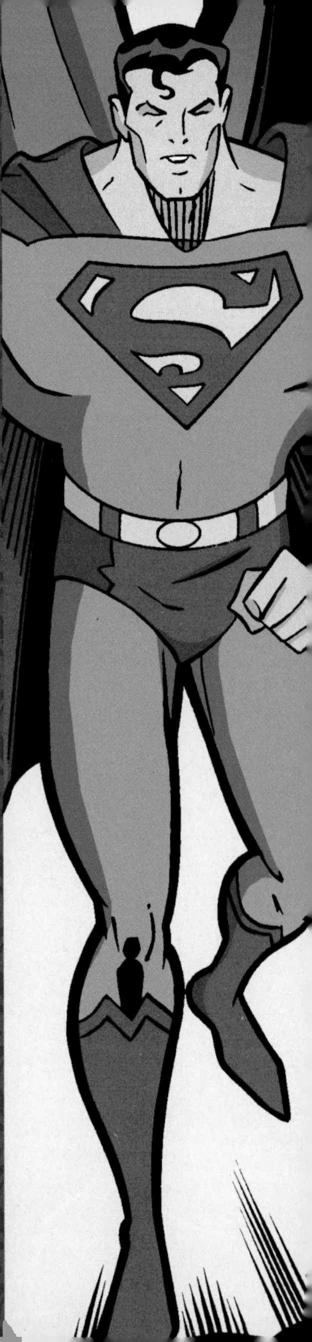

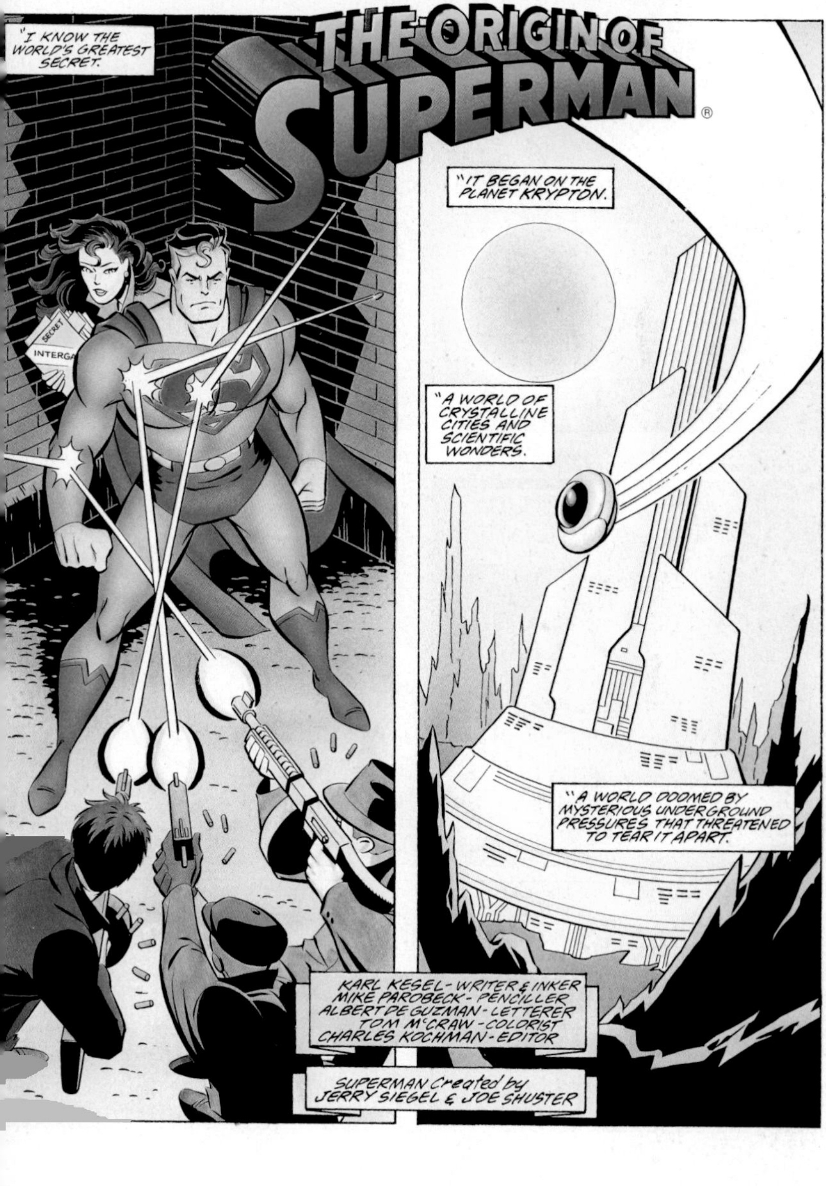

THE ORIGIN OF SUPERMAN®
"I KNOW THE WORLD'S GREATEST SECRET.
SECRET
"IT BEGAN ON THE PLANET KRYPTON.
"A WORLD OF CRYSTALLINE CITIES AND SCIENTIFIC WONDERS.
"A WORLD DOOMED BY MYSTERIOUS UNDERGROUND PRESSURES THAT THREATENED TO TEAR IT APART.
KARL KESEL - WRITER & INKER
MIKE PAROBECK - PENCILLER
ALBERT DE GUZMAN - LETTERER
TOM McCRAW - COLORIST
CHARLES KOCHMAN - EDITOR
SUPERMAN Created by JERRY SIEGEL & JOE SHUSTER

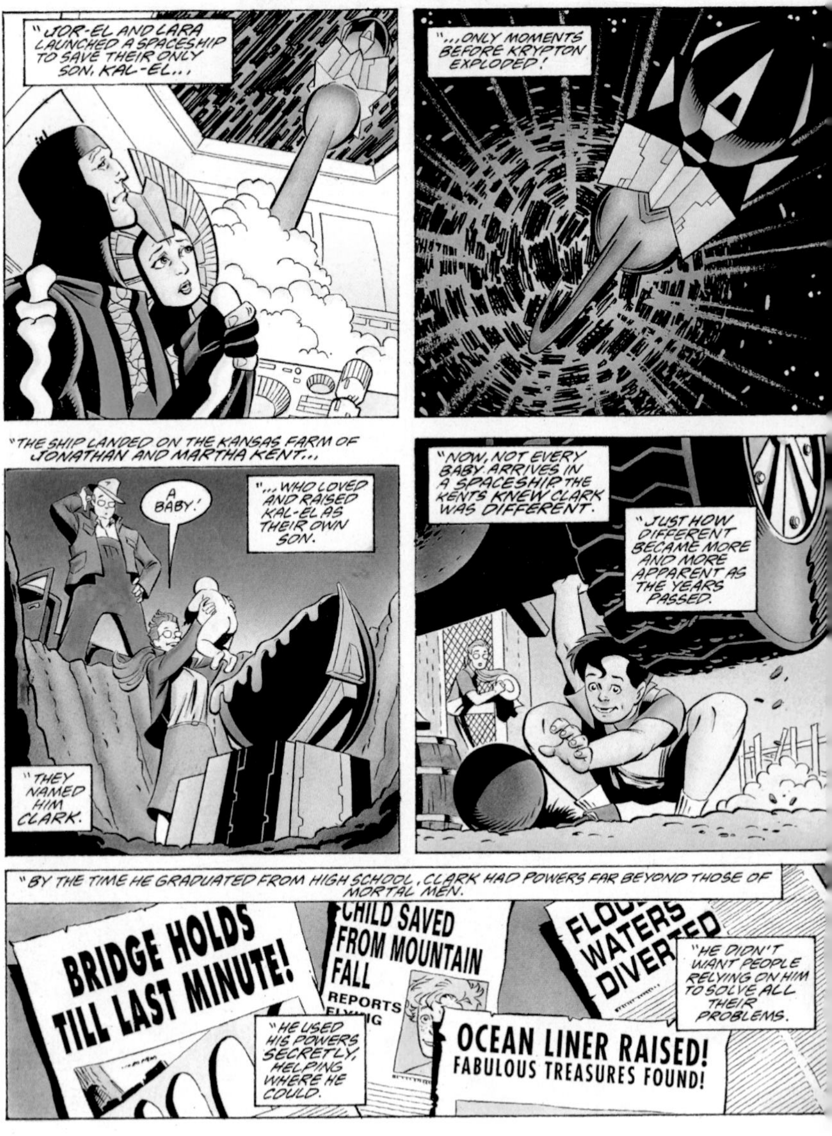
"JOR-EL AND LARA LAUNCHED A SPACESHIP TO SAVE THEIR ONLY SON, KAL-EL...
"...ONLY MOMENTS BEFORE KRYPTON EXPLODED!
"THE SHIP LANDED ON THE KANSAS FARM OF JONATHAN AND MARTHA KENT...
A BABY!
"...WHO LOVED AND RAISED KAL-EL AS THEIR OWN SON.
"THEY NAMED HIM CLARK.
"NOW, NOT EVERY BABY ARRIVES IN A SPACESHIP. THE KENTS KNEW CLARK WAS DIFFERENT.
"JUST HOW DIFFERENT BECAME MORE AND MORE APPARENT AS THE YEARS PASSED.
"BY THE TIME HE GRADUATED FROM HIGH SCHOOL, CLARK HAD POWERS FAR BEYOND THOSE OF MORTAL MEN.
BRIDGE HOLDS TILL LAST MINUTE!
CHILD SAVED FROM MOUNTAIN FALL
REPORTS
WATERS
"HE USED HIS POWERS SECRETLY, HELPING WHERE HE COULD.
"HE DIDN'T WANT PEOPLE RELYING ON HIM TO SOLVE ALL THEIR PROBLEMS.
OCEAN LINER RAISED!
FABULOUS TREASURES FOUND!

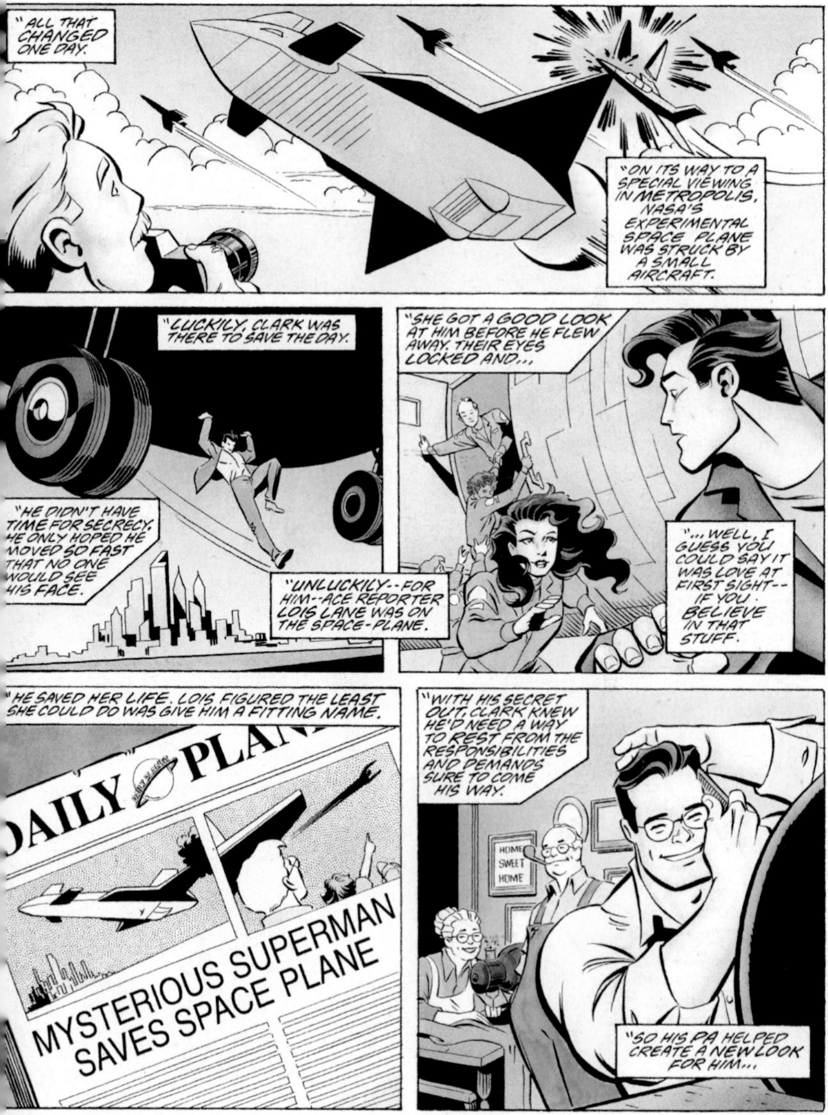
"ALL THAT CHANGED ONE DAY.
"ON ITS WAY TO A SPECIAL VIEWING IN METROPOLIS, NASA'S EXPERIMENTAL SPACE PLANE WAS STRUCK BY A SMALL AIRCRAFT.
"LUCKILY, CLARK WAS THERE TO SAVE THE DAY.
"HE DIDN'T HAVE TIME FOR SECRECY. HE ONLY HOPED HE MOVED SO FAST THAT NO ONE WOULD SEE HIS FACE.
"UNLUCKILY--FOR HIM--ACE REPORTER LOIS LANE WAS ON THE SPACE-PLANE.
"SHE GOT A GOOD LOOK AT HIM BEFORE HE FLEW AWAY. THEIR EYES LOCKED AND...
"...WELL, I GUESS YOU COULD SAY IT WAS LOVE AT FIRST SIGHT--IF YOU BELIEVE IN THAT STUFF.
"HE SAVED HER LIFE. LOIS FIGURED THE LEAST SHE COULD DO WAS GIVE HIM A FITTING NAME.
DAILY PLAN
MYSTERIOUS SUPERMAN SAVES SPACE PLANE
"WITH HIS SECRET OUT, CLARK KNEW HE'D NEED A WAY TO REST FROM THE RESPONSIBILITIES AND DEMANDS SURE TO COME HIS WAY.
HOME SWEET HOME
"SO HIS PA HELPED CREATE A NEW LOOK FOR HIM...

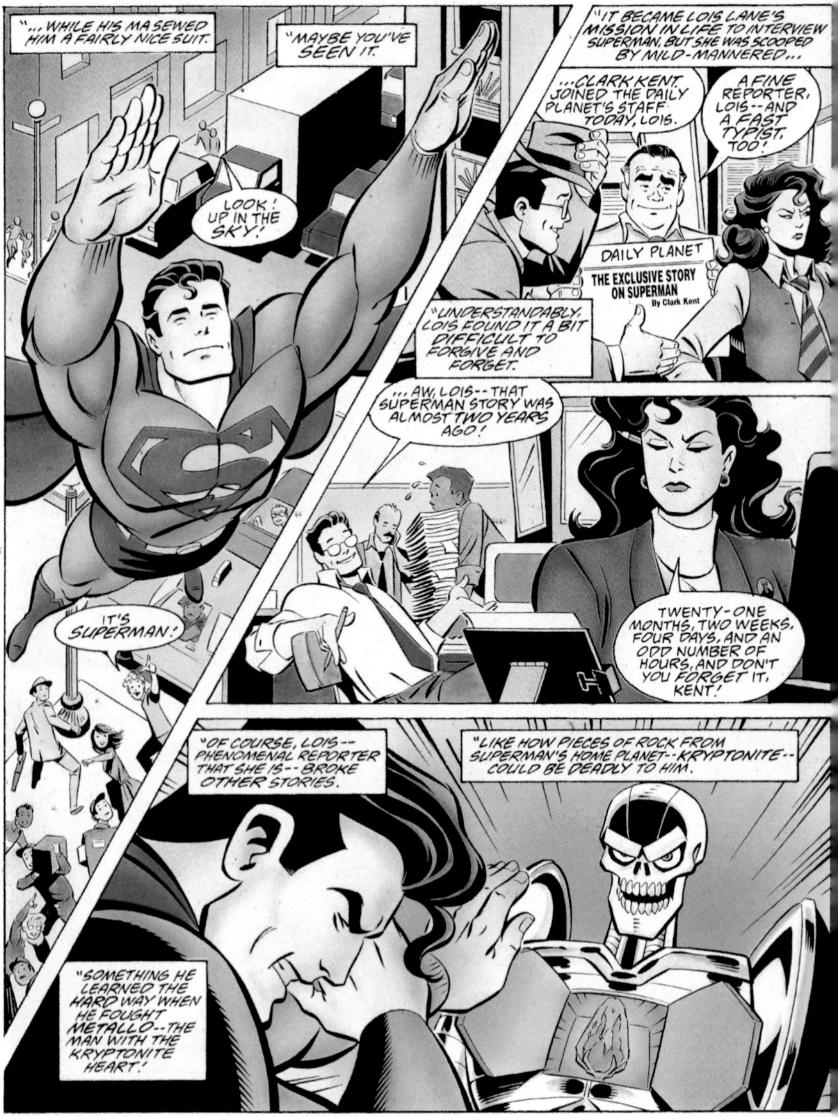
"...WHILE HIS MA SEWED HIM A FAIRLY NICE SUIT.
"MAYBE YOU'VE SEEN IT.
LOOK! UP IN THE SKY!
IT'S SUPERMAN!
"IT BECAME LOIS LANE'S MISSION IN LIFE TO INTERVIEW SUPERMAN. BUT SHE WAS SCOOPED BY MILD-MANNERED...
...CLARK KENT. JOINED THE DAILY PLANET'S STAFF TODAY, LOIS.
A FINE REPORTER, LOIS--AND A FAST TYPIST, TOO!
DAILY PLANET
THE EXCLUSIVE STORY ON SUPERMAN
By Clark Kent
"UNDERSTANDABLY, LOIS FOUND IT A BIT DIFFICULT TO FORGIVE AND FORGET.
...AW, LOIS--THAT SUPERMAN STORY WAS ALMOST TWO YEARS AGO!
TWENTY-ONE MONTHS, TWO WEEKS, FOUR DAYS, AND AN ODD NUMBER OF HOURS, AND DON'T YOU FORGET IT, KENT!
"OF COURSE, LOIS--PHENOMENAL REPORTER THAT SHE IS--BROKE OTHER STORIES.
"LIKE HOW PIECES OF ROCK FROM SUPERMAN'S HOME PLANET--KRYPTONITE--COULD BE DEADLY TO HIM.
"SOMETHING HE LEARNED THE HARD WAY WHEN HE FOUGHT METALLO--THE MAN WITH THE KRYPTONITE HEART!

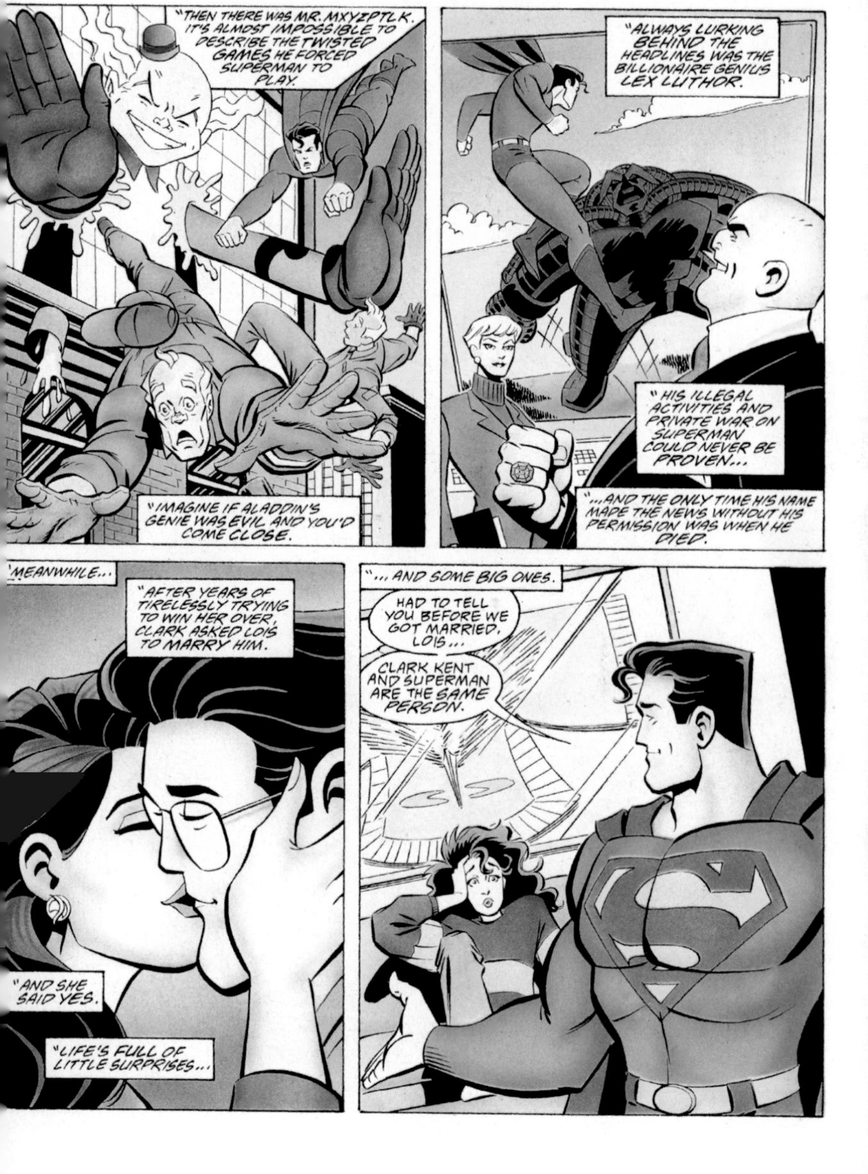
"THEN THERE WAS MR. MXYZPTLK. IT'S ALMOST IMPOSSIBLE TO DESCRIBE THE TWISTED GAMES HE FORCED SUPERMAN TO PLAY.
"IMAGINE IF ALADDIN'S GENIE WAS EVIL AND YOU'D COME CLOSE.
"ALWAYS LURKING BEHIND THE HEADLINES WAS THE BILLIONAIRE GENIUS LEX LUTHOR.
"HIS ILLEGAL ACTIVITIES AND PRIVATE WAR ON SUPERMAN COULD NEVER BE PROVEN...
"...AND THE ONLY TIME HIS NAME MADE THE NEWS WITHOUT HIS PERMISSION WAS WHEN HE DIED.
MEANWHILE...
"AFTER YEARS OF TIRELESSLY TRYING TO WIN HER OVER, CLARK ASKED LOIS TO MARRY HIM.
"AND SHE SAID YES.
"LIFE'S FULL OF LITTLE SURPRISES...
"...AND SOME BIG ONES.
HAD TO TELL YOU BEFORE WE GOT MARRIED, LOIS...
CLARK KENT AND SUPERMAN ARE THE SAME PERSON.

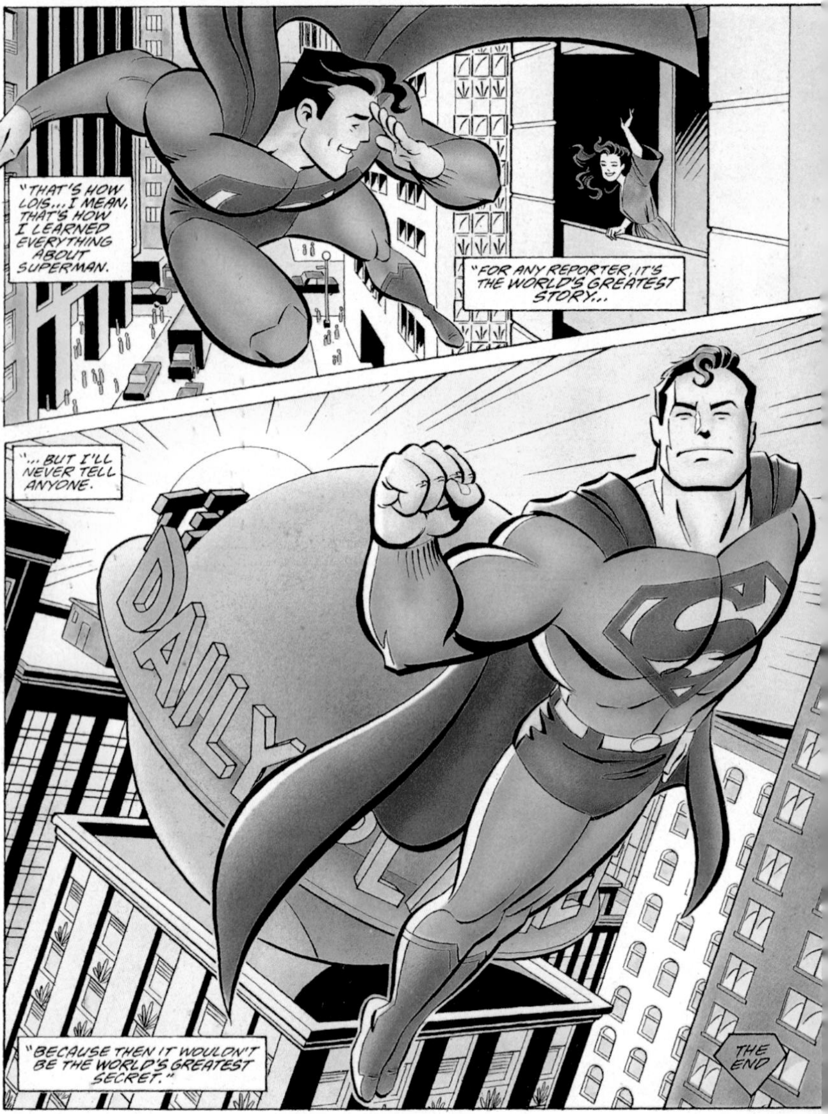
"THAT'S HOW LOIS... I MEAN, THAT'S HOW I LEARNED EVERYTHING ABOUT SUPERMAN.
"FOR ANY REPORTER, IT'S THE WORLD'S GREATEST STORY...
"...BUT I'LL NEVER TELL ANYONE.
DAILY
"BECAUSE THEN IT WOULDN'T BE THE WORLD'S GREATEST SECRET."
THE END

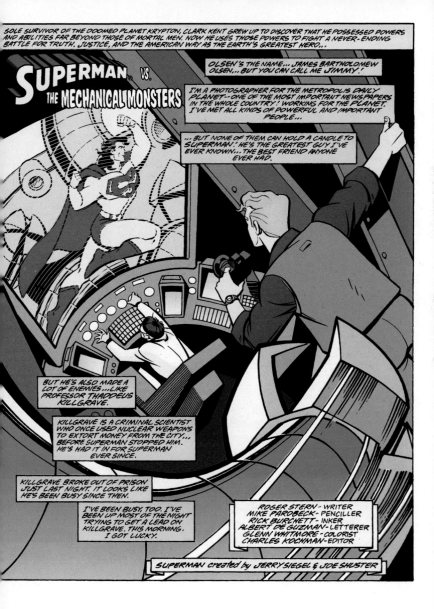

SOLE SURVIVOR OF THE DOOMED PLANET KRYPTON, CLARK KENT GREW UP TO DISCOVER THAT HE POSSESSED POWERS AND ABILITIES FAR BEYOND THOSE OF MORTAL MEN. NOW HE USES THOSE POWERS TO FIGHT A NEVER-ENDING BATTLE FOR TRUTH, JUSTICE, AND THE AMERICAN WAY AS THE EARTH'S GREATEST HERO...

# SUPERMAN vs. THE MECHANICAL MONSTERS

OLSEN'S THE NAME... JAMES BARTHOLOMEW OLSEN... BUT YOU CAN CALL ME JIMMY!

I'M A PHOTOGRAPHER FOR THE METROPOLIS DAILY PLANET--ONE OF THE MOST IMPORTANT NEWSPAPERS IN THE WHOLE COUNTRY! WORKING FOR THE PLANET, I'VE MET ALL KINDS OF POWERFUL AND IMPORTANT PEOPLE...

...BUT NONE OF THEM CAN HOLD A CANDLE TO SUPERMAN! HE'S THE GREATEST GUY I'VE EVER KNOWN... THE BEST FRIEND ANYONE EVER HAD.

BUT HE'S ALSO MADE A LOT OF ENEMIES... LIKE PROFESSOR THADDEUS KILLGRAVE.

KILLGRAVE IS A CRIMINAL SCIENTIST WHO ONCE USED NUCLEAR WEAPONS TO EXTORT MONEY FROM THE CITY... BEFORE SUPERMAN STOPPED HIM. HE'S HAD IT IN FOR SUPERMAN EVER SINCE.

KILLGRAVE BROKE OUT OF PRISON JUST LAST NIGHT. IT LOOKS LIKE HE'S BEEN BUSY SINCE THEN.

I'VE BEEN BUSY, TOO. I'VE BEEN UP MOST OF THE NIGHT TRYING TO GET A LEAD ON KILLGRAVE. THIS MORNING, I GOT LUCKY.

ROGER STERN - WRITER
MIKE PAROBECK - PENCILLER
RICK BURCHETT - INKER
ALBERT DE GUZMAN - LETTERER
GLENN WHITMORE - COLORIST
CHARLES KOCHMAN - EDITOR

SUPERMAN created by JERRY SIEGEL & JOE SHUSTER

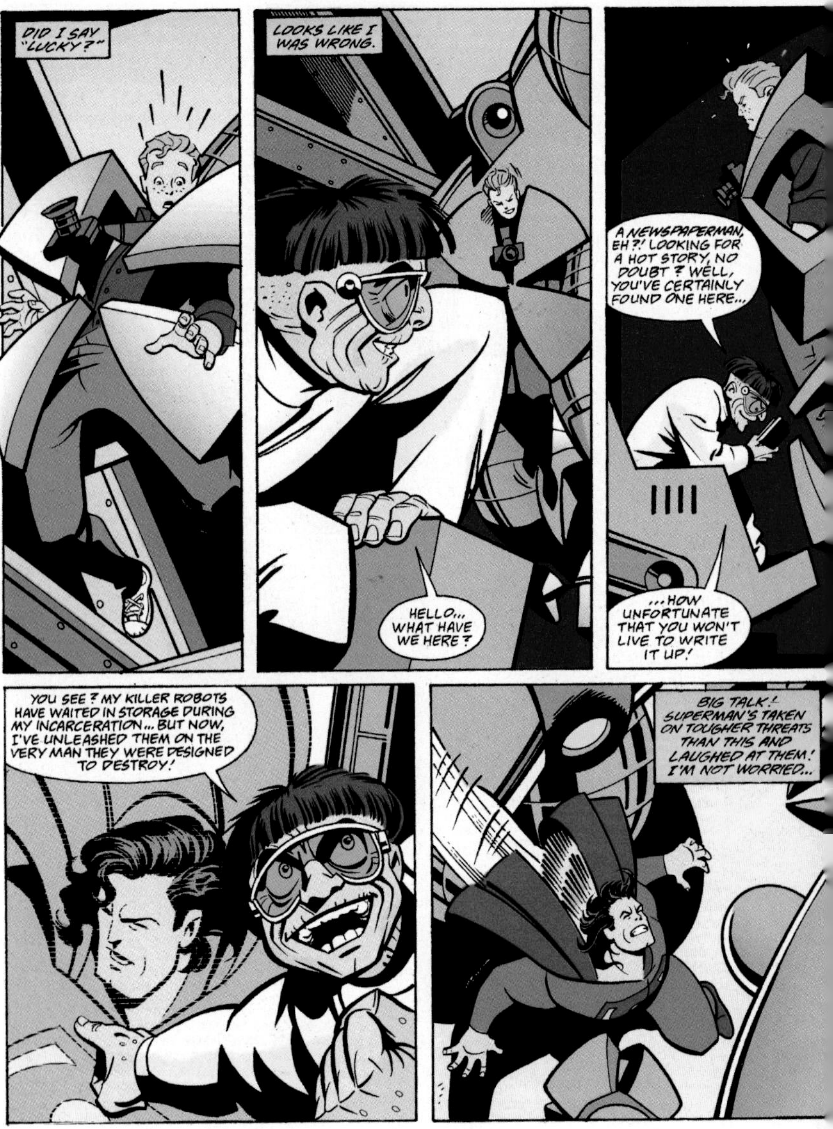
DID I SAY "LUCKY?"
LOOKS LIKE I WAS WRONG.
HELLO... WHAT HAVE WE HERE?
A NEWSPAPERMAN, EH?! LOOKING FOR A HOT STORY, NO DOUBT? WELL, YOU'VE CERTAINLY FOUND ONE HERE...
...HOW UNFORTUNATE THAT YOU WON'T LIVE TO WRITE IT UP!
YOU SEE? MY KILLER ROBOTS HAVE WAITED IN STORAGE DURING MY INCARCERATION... BUT NOW, I'VE UNLEASHED THEM ON THE VERY MAN THEY WERE DESIGNED TO DESTROY!
BIG TALK! SUPERMAN'S TAKEN ON TOUGHER THREATS THAN THIS AND LAUGHED AT THEM! I'M NOT WORRIED...

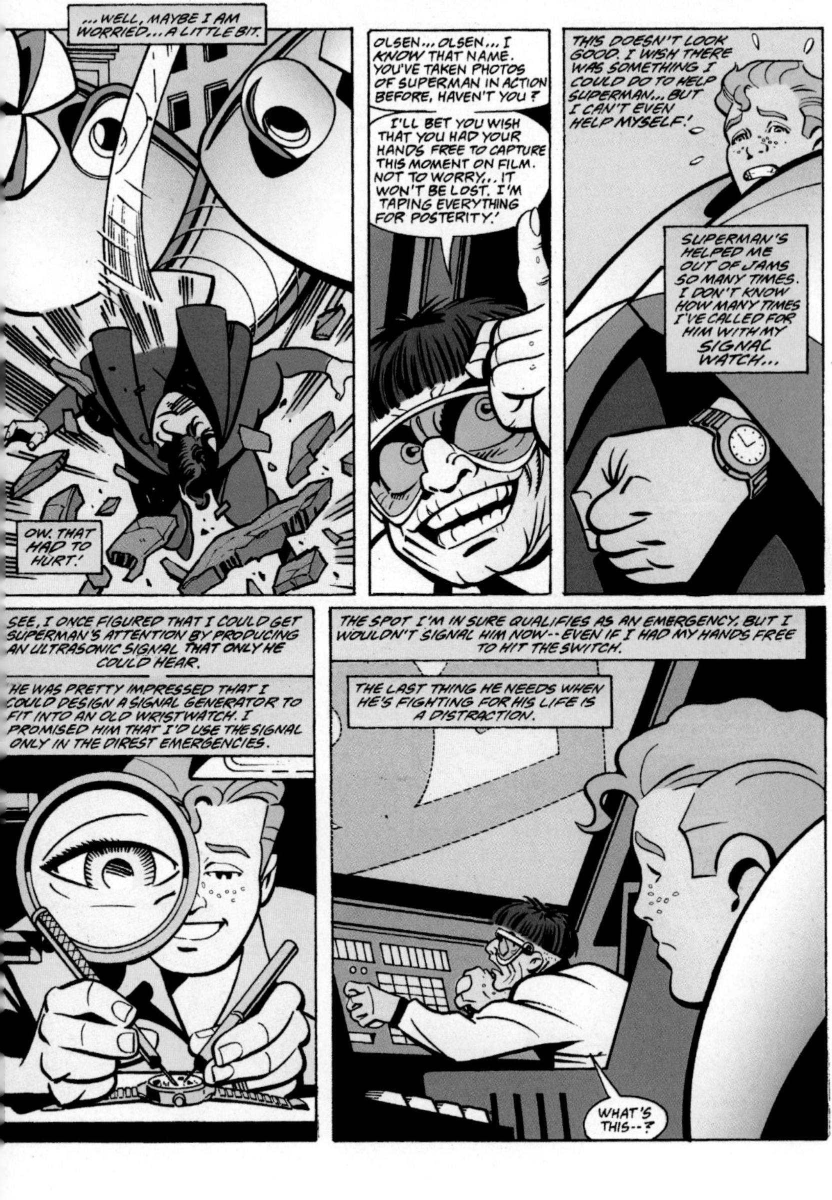
...WELL, MAYBE I AM WORRIED... A LITTLE BIT.
OW. THAT HAD TO HURT!
OLSEN... OLSEN... I KNOW THAT NAME. YOU'VE TAKEN PHOTOS OF SUPERMAN IN ACTION BEFORE, HAVEN'T YOU?
I'LL BET YOU WISH THAT YOU HAD YOUR HANDS FREE TO CAPTURE THIS MOMENT ON FILM. NOT TO WORRY... IT WON'T BE LOST. I'M TAPING EVERYTHING FOR POSTERITY!
THIS DOESN'T LOOK GOOD. I WISH THERE WAS SOMETHING I COULD DO TO HELP SUPERMAN... BUT I CAN'T EVEN HELP MYSELF!
SUPERMAN'S HELPED ME OUT OF JAMS SO MANY TIMES. I DON'T KNOW HOW MANY TIMES I'VE CALLED FOR HIM WITH MY SIGNAL WATCH...
SEE, I ONCE FIGURED THAT I COULD GET SUPERMAN'S ATTENTION BY PRODUCING AN ULTRASONIC SIGNAL THAT ONLY HE COULD HEAR.
HE WAS PRETTY IMPRESSED THAT I COULD DESIGN A SIGNAL GENERATOR TO FIT INTO AN OLD WRISTWATCH. I PROMISED HIM THAT I'D USE THE SIGNAL ONLY IN THE DIREST EMERGENCIES.
THE SPOT I'M IN SURE QUALIFIES AS AN EMERGENCY, BUT I WOULDN'T SIGNAL HIM NOW--EVEN IF I HAD MY HANDS FREE TO HIT THE SWITCH.
THE LAST THING HE NEEDS WHEN HE'S FIGHTING FOR HIS LIFE IS A DISTRACTION.
WHAT'S THIS--?

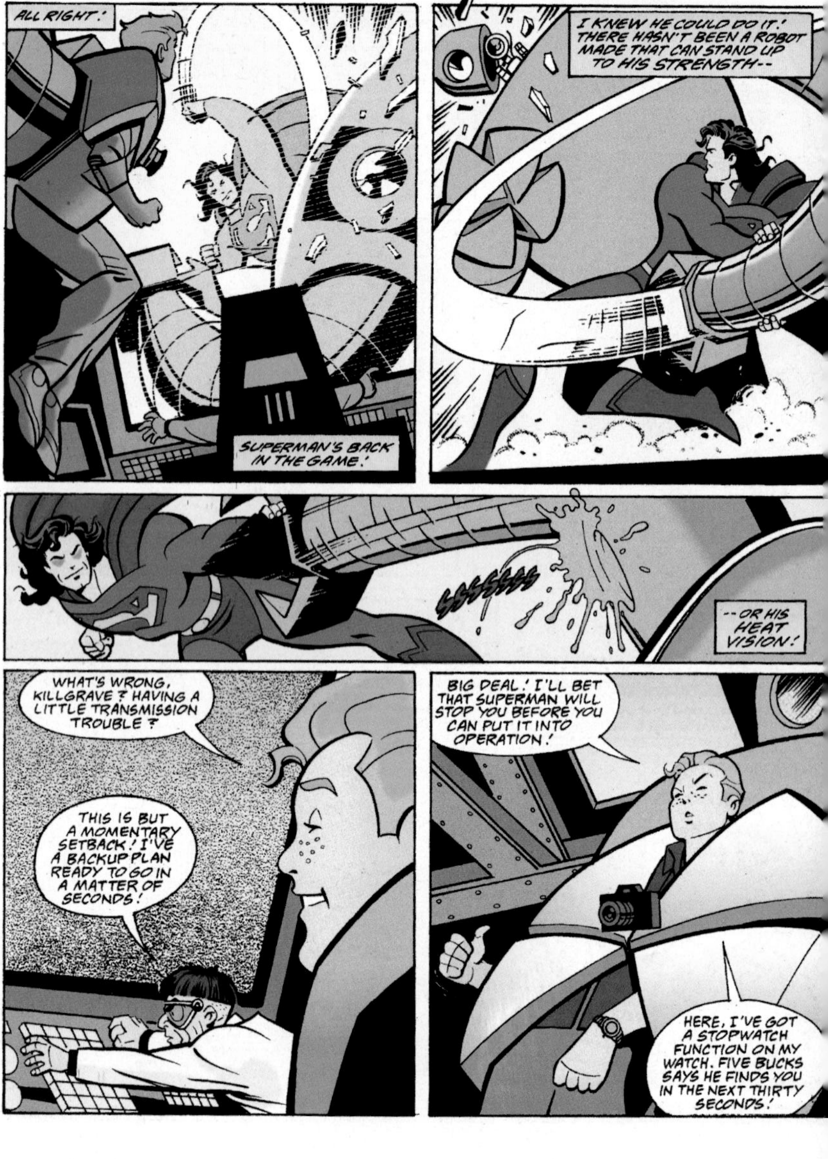
ALL RIGHT!
SUPERMAN'S BACK IN THE GAME!
I KNEW HE COULD DO IT! THERE HASN'T BEEN A ROBOT MADE THAT CAN STAND UP TO HIS STRENGTH--
SSSSSSS
--OR HIS HEAT VISION!
WHAT'S WRONG, KILLGRAVE? HAVING A LITTLE TRANSMISSION TROUBLE?
THIS IS BUT A MOMENTARY SETBACK! I'VE A BACKUP PLAN READY TO GO IN A MATTER OF SECONDS!
BIG DEAL! I'LL BET THAT SUPERMAN WILL STOP YOU BEFORE YOU CAN PUT IT INTO OPERATION!
HERE, I'VE GOT A STOPWATCH FUNCTION ON MY WATCH. FIVE BUCKS SAYS HE FINDS YOU IN THE NEXT THIRTY SECONDS!

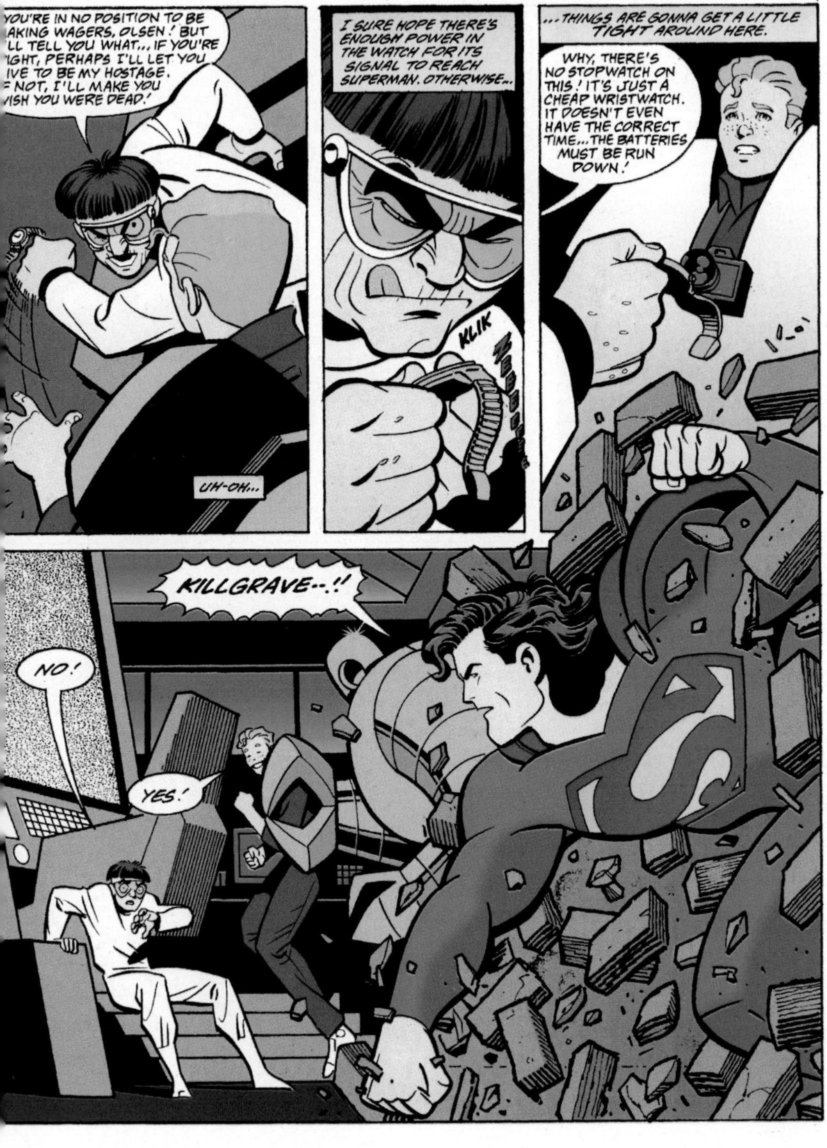
YOU'RE IN NO POSITION TO BE MAKING WAGERS, OLSEN! BUT I'LL TELL YOU WHAT... IF YOU'RE RIGHT, PERHAPS I'LL LET YOU LIVE TO BE MY HOSTAGE. IF NOT, I'LL MAKE YOU WISH YOU WERE DEAD!
UH-OH...
I SURE HOPE THERE'S ENOUGH POWER IN THE WATCH FOR ITS SIGNAL TO REACH SUPERMAN. OTHERWISE...
KLIK
...THINGS ARE GONNA GET A LITTLE TIGHT AROUND HERE.
WHY, THERE'S NO STOPWATCH ON THIS! IT'S JUST A CHEAP WRISTWATCH. IT DOESN'T EVEN HAVE THE CORRECT TIME... THE BATTERIES MUST BE RUN DOWN!
KILLGRAVE--!!
NO!
YES!

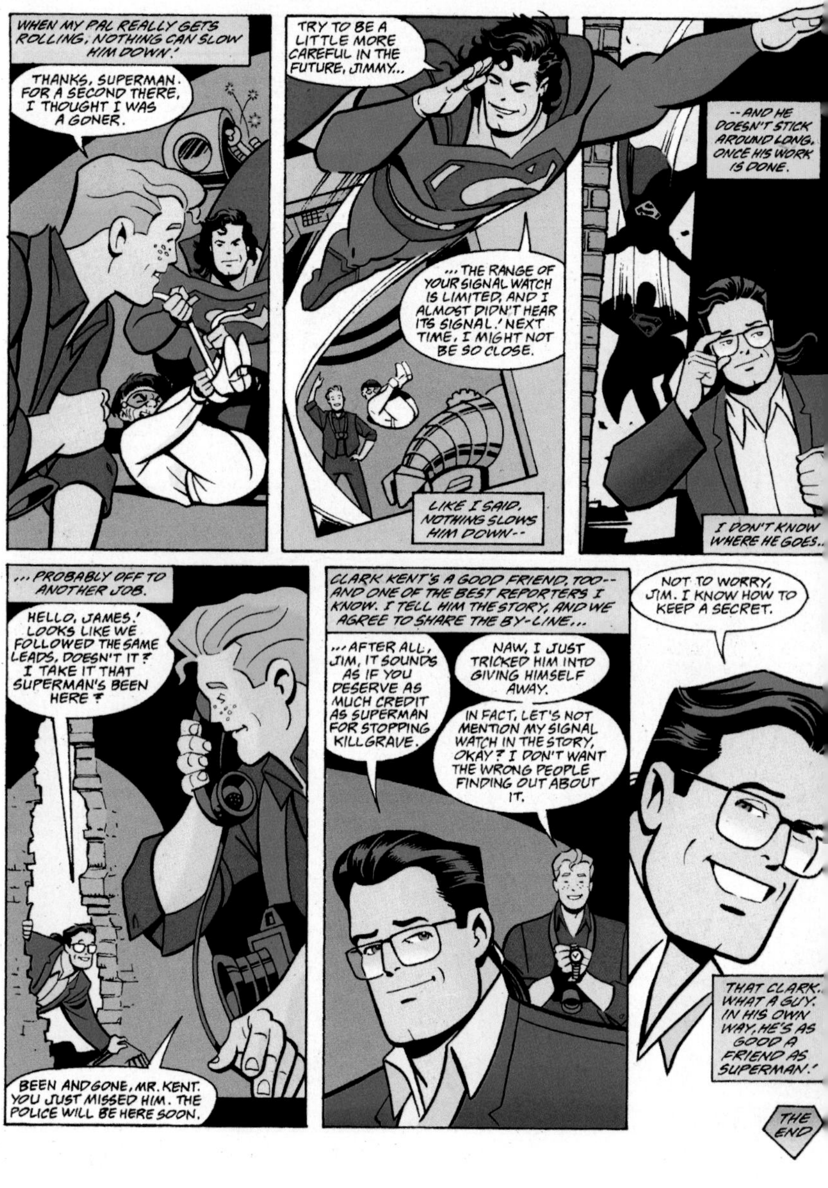
WHEN MY PAL REALLY GETS ROLLING, NOTHING CAN SLOW HIM DOWN!
THANKS, SUPERMAN. FOR A SECOND THERE, I THOUGHT I WAS A GONER.
TRY TO BE A LITTLE MORE CAREFUL IN THE FUTURE, JIMMY...
...THE RANGE OF YOUR SIGNAL WATCH IS LIMITED, AND I ALMOST DIDN'T HEAR ITS SIGNAL! NEXT TIME, I MIGHT NOT BE SO CLOSE.
LIKE I SAID, NOTHING SLOWS HIM DOWN--
--AND HE DOESN'T STICK AROUND LONG, ONCE HIS WORK IS DONE.
I DON'T KNOW WHERE HE GOES...
...PROBABLY OFF TO ANOTHER JOB.
HELLO, JAMES! LOOKS LIKE WE FOLLOWED THE SAME LEADS, DOESN'T IT? I TAKE IT THAT SUPERMAN'S BEEN HERE?
BEEN AND GONE, MR. KENT. YOU JUST MISSED HIM. THE POLICE WILL BE HERE SOON.
CLARK KENT'S A GOOD FRIEND, TOO--AND ONE OF THE BEST REPORTERS I KNOW. I TELL HIM THE STORY, AND WE AGREE TO SHARE THE BY-LINE...
...AFTER ALL, JIM, IT SOUNDS AS IF YOU DESERVE AS MUCH CREDIT AS SUPERMAN FOR STOPPING KILLGRAVE.
NAW, I JUST TRICKED HIM INTO GIVING HIMSELF AWAY.
IN FACT, LET'S NOT MENTION MY SIGNAL WATCH IN THE STORY, OKAY? I DON'T WANT THE WRONG PEOPLE FINDING OUT ABOUT IT.
NOT TO WORRY, JIM. I KNOW HOW TO KEEP A SECRET.
THAT CLARK. WHAT A GUY. IN HIS OWN WAY, HE'S AS GOOD A FRIEND AS SUPERMAN!
THE END

SOLE SURVIVOR OF THE DOOMED PLANET KRYPTON, CLARK KENT GREW UP TO DISCOVER THAT HE POSSESSED POWERS AND ABILITIES FAR BEYOND THOSE OF MORTAL MEN. NOW HE USES THOSE POWERS TO FIGHT A NEVER-ENDING BATTLE FOR TRUTH, JUSTICE, AND THE GOOD OF ALL HUMANITY AS THE EARTH'S GREATEST HERO...

# SUPERMAN IN ALL MX'D UP

CAN YOU *IMAGINE* THE CHIEF SAYING HE DIDN'T WANT ANY MORE *CARNIVAL* STORIES....

...ESPECIALLY FROM HIS *TOP REPORTERS* WHO SHOULD BE DELIVERING *REAL NEWS!*

WHAT A *GRUMP*, HUH, CLARK! SAYING ALL THE *CARNIVAL* STORIES HAD BEEN WRITTEN!

AND HE DIDN'T EVEN *CARE* THAT THIS IS ONE OF THE *FINEST* TRAVELING CARNIVALS IN THE COUNTRY!

BUT WE CAN'T *ALWAYS* BE DELIVERING HARD-HITTING NEWS. SOMETIMES IT'S NICE TO HAVE A *DAY OFF.*

C'MON, LOIS. LET'S TRY THE *FERRIS WHEEL!*

WE CAN SEE THE *WHOLE PARK!*

NOBODY SAYS A *REPORTER* HAS TO WORK ALL THE TIME.

IT'S KINDA *FUN* JUST BEING HERE, ISN'T IT?

THE *OCTOPUS!* AIRPLANE RIDES! THE *CAROUSEL!*

IT EVEN HAS A *HOUSE OF MIRRORS!*

SUPERMAN *Created by* JERRY SIEGEL & JOE SHUSTER

LOUISE SIMONSON
WRITER

MIKE PAROBECK
PENCILLER

RICK BURCHETT
INKER

ALBERT DE GUZMAN
LETTERER

GLENN WHITMORE
COLORIST

CHARLES KOCHMAN
EDITOR

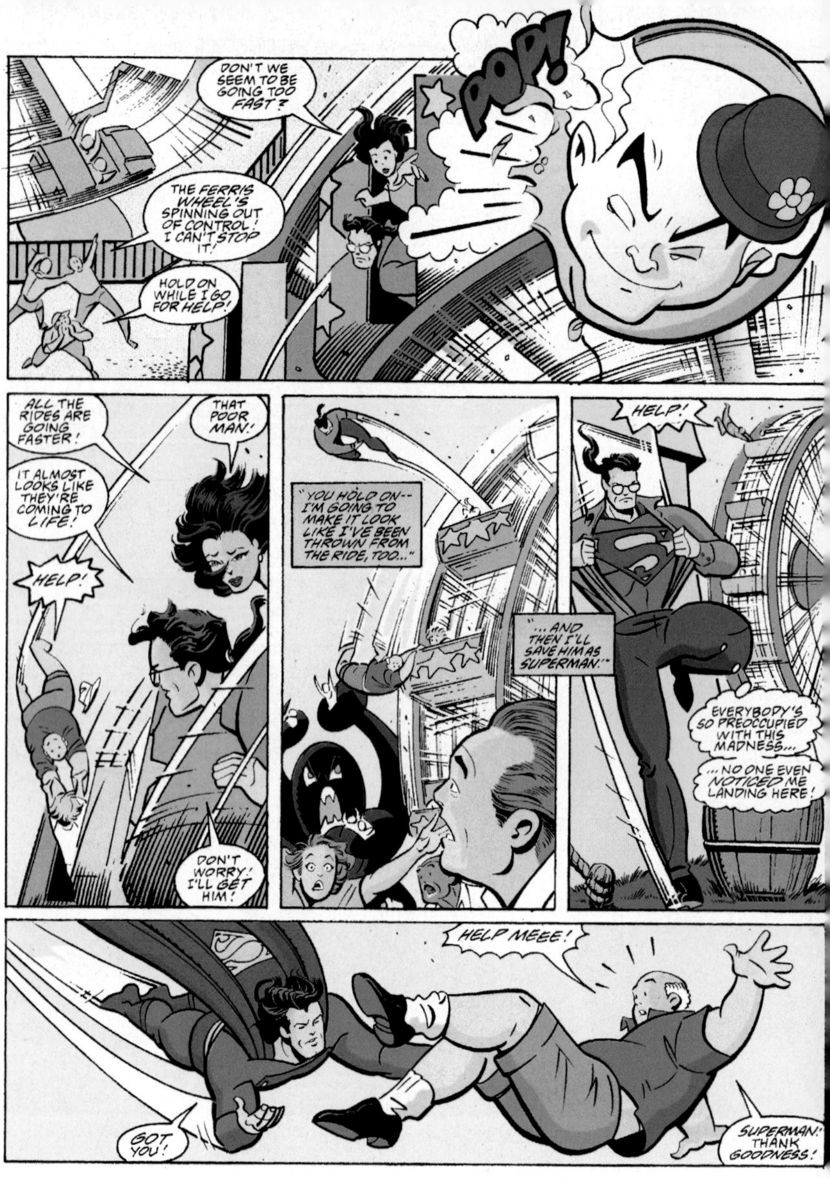
DON'T WE SEEM TO BE GOING TOO FAST?
THE FERRIS WHEEL'S SPINNING OUT OF CONTROL! I CAN'T STOP IT!
HOLD ON WHILE I GO FOR HELP!
POP!
ALL THE RIDES ARE GOING FASTER!
THAT POOR MAN!
IT ALMOST LOOKS LIKE THEY'RE COMING TO LIFE!
HELP!
DON'T WORRY! I'LL GET HIM!
"YOU HOLD ON-- I'M GOING TO MAKE IT LOOK LIKE I'VE BEEN THROWN FROM THE RIDE, TOO..."
"...AND THEN I'LL SAVE HIM AS SUPERMAN."
HELP!
EVERYBODY'S SO PREOCCUPIED WITH THIS MADNESS...
...NO ONE EVEN NOTICED ME LANDING HERE!
HELP MEEE!
GOT YOU!
SUPERMAN! THANK GOODNESS!

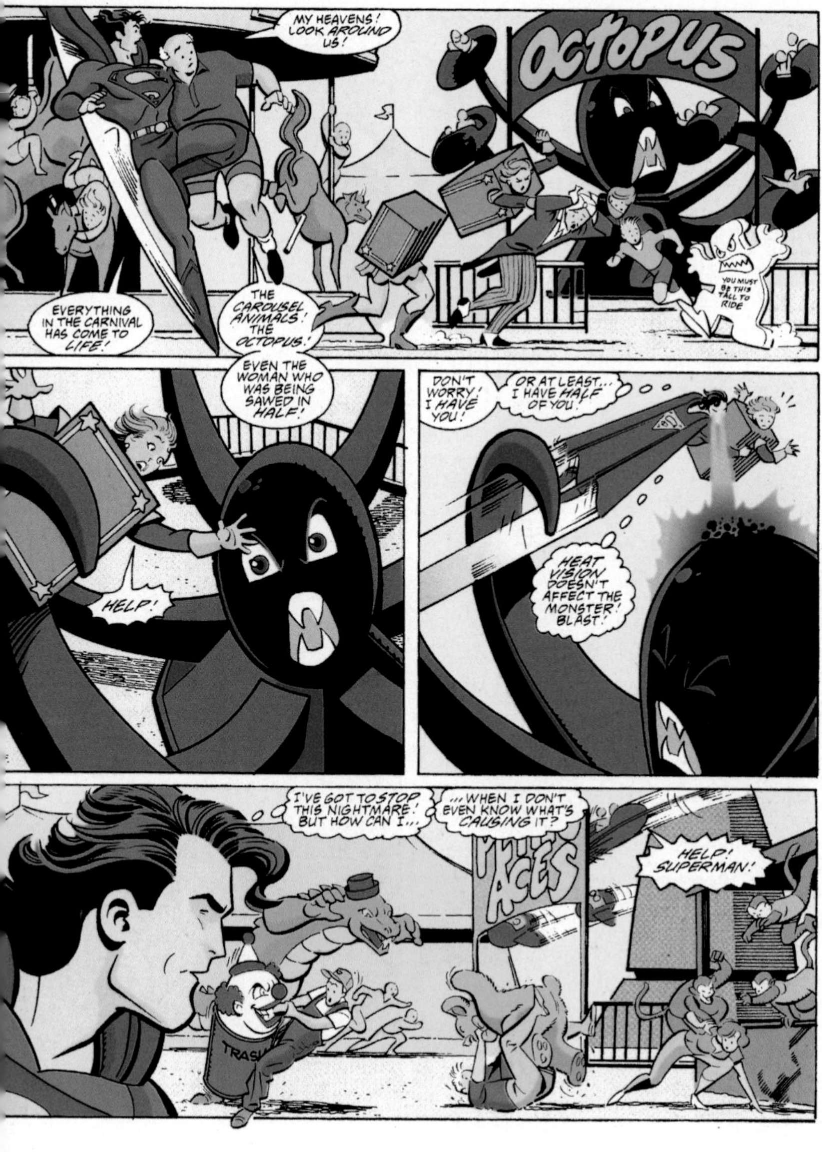

MY HEAVENS! LOOK AROUND US!
OCTOPUS
EVERYTHING IN THE CARNIVAL HAS COME TO LIFE!
THE CAROUSEL ANIMALS! THE OCTOPUS!
YOU MUST BE THIS TALL TO RIDE
EVEN THE WOMAN WHO WAS BEING SAWED IN HALF!
HELP!
DON'T WORRY! I HAVE YOU!
OR AT LEAST... I HAVE HALF OF YOU!
HEAT VISION DOESN'T AFFECT THE MONSTER! BLAST!
I'VE GOT TO STOP THIS NIGHTMARE! BUT HOW CAN I...
...WHEN I DON'T EVEN KNOW WHAT'S CAUSING IT?
ACES
HELP! SUPERMAN!

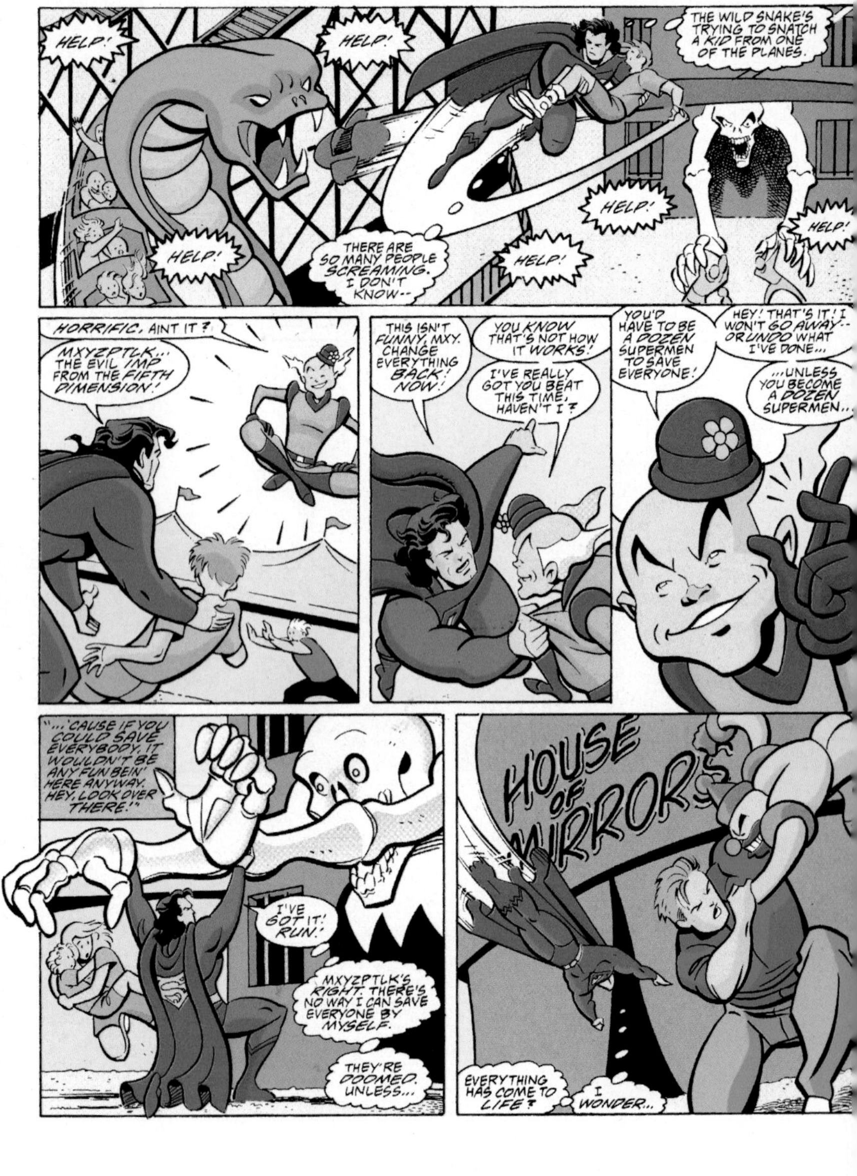
HELP!
HELP!
THE WILD SNAKE'S TRYING TO SNATCH A KID FROM ONE OF THE PLANES.
HELP!
HELP!
HELP!
THERE ARE SO MANY PEOPLE SCREAMING. I DON'T KNOW--
HELP!
HORRIFIC, AINT IT?
MXYZPTLK... THE EVIL IMP FROM THE FIFTH DIMENSION!
THIS ISN'T FUNNY, MXY. CHANGE EVERYTHING BACK! NOW!
YOU KNOW THAT'S NOT HOW IT WORKS!
I'VE REALLY GOT YOU BEAT THIS TIME, HAVEN'T I?
YOU'D HAVE TO BE A DOZEN SUPERMEN TO SAVE EVERYONE!
HEY! THAT'S IT! I WON'T GO AWAY--OR UNDO WHAT I'VE DONE...
...UNLESS YOU BECOME A DOZEN SUPERMEN...
"...'CAUSE IF YOU COULD SAVE EVERYBODY, IT WOULDN'T BE ANY FUN BEIN' HERE ANYWAY. HEY, LOOK OVER THERE!"
I'VE GOT IT! RUN!
MXYZPTLK'S RIGHT. THERE'S NO WAY I CAN SAVE EVERYONE BY MYSELF.
THEY'RE DOOMED. UNLESS...
HOUSE OF MIRRORS
EVERYTHING HAS COME TO LIFE?
I WONDER...

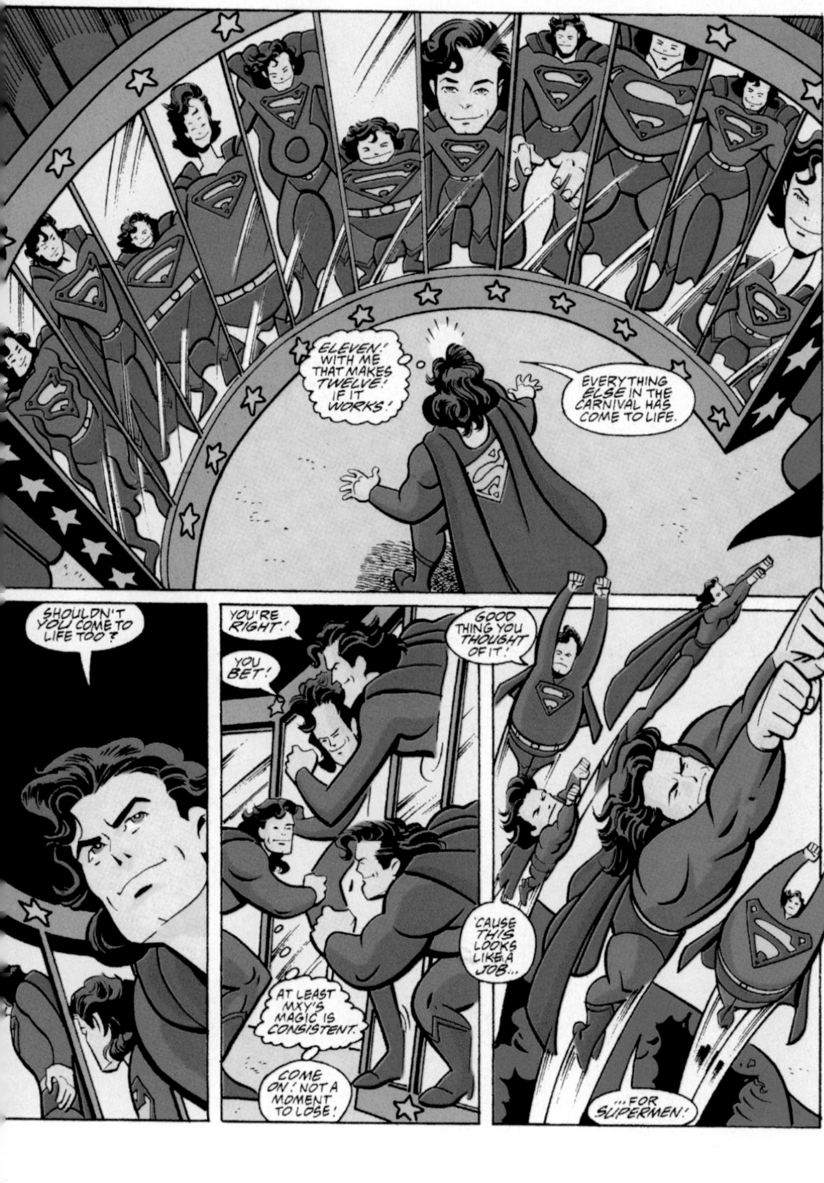
ELEVEN! WITH ME THAT MAKES TWELVE! IF IT WORKS!
EVERYTHING ELSE IN THE CARNIVAL HAS COME TO LIFE.
SHOULDN'T YOU COME TO LIFE TOO?
YOU'RE RIGHT!
YOU BET!
AT LEAST MXY'S MAGIC IS CONSISTENT.
COME ON! NOT A MOMENT TO LOSE!
GOOD THING YOU THOUGHT OF IT!
'CAUSE THIS LOOKS LIKE A JOB...
...FOR SUPERMEN!

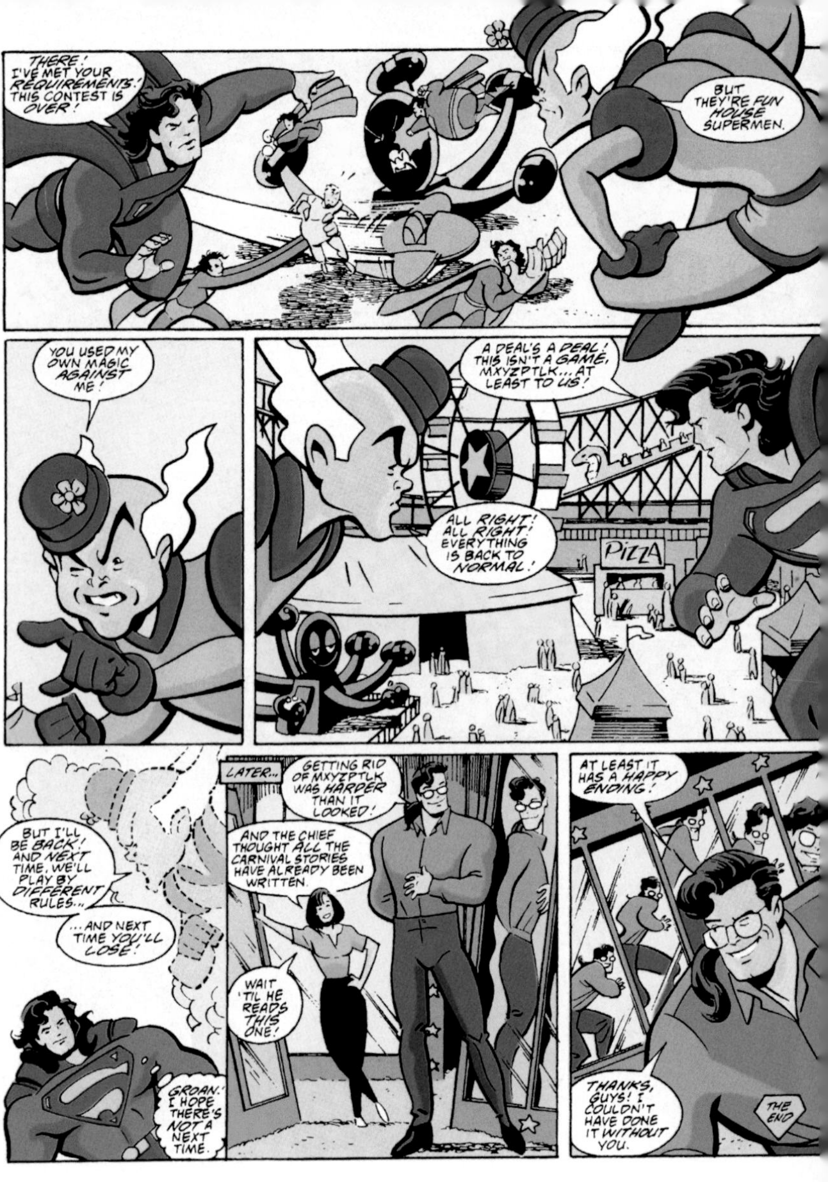
THERE! I'VE MET YOUR REQUIREMENTS! THIS CONTEST IS OVER!
BUT THEY'RE FUN HOUSE SUPERMEN.
YOU USED MY OWN MAGIC AGAINST ME!
A DEAL'S A DEAL! THIS ISN'T A GAME, MXYZPTLK... AT LEAST TO US!
ALL RIGHT! ALL RIGHT! EVERYTHING IS BACK TO NORMAL!
PIZZA
BUT I'LL BE BACK! AND NEXT TIME, WE'LL PLAY BY DIFFERENT RULES...
...AND NEXT TIME YOU'LL LOSE!
GROAN! I HOPE THERE'S NOT A NEXT TIME.
LATER...
GETTING RID OF MXYZPTLK WAS HARDER THAN IT LOOKED!
AND THE CHIEF THOUGHT ALL THE CARNIVAL STORIES HAVE ALREADY BEEN WRITTEN.
WAIT 'TIL HE READS THIS ONE!
AT LEAST IT HAS A HAPPY ENDING!
THANKS, GUYS! I COULDN'T HAVE DONE IT WITHOUT YOU.
THE END

SOLE SURVIVOR OF THE DOOMED PLANET KRYPTON, CLARK KENT GREW UP TO DISCOVER THAT HE POSSESSED POWERS AND ABILITIES FAR BEYOND THOSE OF MORTAL MEN. NOW HE USES THOSE POWERS TO FIGHT A NEVER-ENDING BATTLE FOR TRUTH, JUSTICE, AND THE GOOD OF ALL HUMANITY AS THE EARTH'S GREATEST HERO...

SUPERMAN. IN:
THE DOOMSDAY SOLUTION

"IT'S SOMETHING I'LL NEVER FORGET!"

"I WAS YOUNGER, STILL LIVING ON THE FARM WHERE I GREW UP."

THE CORN, ALMOST READY FOR HARVEST, TOWERED OVER ME.

"A MENACING GROWLING SOUND--

"--UNLIKE ONE I HAD EVER HEARD--

"--WAS DRAWING ME... PULLING ME INTO THAT CORNFIELD.

"I WAS TERRIFIED..

"--WITH GOOD REASON.

"A POWERFUL MONSTER BURST RIGHT OUT OF THE GROUND WITH A ROAR MORE FEROCIOUS THAN ANY LION.

"IT WAS DOOMSDAY... AND HE WAS AFTER ME!"

SUPERMAN Created by
JERRY SIEGEL & JOE SHUSTER

DAN JURGENS - WRITER ★ MIKE PAROBECK & RICK BURCHETT - ARTISTS
GLENN WHITMORE - COLORIST ★ ALBERT DEGUZMAN - LETTERER ★ CHARLES KOCHMAN - EDITOR

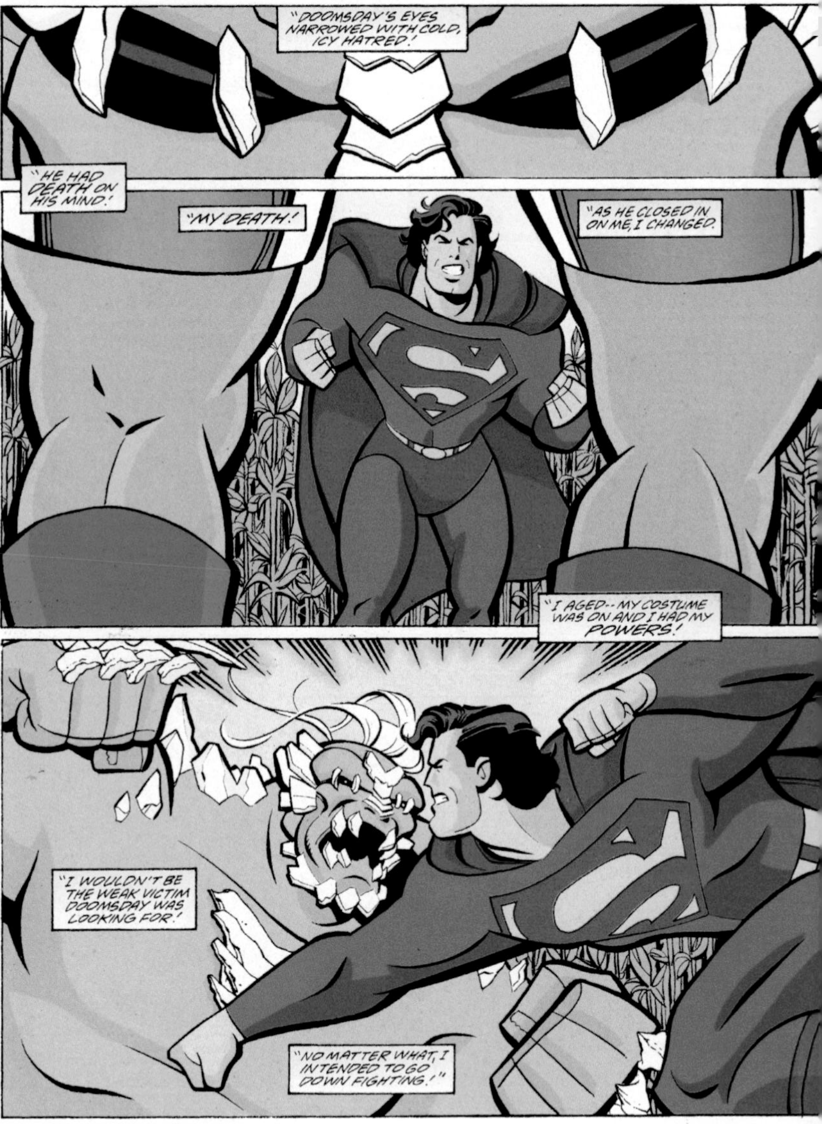

"DOOMSDAY'S EYES NARROWED WITH COLD, ICY HATRED.'
"HE HAD DEATH ON HIS MIND.'
"MY DEATH.'
"AS HE CLOSED IN ON ME, I CHANGED.
"I AGED-- MY COSTUME WAS ON AND I HAD MY POWERS!
"I WOULDN'T BE THE WEAK VICTIM DOOMSDAY WAS LOOKING FOR.'
"NO MATTER WHAT, I INTENDED TO GO DOWN FIGHTING.'"

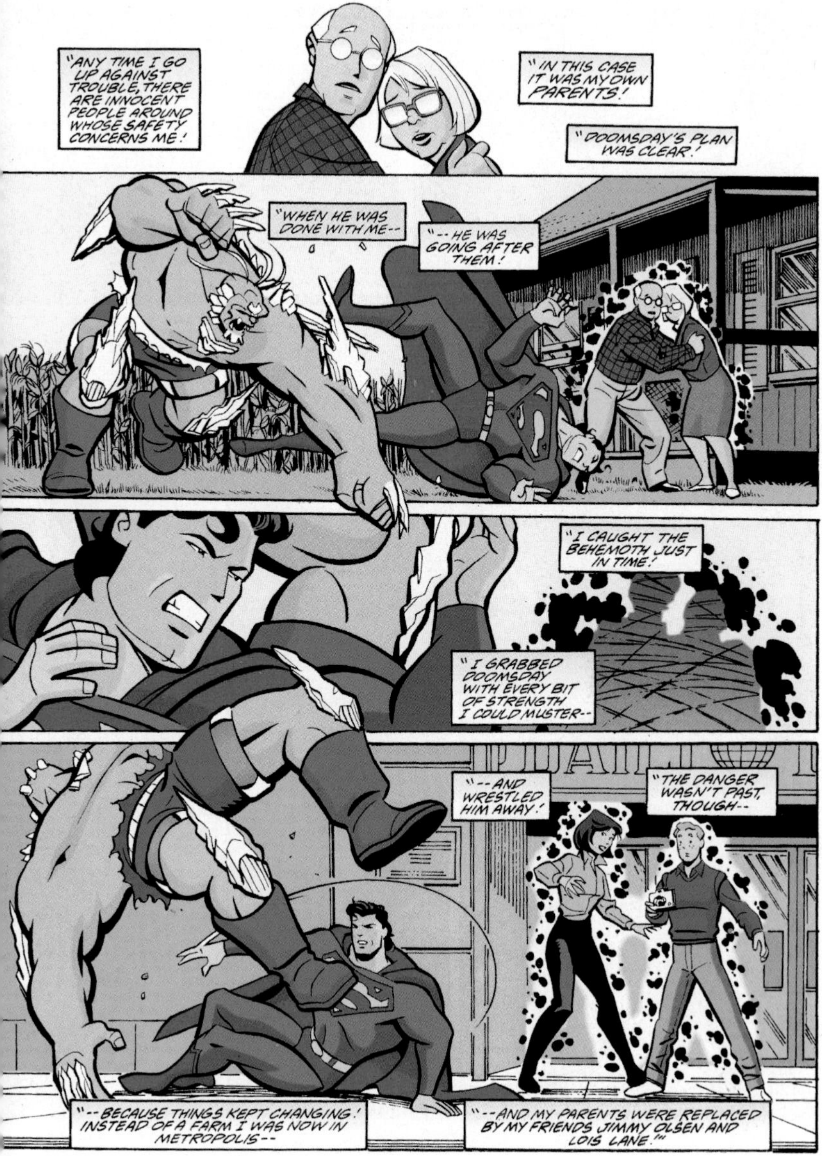
"ANY TIME I GO UP AGAINST TROUBLE, THERE ARE INNOCENT PEOPLE AROUND WHOSE SAFETY CONCERNS ME!
"IN THIS CASE IT WAS MY OWN PARENTS!
"DOOMSDAY'S PLAN WAS CLEAR!
"WHEN HE WAS DONE WITH ME--
"--HE WAS GOING AFTER THEM!
"I CAUGHT THE BEHEMOTH JUST IN TIME!
"I GRABBED DOOMSDAY WITH EVERY BIT OF STRENGTH I COULD MUSTER--
"--AND WRESTLED HIM AWAY!
"THE DANGER WASN'T PAST, THOUGH--
"--BECAUSE THINGS KEPT CHANGING! INSTEAD OF A FARM I WAS NOW IN METROPOLIS--
"--AND MY PARENTS WERE REPLACED BY MY FRIENDS JIMMY OLSEN AND LOIS LANE."

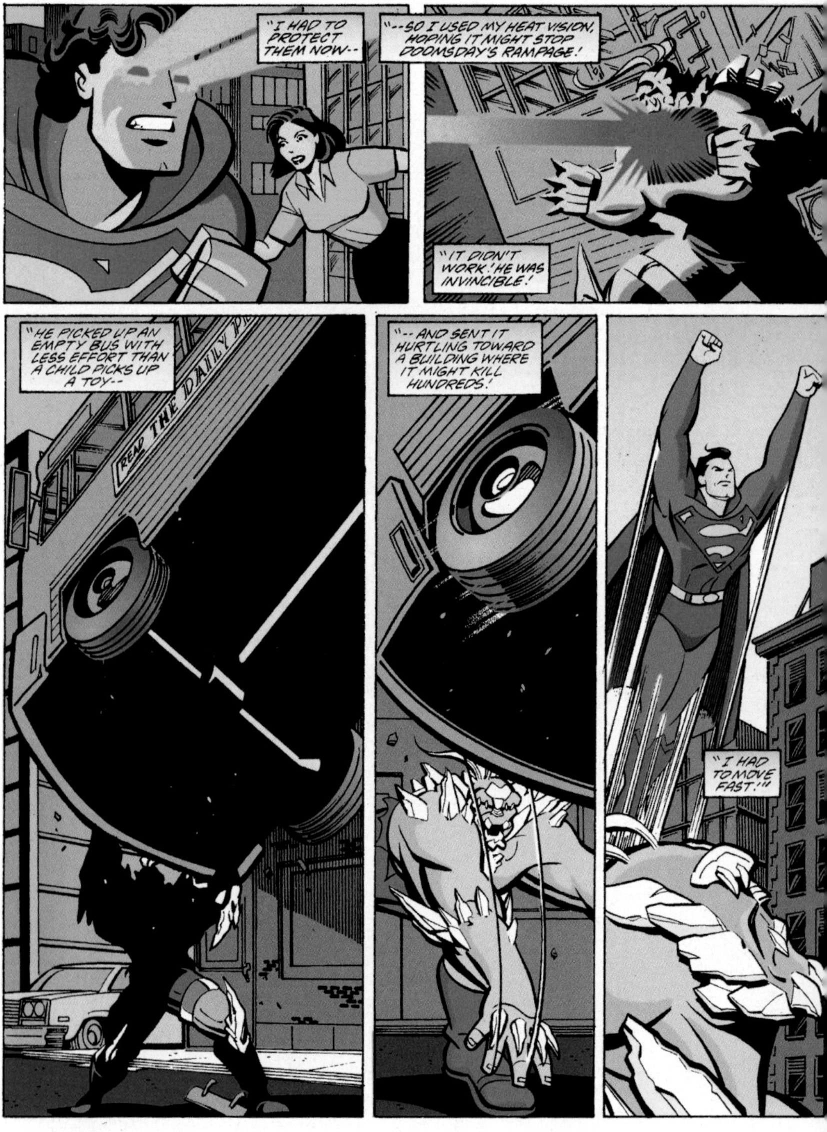
"I HAD TO PROTECT THEM NOW--
"--SO I USED MY HEAT VISION, HOPING IT MIGHT STOP DOOMSDAY'S RAMPAGE!
"IT DIDN'T WORK! HE WAS INVINCIBLE!
"HE PICKED UP AN EMPTY BUS WITH LESS EFFORT THAN A CHILD PICKS UP A TOY--
READ THE DAILY
"--AND SENT IT HURTLING TOWARD A BUILDING WHERE IT MIGHT KILL HUNDREDS!
"I HAD TO MOVE FAST!"

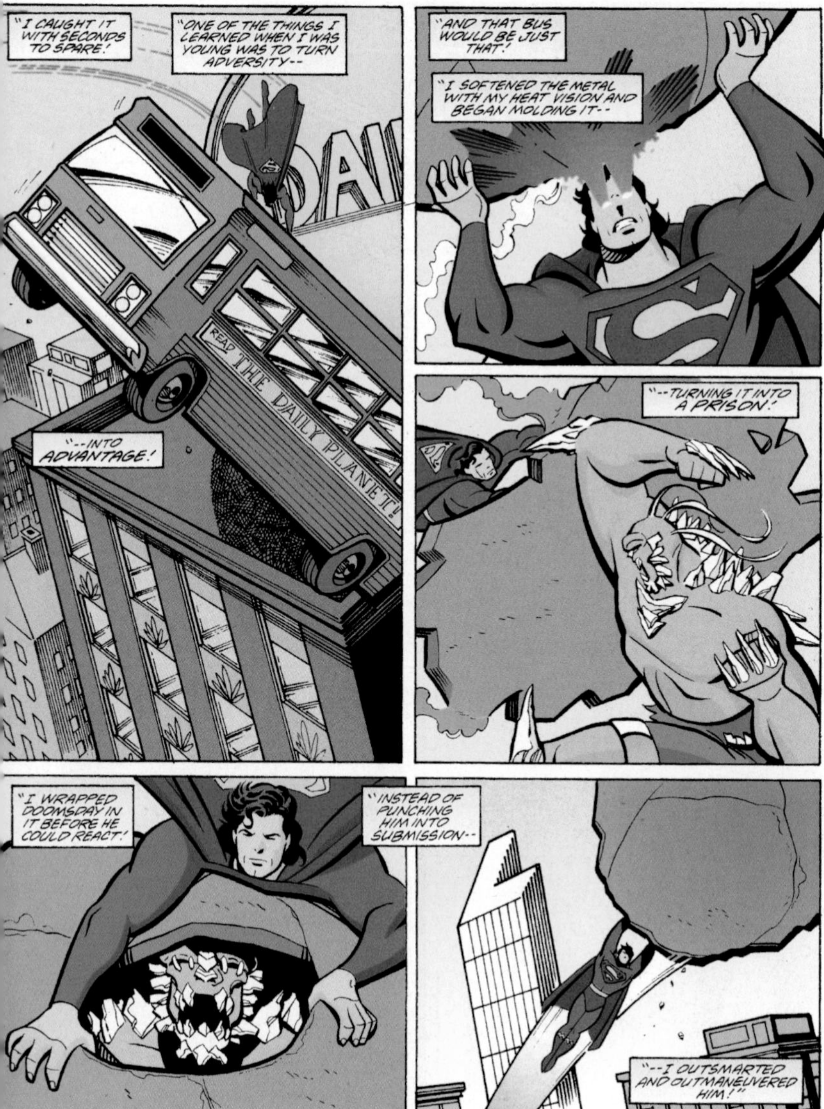
"I CAUGHT IT WITH SECONDS TO SPARE!
"ONE OF THE THINGS I LEARNED WHEN I WAS YOUNG WAS TO TURN ADVERSITY--
"--INTO ADVANTAGE!
READ THE DAILY PLANET!
"AND THAT BUS WOULD BE JUST THAT!
"I SOFTENED THE METAL WITH MY HEAT VISION AND BEGAN MOLDING IT--
"--TURNING IT INTO A PRISON!
"I WRAPPED DOOMSDAY IN IT BEFORE HE COULD REACT!
"INSTEAD OF PUNCHING HIM INTO SUBMISSION--
"--I OUTSMARTED AND OUTMANEUVERED HIM!"

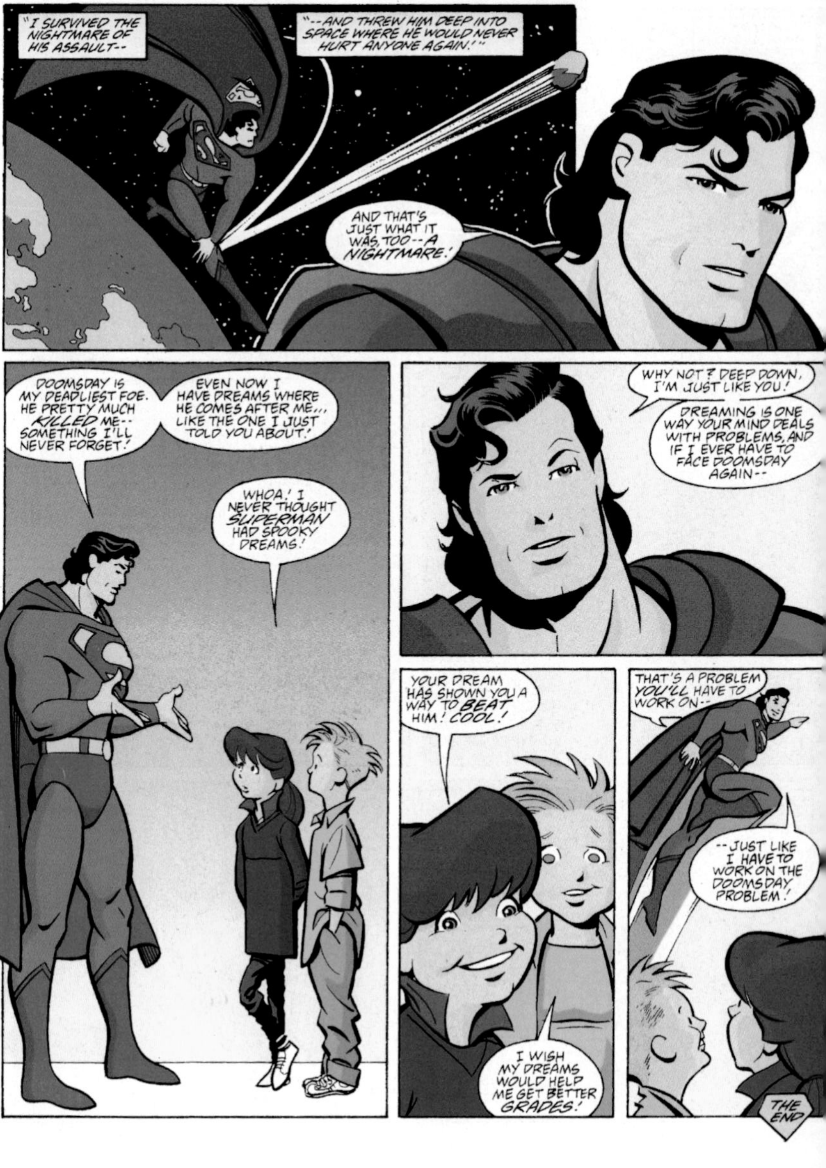
"I SURVIVED THE NIGHTMARE OF HIS ASSAULT--
"--AND THREW HIM DEEP INTO SPACE WHERE HE WOULD NEVER HURT ANYONE AGAIN!"
AND THAT'S JUST WHAT IT WAS, TOO--A NIGHTMARE!
DOOMSDAY IS MY DEADLIEST FOE. HE PRETTY MUCH KILLED ME--SOMETHING I'LL NEVER FORGET!
EVEN NOW I HAVE DREAMS WHERE HE COMES AFTER ME... LIKE THE ONE I JUST TOLD YOU ABOUT!
WHOA! I NEVER THOUGHT SUPERMAN HAD SPOOKY DREAMS!
WHY NOT? DEEP DOWN, I'M JUST LIKE YOU!
DREAMING IS ONE WAY YOUR MIND DEALS WITH PROBLEMS, AND IF I EVER HAVE TO FACE DOOMSDAY AGAIN--
YOUR DREAM HAS SHOWN YOU A WAY TO BEAT HIM! COOL!
I WISH MY DREAMS WOULD HELP ME GET BETTER GRADES!
THAT'S A PROBLEM YOU'LL HAVE TO WORK ON--
--JUST LIKE I HAVE TO WORK ON THE DOOMSDAY PROBLEM!
THE END

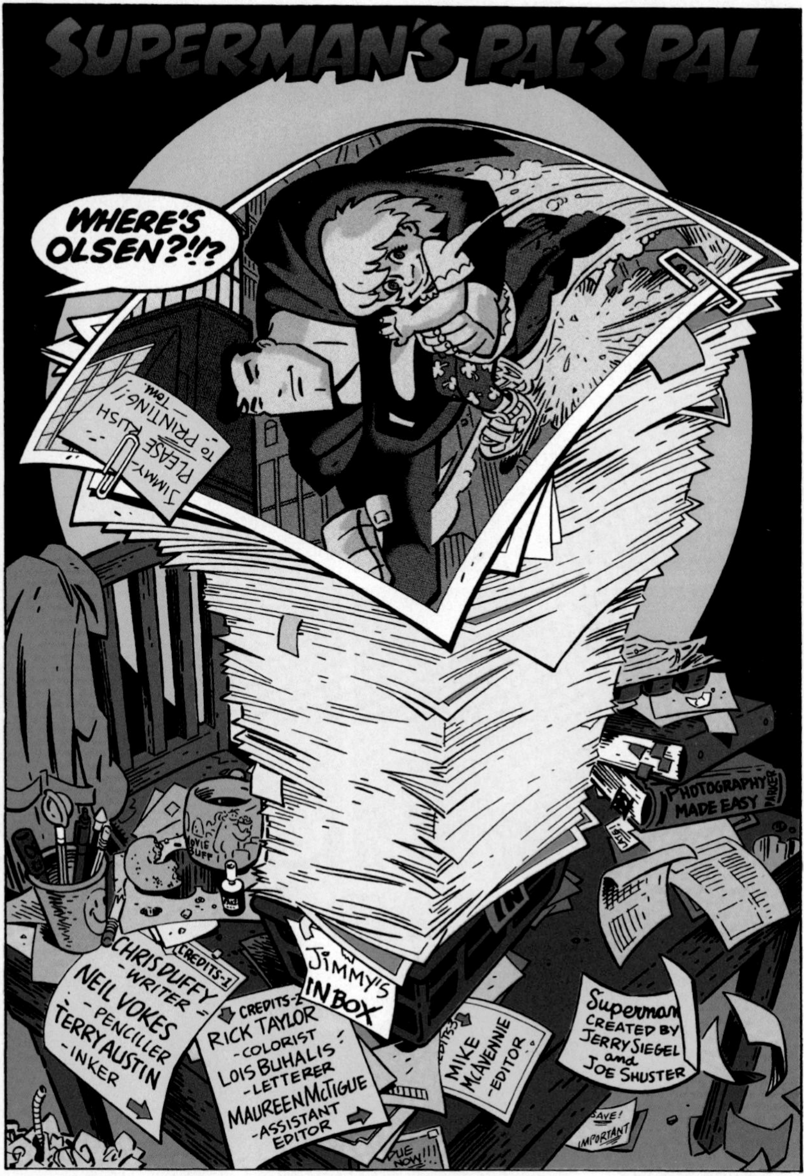

SUPERMAN'S PAL'S PAL
WHERE'S OLSEN?!!?
JIMMY- PLEASE RUSH TO PRINTING!! -TOM.
CREDITS-1
CHRIS DUFFY -WRITER
NEIL VOKES -PENCILLER
TERRY AUSTIN -INKER
CREDITS-2
RICK TAYLOR -COLORIST
LOIS BUHALIS -LETTERER
MAUREEN McTIGUE -ASSISTANT EDITOR
JIMMY'S IN BOX
MIKE McAVENNIE -EDITOR
Superman CREATED BY JERRY SIEGEL and JOE SHUSTER
PHOTOGRAPHY MADE EASY
PARKER
SAVE! IMPORTANT
DUE NOW!!!

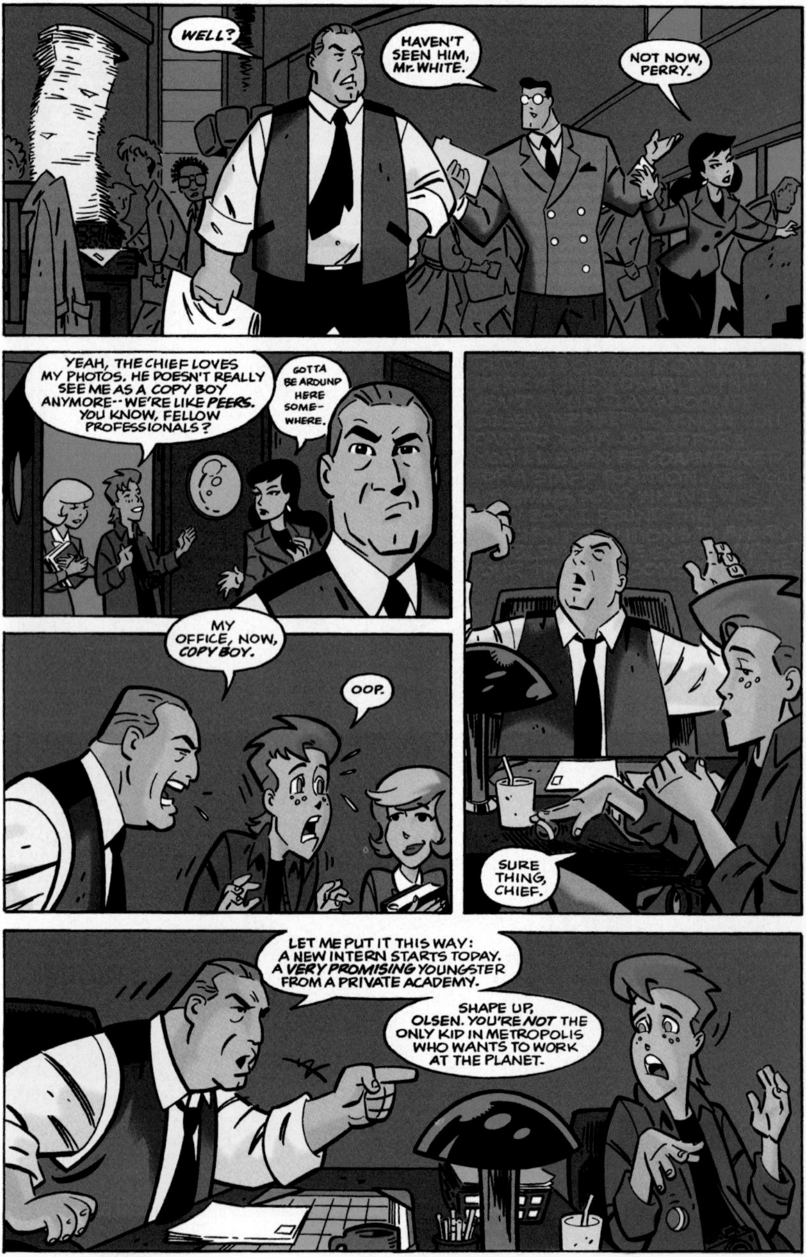
WELL?
HAVEN'T SEEN HIM, Mr. WHITE.
NOT NOW, PERRY.
YEAH, THE CHIEF LOVES MY PHOTOS. HE DOESN'T REALLY SEE ME AS A COPY BOY ANYMORE-- WE'RE LIKE PEERS. YOU KNOW, FELLOW PROFESSIONALS?
GOTTA BE AROUND HERE SOME-WHERE.
MY OFFICE, NOW, COPY BOY.
OOP.
SURE THING, CHIEF.
LET ME PUT IT THIS WAY: A NEW INTERN STARTS TODAY. A VERY PROMISING YOUNGSTER FROM A PRIVATE ACADEMY.
SHAPE UP, OLSEN. YOU'RE NOT THE ONLY KID IN METROPOLIS WHO WANTS TO WORK AT THE PLANET.

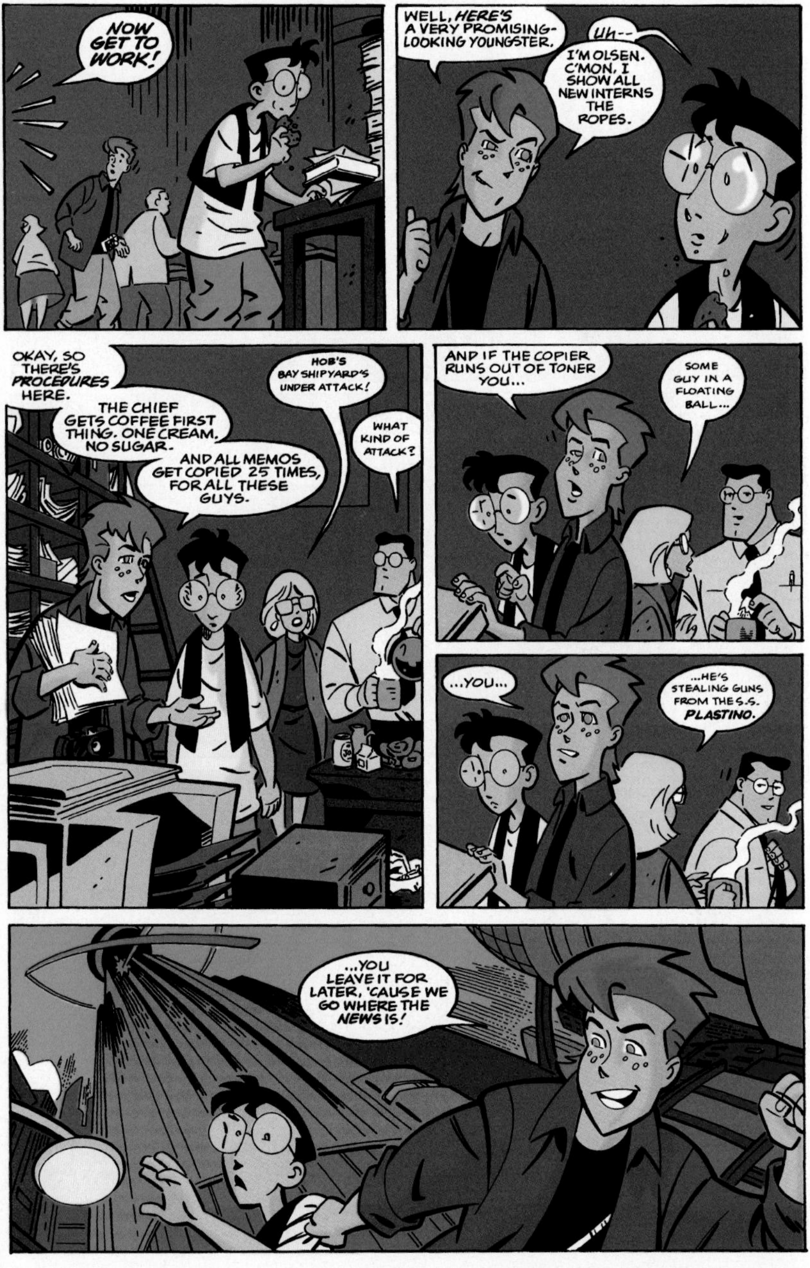
NOW GET TO WORK!
WELL, HERE'S A VERY PROMISING-LOOKING YOUNGSTER.
Uh--
I'M OLSEN. C'MON, I SHOW ALL NEW INTERNS THE ROPES.
OKAY, SO THERE'S PROCEDURES HERE.
THE CHIEF GETS COFFEE FIRST THING. ONE CREAM. NO SUGAR.
AND ALL MEMOS GET COPIED 25 TIMES, FOR ALL THESE GUYS.
HOB'S BAY SHIPYARD'S UNDER ATTACK!
WHAT KIND OF ATTACK?
AND IF THE COPIER RUNS OUT OF TONER YOU...
SOME GUY IN A FLOATING BALL...
...YOU...
...HE'S STEALING GUNS FROM THE S.S. PLASTINO.
...YOU LEAVE IT FOR LATER, 'CAUSE WE GO WHERE THE NEWS IS!

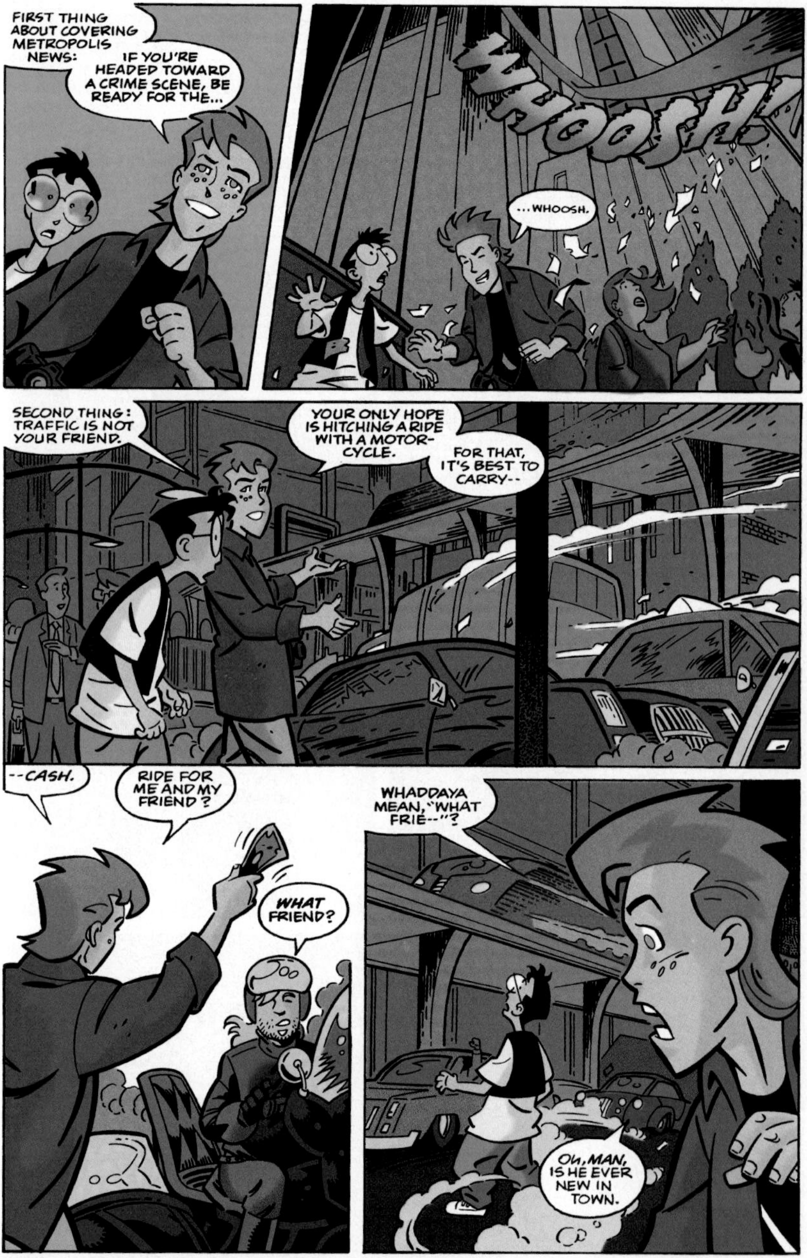
FIRST THING ABOUT COVERING METROPOLIS NEWS: IF YOU'RE HEADED TOWARD A CRIME SCENE, BE READY FOR THE...
WHOOSH!
...WHOOSH.
SECOND THING: TRAFFIC IS NOT YOUR FRIEND.
YOUR ONLY HOPE IS HITCHING A RIDE WITH A MOTOR-CYCLE.
FOR THAT, IT'S BEST TO CARRY--
--CASH.
RIDE FOR ME AND MY FRIEND?
WHAT FRIEND?
WHADDAYA MEAN, "WHAT FRIE--"?
OH, MAN, IS HE EVER NEW IN TOWN.

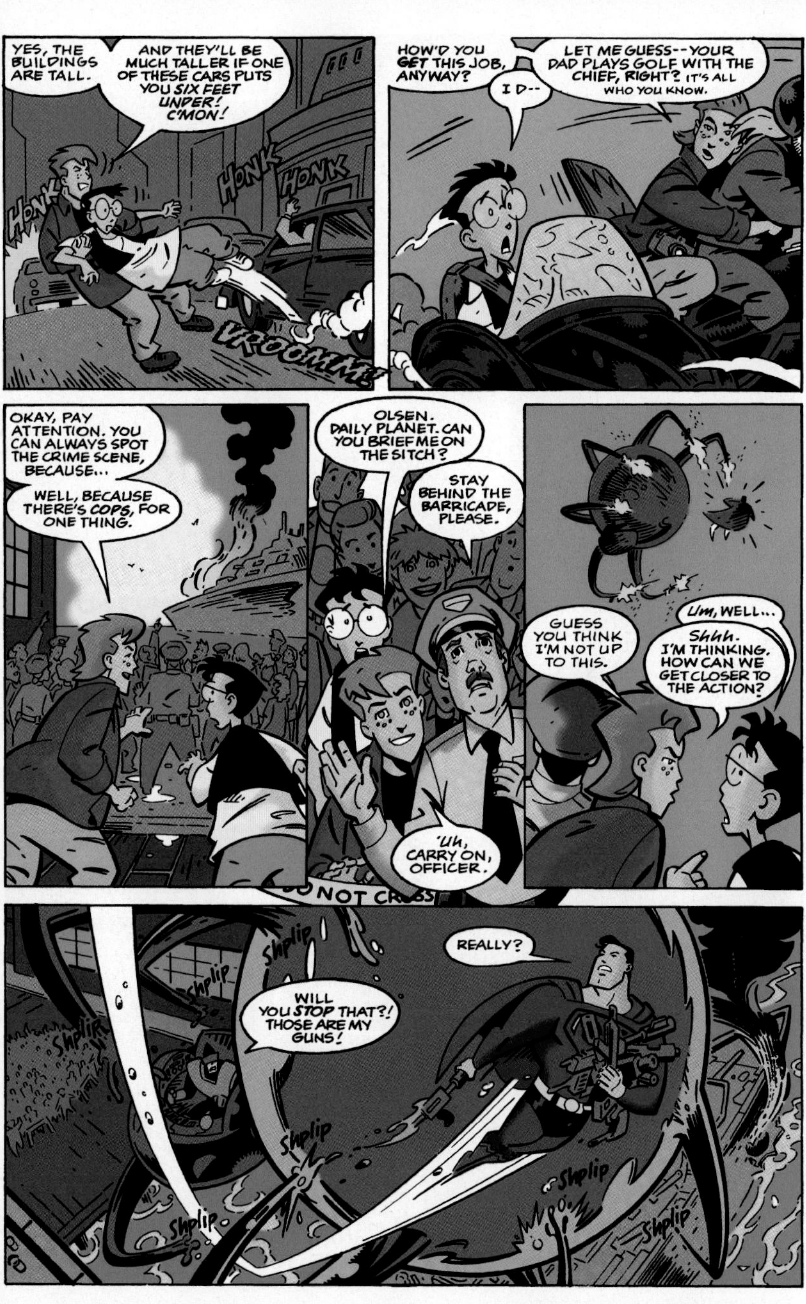
YES, THE BUILDINGS ARE TALL.
AND THEY'LL BE MUCH TALLER IF ONE OF THESE CARS PUTS YOU SIX FEET UNDER! C'MON!
HONK
HONK
HONK
VROOMMM!
HOW'D YOU GET THIS JOB, ANYWAY?
I D--
LET ME GUESS--YOUR DAD PLAYS GOLF WITH THE CHIEF, RIGHT? IT'S ALL WHO YOU KNOW.
OKAY, PAY ATTENTION. YOU CAN ALWAYS SPOT THE CRIME SCENE, BECAUSE...
WELL, BECAUSE THERE'S COPS, FOR ONE THING.
OLSEN. DAILY PLANET. CAN YOU BRIEF ME ON THE SITCH?
STAY BEHIND THE BARRICADE, PLEASE.
'UH, CARRY ON, OFFICER.
DO NOT CROSS
GUESS YOU THINK I'M NOT UP TO THIS.
UM, WELL...
SHHH. I'M THINKING. HOW CAN WE GET CLOSER TO THE ACTION?
SHPLIP
SHPLIP
SHPLIR
REALLY?
WILL YOU STOP THAT?! THOSE ARE MY GUNS!
SHPLIP
SHPLIP
SHPLIP
SHPLIP

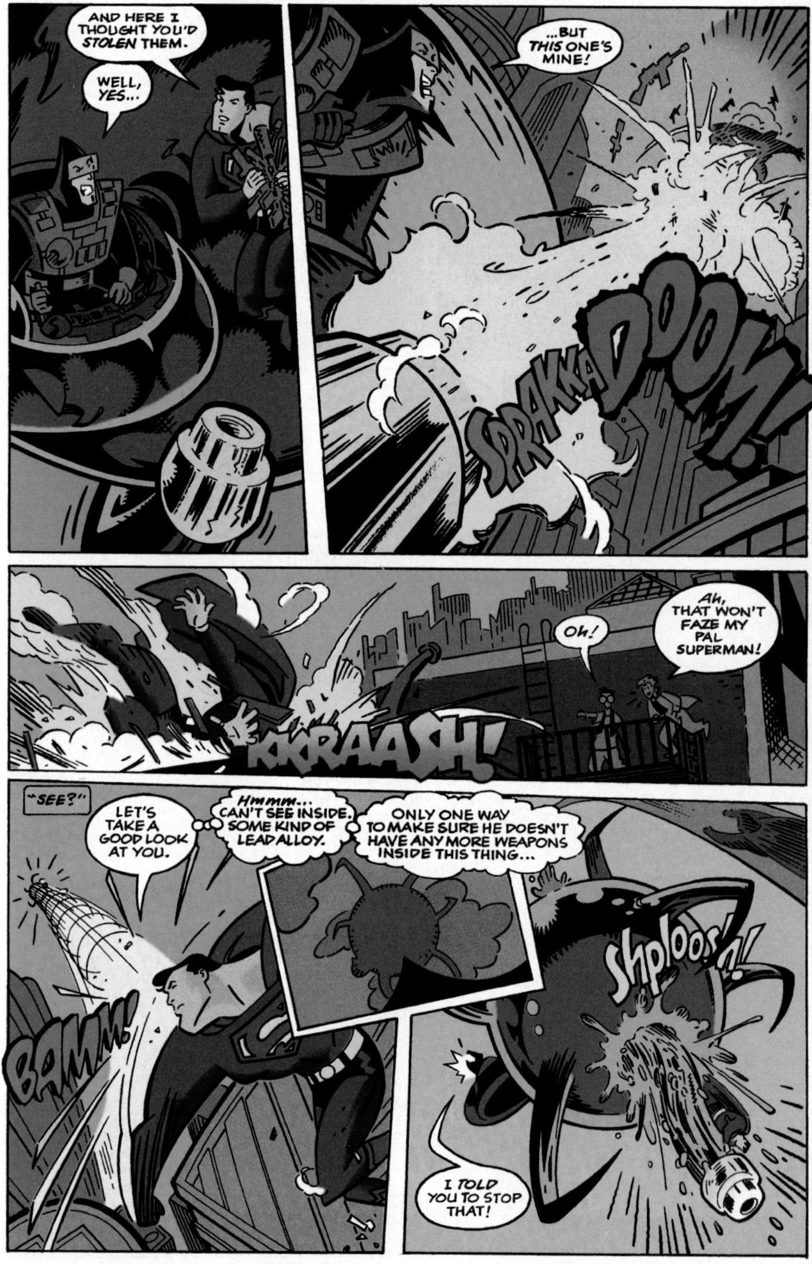
AND HERE I THOUGHT YOU'D STOLEN THEM.
WELL, YES...
...BUT THIS ONE'S MINE!
SPRAKKADOOM!!
Oh!
Ah, THAT WON'T FAZE MY PAL SUPERMAN!
KKRAASH!
"SEE?"
LET'S TAKE A GOOD LOOK AT YOU.
Hmmm... CAN'T SEE INSIDE. SOME KIND OF LEAD ALLOY.
ONLY ONE WAY TO MAKE SURE HE DOESN'T HAVE ANY MORE WEAPONS INSIDE THIS THING...
BAMM!
Shploosh!
I TOLD YOU TO STOP THAT!

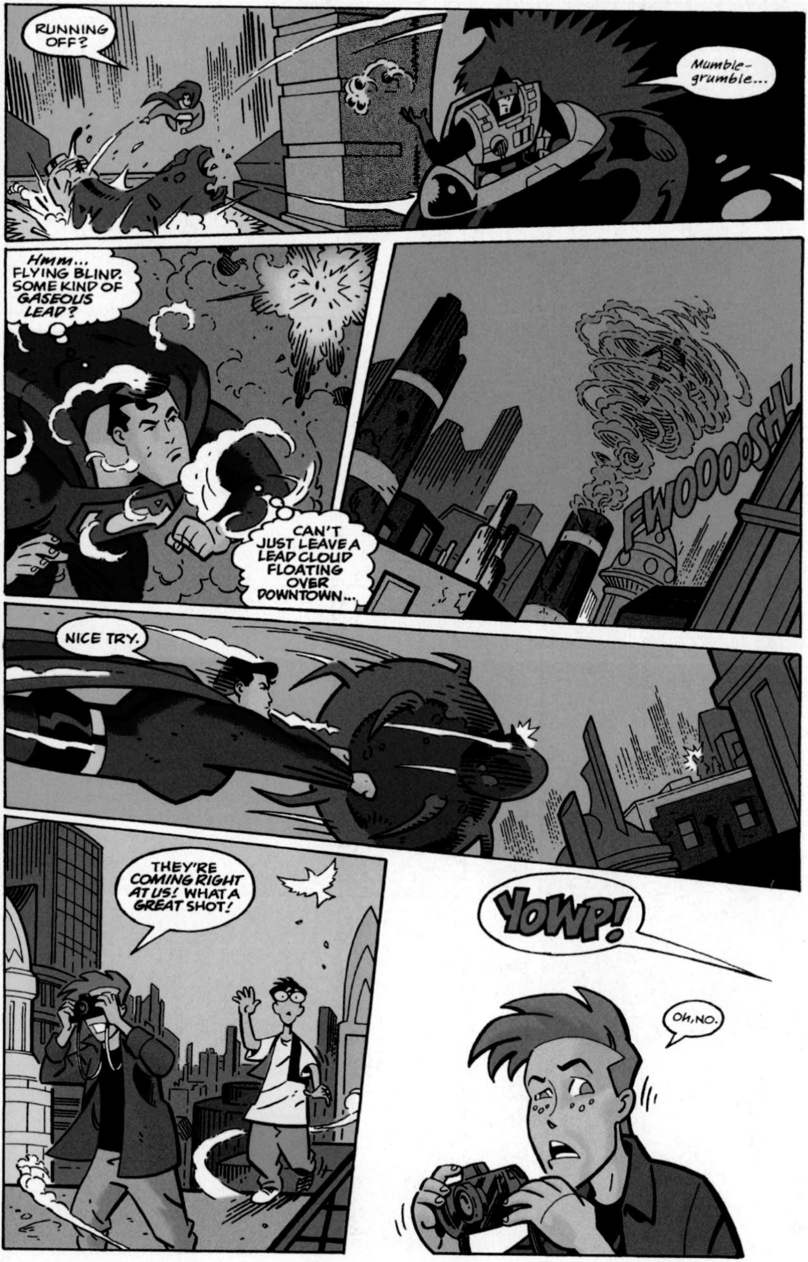
RUNNING OFF?
Mumble-grumble...
Hmm... FLYING BLIND. SOME KIND OF GASEOUS LEAD?
CAN'T JUST LEAVE A LEAD CLOUD FLOATING OVER DOWNTOWN...
FWOOOOOSH!
NICE TRY.
THEY'RE COMING RIGHT AT US! WHAT A GREAT SHOT!
YOWP!
OH, NO.

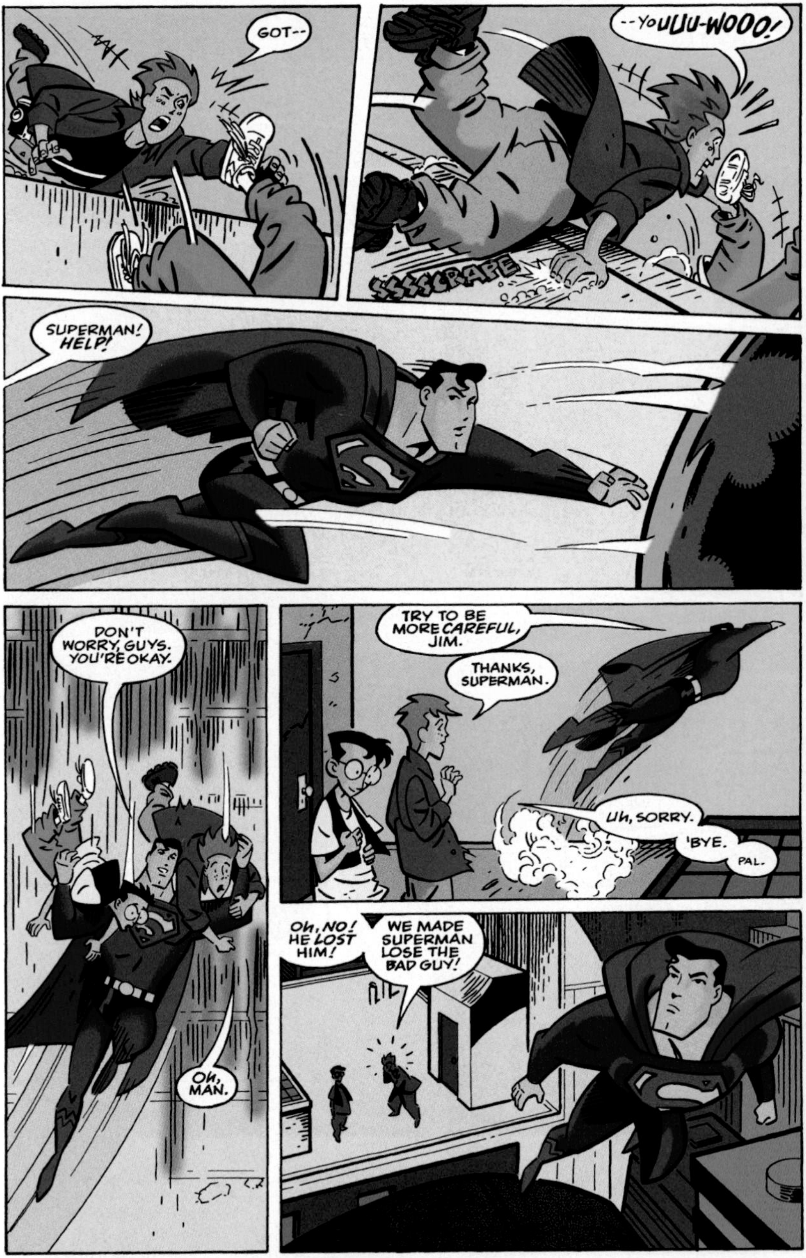
GOT--
--YOUUU-WOOO!
SSSSCRAPE
SUPERMAN! HELP!
DON'T WORRY, GUYS. YOU'RE OKAY.
OH, MAN.
TRY TO BE MORE CAREFUL, JIM.
THANKS, SUPERMAN.
UH, SORRY.
'BYE.
PAL.
OH, NO! HE LOST HIM!
WE MADE SUPERMAN LOSE THE BAD GUY!

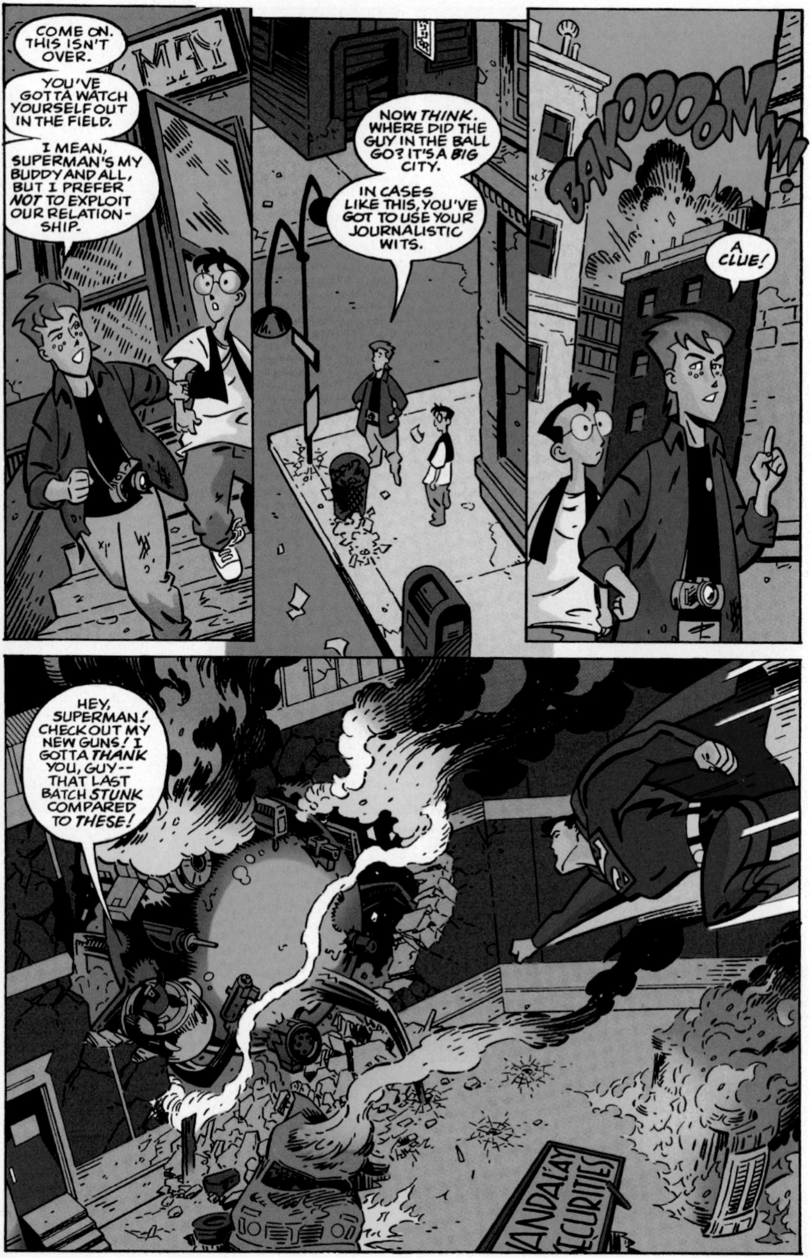
COME ON. THIS ISN'T OVER.
YOU'VE GOTTA WATCH YOURSELF OUT IN THE FIELD.
I MEAN, SUPERMAN'S MY BUDDY AND ALL, BUT I PREFER NOT TO EXPLOIT OUR RELATIONSHIP.
NOW THINK. WHERE DID THE GUY IN THE BALL GO? IT'S A BIG CITY.
IN CASES LIKE THIS, YOU'VE GOT TO USE YOUR JOURNALISTIC WITS.
BAKOOOOOM!!
A CLUE!
HEY, SUPERMAN! CHECK OUT MY NEW GUNS! I GOTTA THANK YOU, GUY-- THAT LAST BATCH STUNK COMPARED TO THESE!
VANDALAY SECURITIES

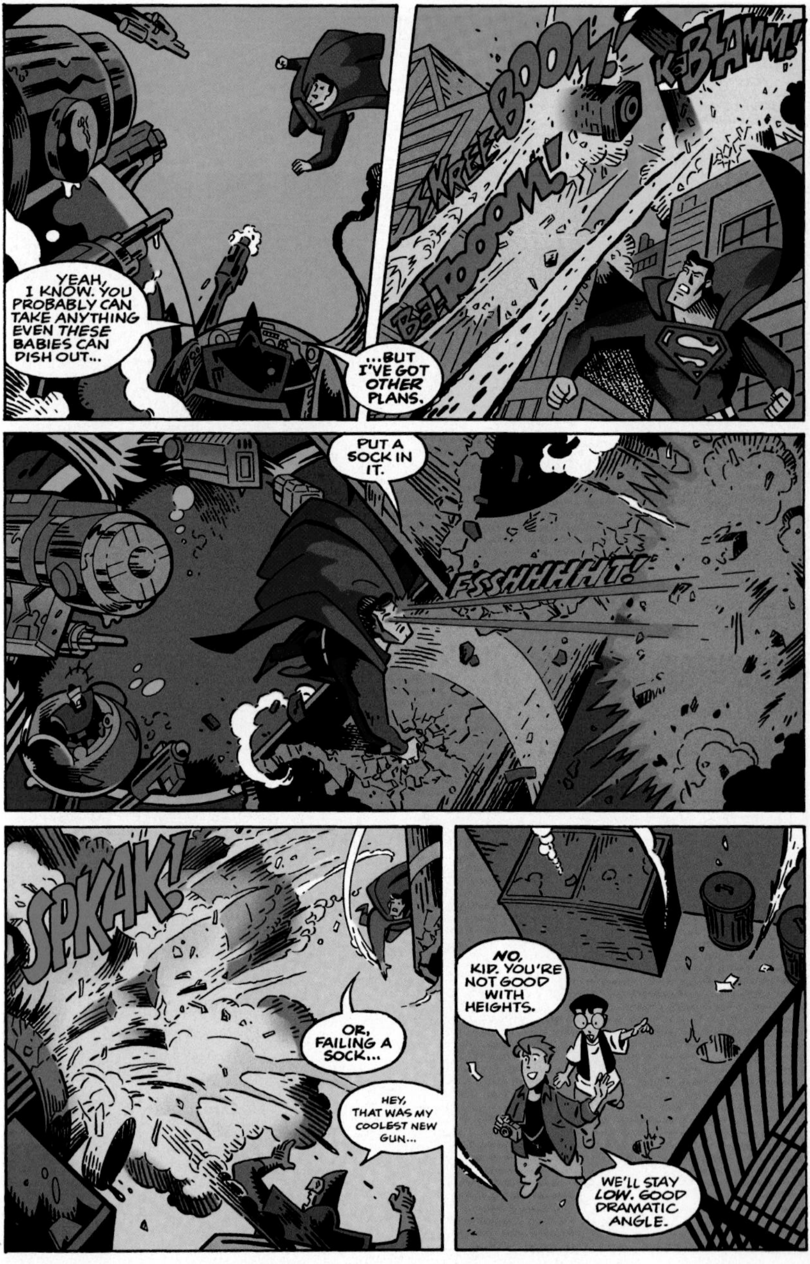
YEAH, I KNOW. YOU PROBABLY CAN TAKE ANYTHING EVEN THESE BABIES CAN DISH OUT...
...BUT I'VE GOT OTHER PLANS.
SKREE-BOOM!
K-BLAMM!
BE-TOOOOM!
PUT A SOCK IN IT.
FSSHHHHHT!
SPKAK!
OR, FAILING A SOCK...
HEY, THAT WAS MY COOLEST NEW GUN...
NO, KID. YOU'RE NOT GOOD WITH HEIGHTS.
WE'LL STAY LOW. GOOD DRAMATIC ANGLE.

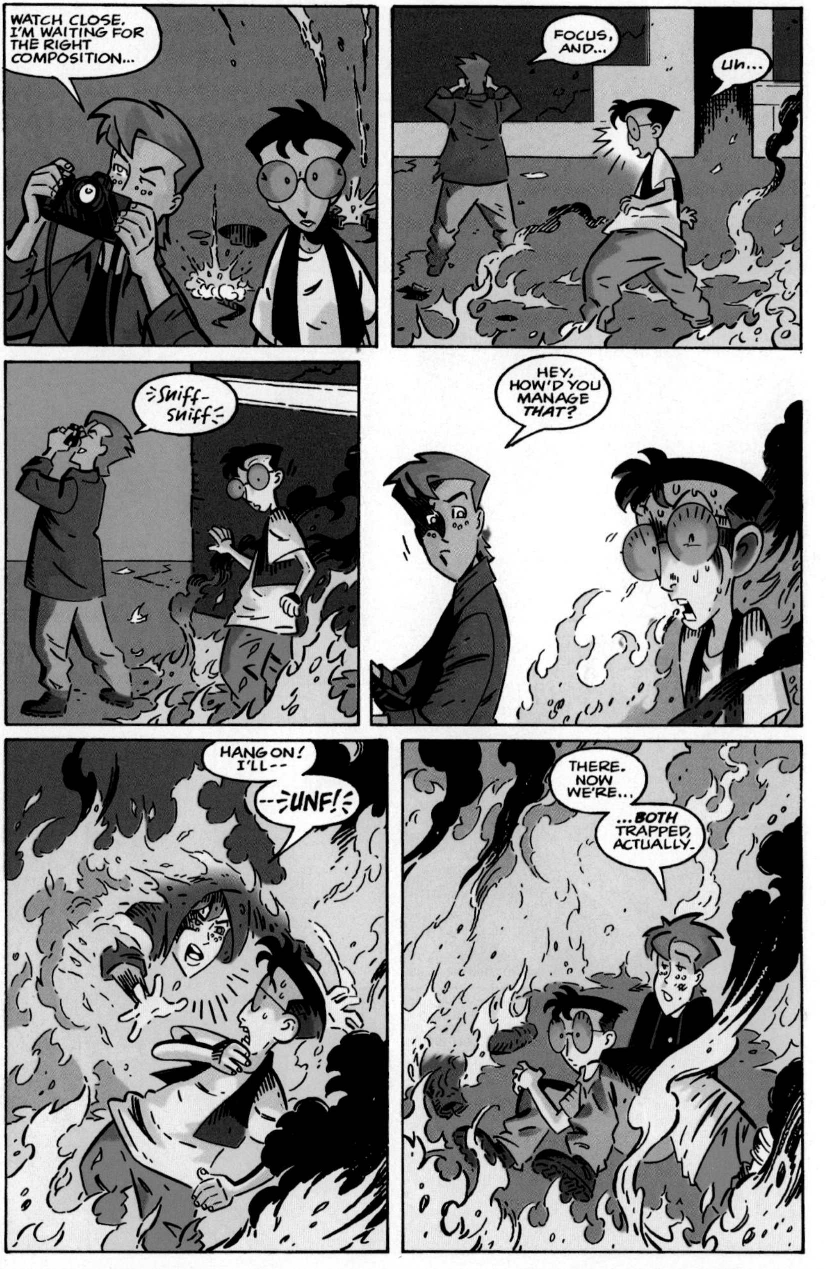
WATCH CLOSE. I'M WAITING FOR THE RIGHT COMPOSITION...
FOCUS, AND...
Uh...
SNIFF-SNIFF
HEY, HOW'D YOU MANAGE *THAT*?
HANG ON! I'LL--
--UNF!
THERE. NOW WE'RE...
...*BOTH* TRAPPED, ACTUALLY.

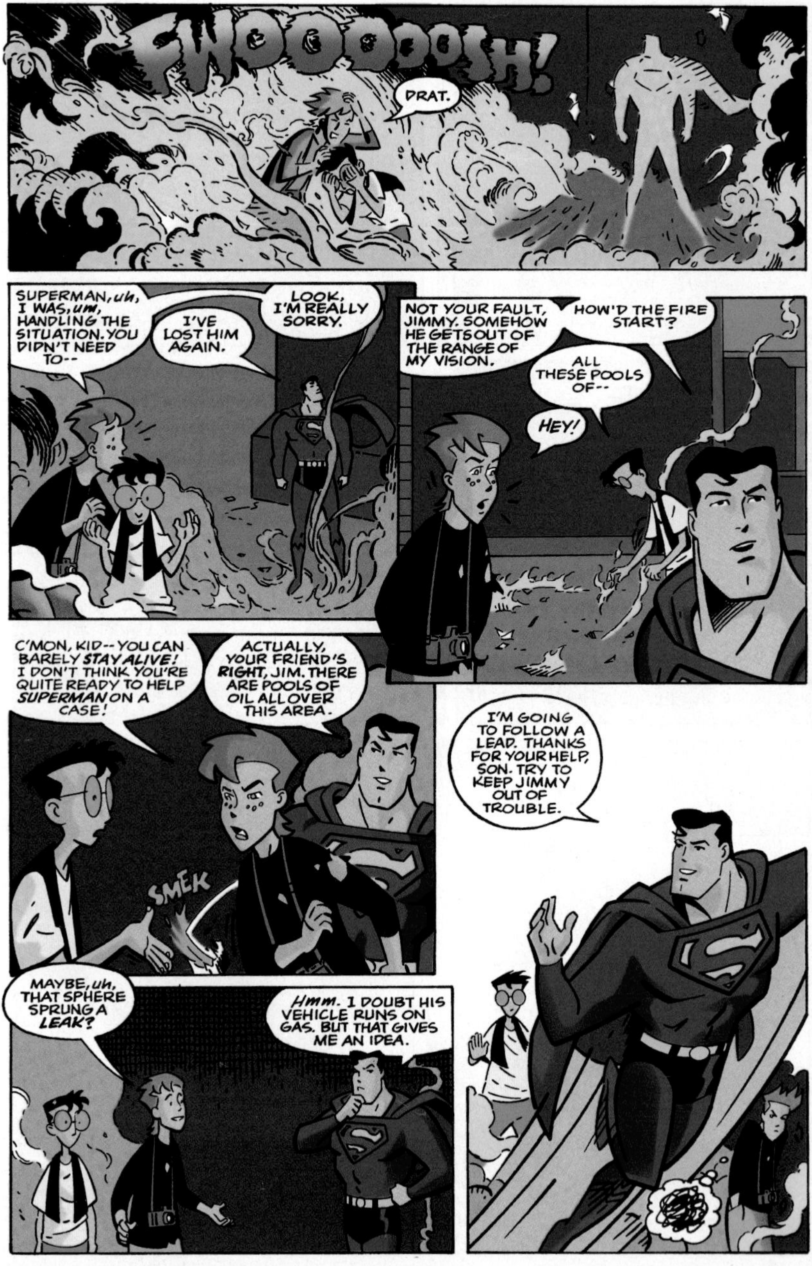
FWOOOOOSH!
DRAT.
SUPERMAN, uh, I WAS, um, HANDLING THE SITUATION. YOU DIDN'T NEED TO--
I'VE LOST HIM AGAIN.
LOOK, I'M REALLY SORRY.
NOT YOUR FAULT, JIMMY. SOMEHOW HE GETS OUT OF THE RANGE OF MY VISION.
HOW'D THE FIRE START?
ALL THESE POOLS OF--
HEY!
C'MON, KID-- YOU CAN BARELY STAY ALIVE! I DON'T THINK YOU'RE QUITE READY TO HELP SUPERMAN ON A CASE!
ACTUALLY, YOUR FRIEND'S RIGHT, JIM. THERE ARE POOLS OF OIL ALL OVER THIS AREA.
SMEK
I'M GOING TO FOLLOW A LEAD. THANKS FOR YOUR HELP, SON. TRY TO KEEP JIMMY OUT OF TROUBLE.
MAYBE, uh, THAT SPHERE SPRUNG A LEAK?
Hmm. I DOUBT HIS VEHICLE RUNS ON GAS. BUT THAT GIVES ME AN IDEA.

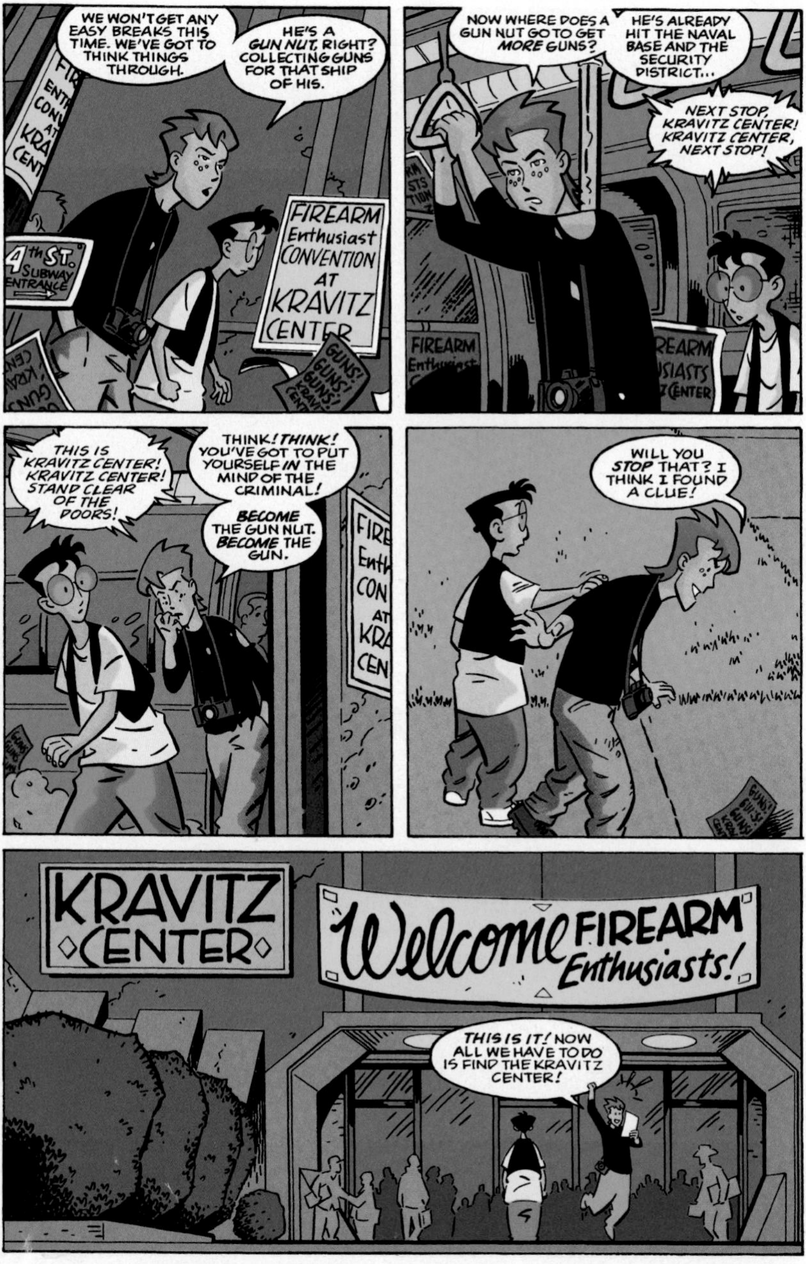
WE WON'T GET ANY EASY BREAKS THIS TIME. WE'VE GOT TO THINK THINGS THROUGH.
HE'S A GUN NUT, RIGHT? COLLECTING GUNS FOR THAT SHIP OF HIS.
4th ST. SUBWAY ENTRANCE
FIREARM Enthusiast CONVENTION AT KRAVITZ CENTER
NOW WHERE DOES A GUN NUT GO TO GET MORE GUNS?
HE'S ALREADY HIT THE NAVAL BASE AND THE SECURITY DISTRICT...
NEXT STOP, KRAVITZ CENTER! KRAVITZ CENTER, NEXT STOP!
THIS IS KRAVITZ CENTER! KRAVITZ CENTER! STAND CLEAR OF THE DOORS!
THINK! THINK! YOU'VE GOT TO PUT YOURSELF IN THE MIND OF THE CRIMINAL!
BECOME THE GUN NUT. BECOME THE GUN.
WILL YOU STOP THAT? I THINK I FOUND A CLUE!
KRAVITZ CENTER
Welcome FIREARM Enthusiasts!
THIS IS IT! NOW ALL WE HAVE TO DO IS FIND THE KRAVITZ CENTER!

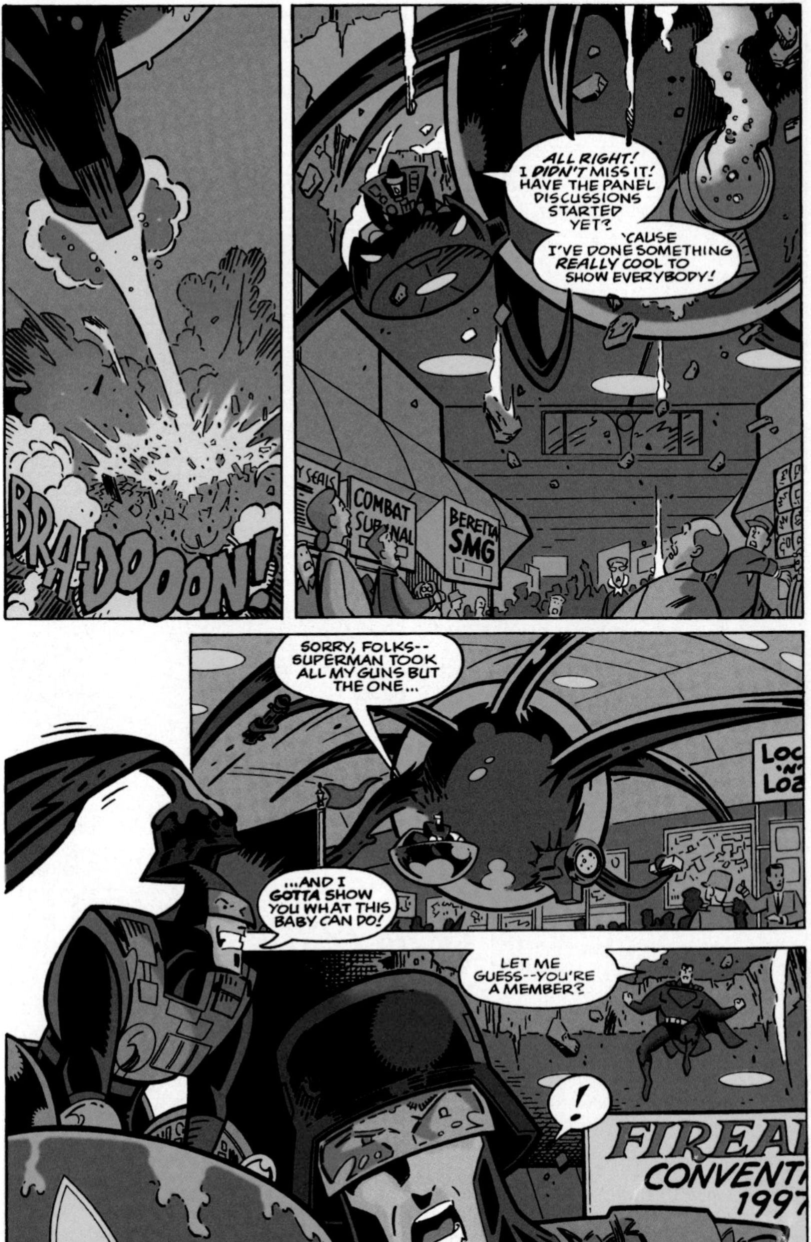
BRA-DOOOON!
ALL RIGHT! I DIDN'T MISS IT! HAVE THE PANEL DISCUSSIONS STARTED YET?
'CAUSE I'VE DONE SOMETHING REALLY COOL TO SHOW EVERYBODY!
COMBAT SURVIVAL
BERETTA SMG
SORRY, FOLKS-- SUPERMAN TOOK ALL MY GUNS BUT THE ONE...
...AND I GOTTA SHOW YOU WHAT THIS BABY CAN DO!
LET ME GUESS--YOU'RE A MEMBER?
!
CONVENT
199

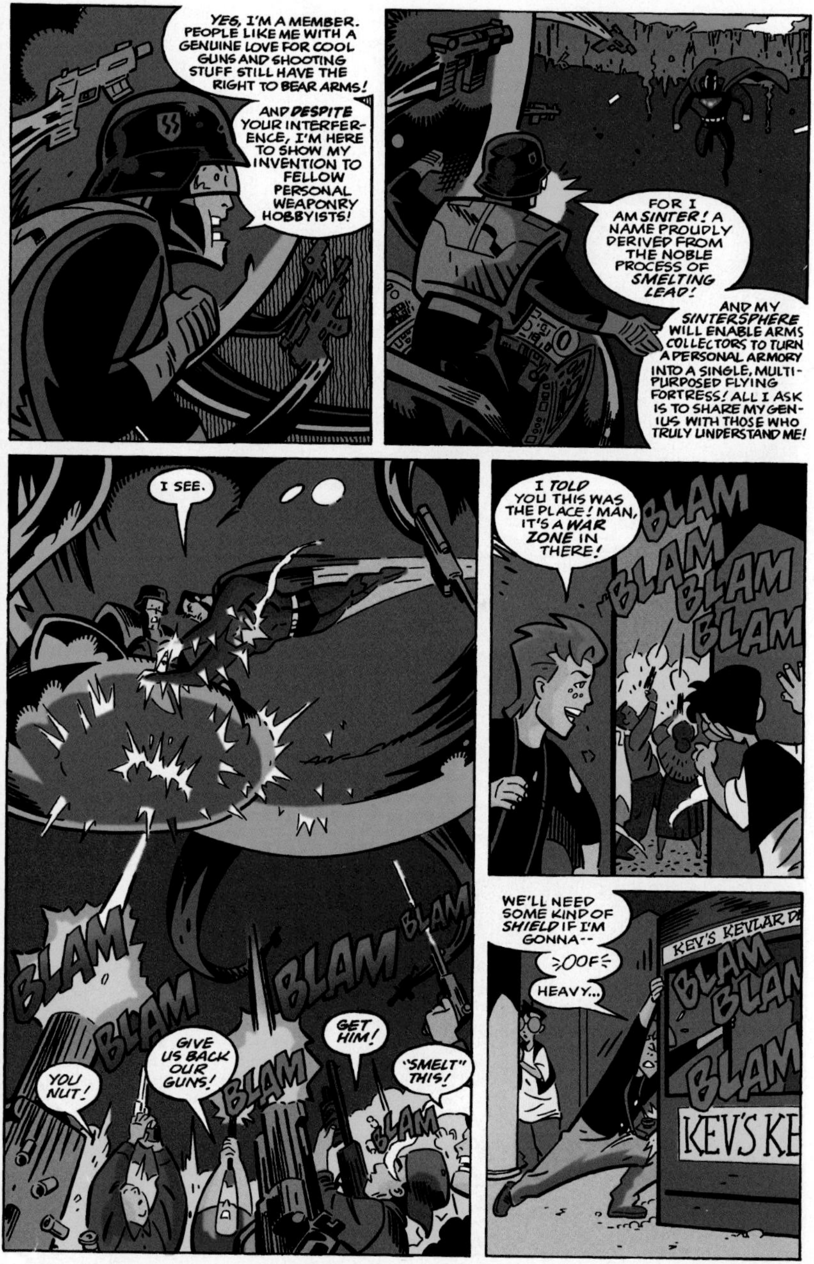
YES, I'M A MEMBER. PEOPLE LIKE ME WITH A GENUINE LOVE FOR COOL GUNS AND SHOOTING STUFF STILL HAVE THE RIGHT TO BEAR ARMS!
AND DESPITE YOUR INTERFERENCE, I'M HERE TO SHOW MY INVENTION TO FELLOW PERSONAL WEAPONRY HOBBYISTS!
FOR I AM SINTER! A NAME PROUDLY DERIVED FROM THE NOBLE PROCESS OF SMELTING LEAD!
AND MY SINTERSPHERE WILL ENABLE ARMS COLLECTORS TO TURN A PERSONAL ARMORY INTO A SINGLE, MULTI-PURPOSED FLYING FORTRESS! ALL I ASK IS TO SHARE MY GENIUS WITH THOSE WHO TRULY UNDERSTAND ME!
I SEE.
BLAM
BLAM
BLAM
BLAM
YOU NUT!
GIVE US BACK OUR GUNS!
BLAM
GET HIM!
"SMELT" THIS!
BLAM
I TOLD YOU THIS WAS THE PLACE! MAN, IT'S A WAR ZONE IN THERE!
BLAM
BLAM
BLAM
BLAM
BLAM
WE'LL NEED SOME KIND OF SHIELD IF I'M GONNA--
OOF
HEAVY...
KEV'S KEVLAR D
BLAM
BLAM
BLAM
KEV'S KE

BLAM BLAM BLAM BLAM

HOLD MY CAMERA FOR A SECOND.

STOP WASTING FILM!

LOOK, IF YOU'RE GONNA LEARN *ANYTHING,* YOU HAVE TO HELP ME, OKAY? JUST DON'T *TOUCH* ANYTHING, ALL RIGHT?

BLAM BLAM

Pckzzt Pckzzt Pckzzt

I JUST WANNA-- *HEY!*

OKA-

HEY, WHY'D ALL THE FIRING STOP?

*Ahh,* SUPERMAN BUSTED THE GUY'S GUNS AND CHASED HIM OFF.

I BETTER GET *REIMBURSED* FOR MY GUNS, THAT'S ALL I CAN SAY.

HAPP IS A LUZ

SHOC EM!

YOU TURNED THEM ALL AGAINST ME!

YOU'LL PAY! METROPOLIS WILL PAY!

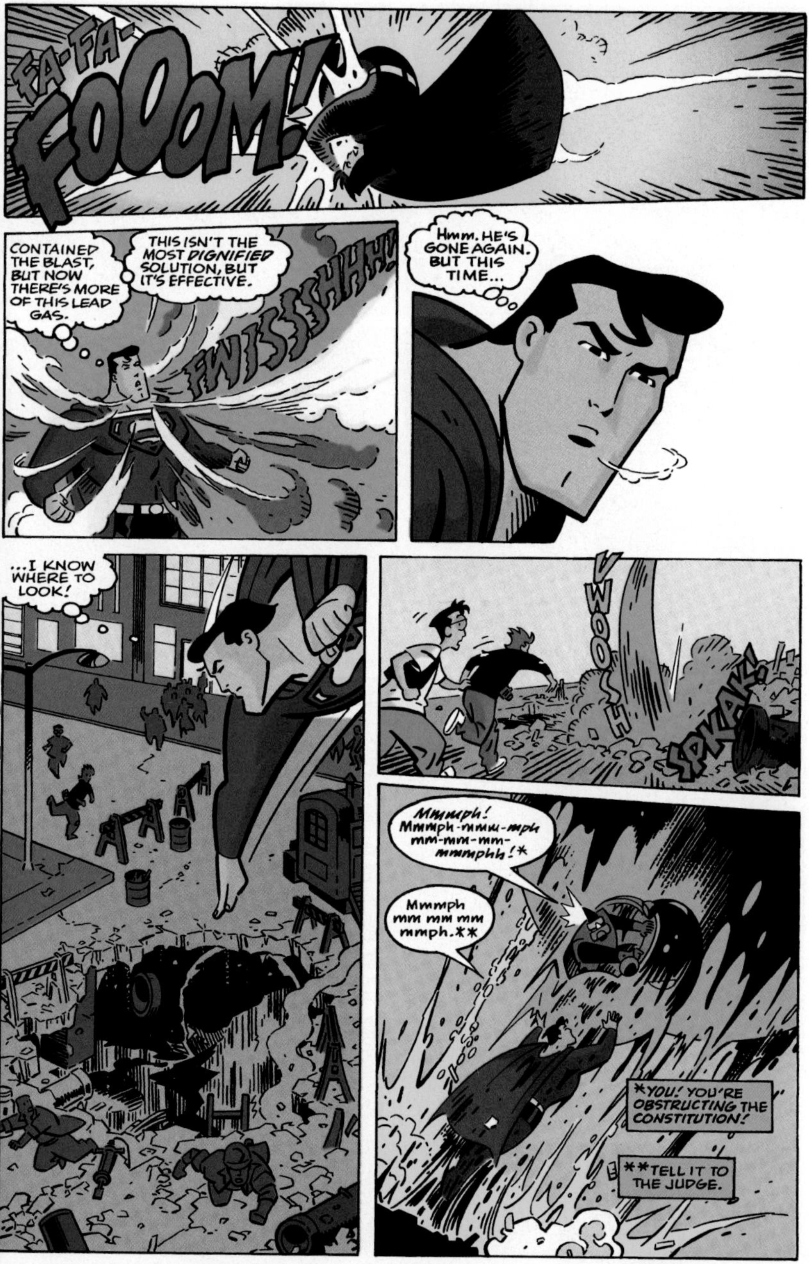

FA-FA-FOOOM!!
CONTAINED THE BLAST, BUT NOW THERE'S MORE OF THIS LEAD GAS.
THIS ISN'T THE MOST DIGNIFIED SOLUTION, BUT IT'S EFFECTIVE.
FWISSSSHHH!
Hmm. HE'S GONE AGAIN. BUT THIS TIME...
...I KNOW WHERE TO LOOK!
VWOOOSH
SPKAK!!
Mmmph! Mmmph-mmm-mph mm-mm-mm-mmmphh!*
Mmmph mm mm mm mmph.**
*YOU! YOU'RE OBSTRUCTING THE CONSTITUTION!
**TELL IT TO THE JUDGE.

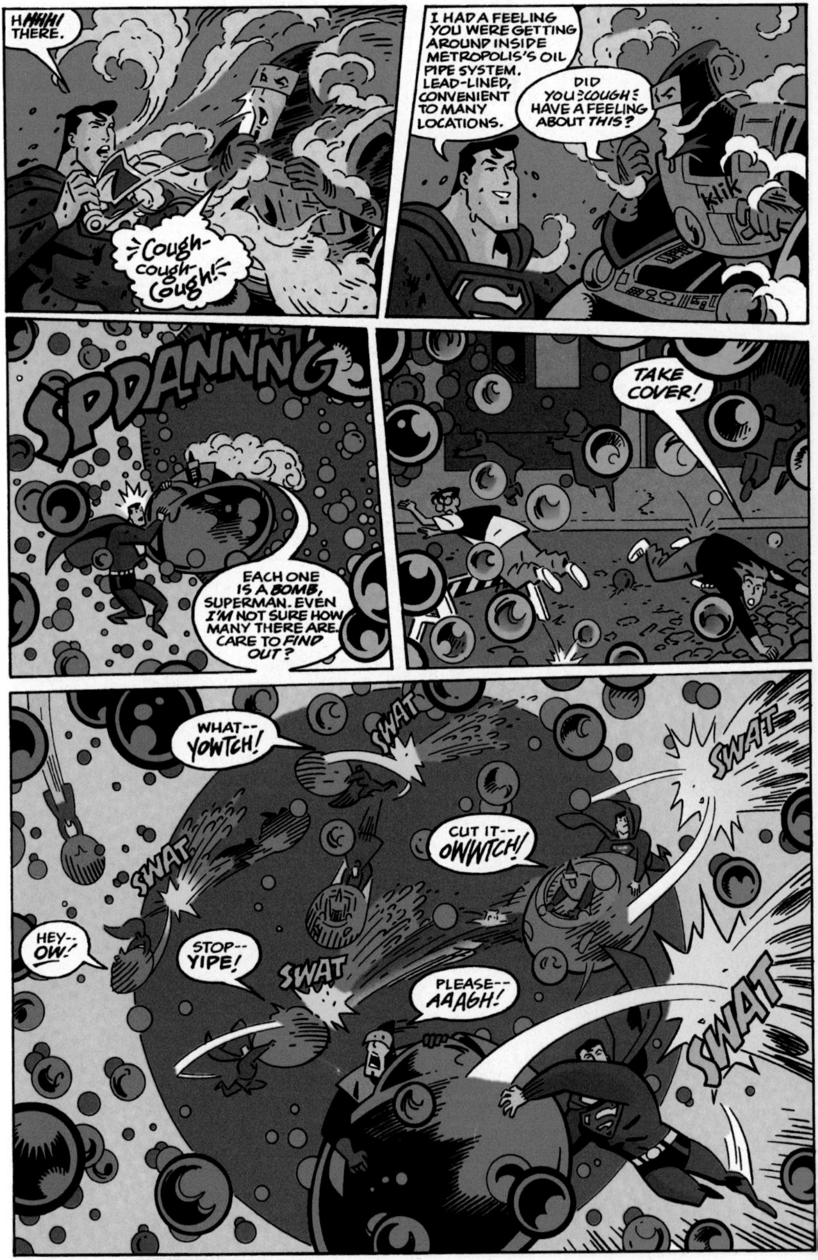

HHHH! THERE.
Cough-cough-Cough!
I HAD A FEELING YOU WERE GETTING AROUND INSIDE METROPOLIS'S OIL PIPE SYSTEM. LEAD-LINED, CONVENIENT TO MANY LOCATIONS.
DID YOU COUGH HAVE A FEELING ABOUT THIS?
klik
SPDANNNG
EACH ONE IS A BOMB, SUPERMAN. EVEN I'M NOT SURE HOW MANY THERE ARE. CARE TO FIND OUT?
TAKE COVER!
WHAT-- YOWTCH!
SWAT
SWAT
CUT IT-- OWWTCH!
SWAT
HEY-- OW!
STOP-- YIPE!
SWAT
PLEASE-- AAAGH!
SWAT

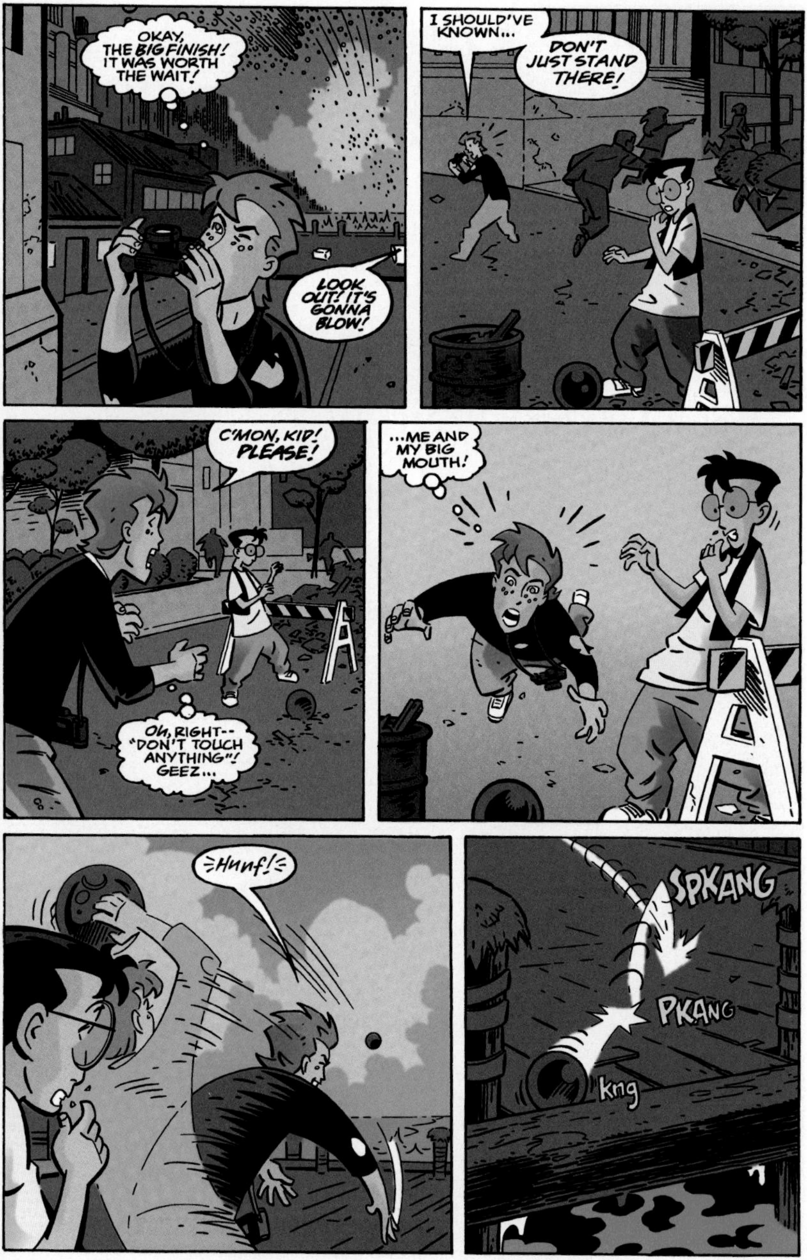
OKAY, THE BIG FINISH! IT WAS WORTH THE WAIT!
LOOK OUT! IT'S GONNA BLOW!
I SHOULD'VE KNOWN...
DON'T JUST STAND THERE!
C'MON, KID! PLEASE!
OH, RIGHT-- "DON'T TOUCH ANYTHING"! GEEZ...
...ME AND MY BIG MOUTH!
Hunf!
SPKANG
PKANG
kng

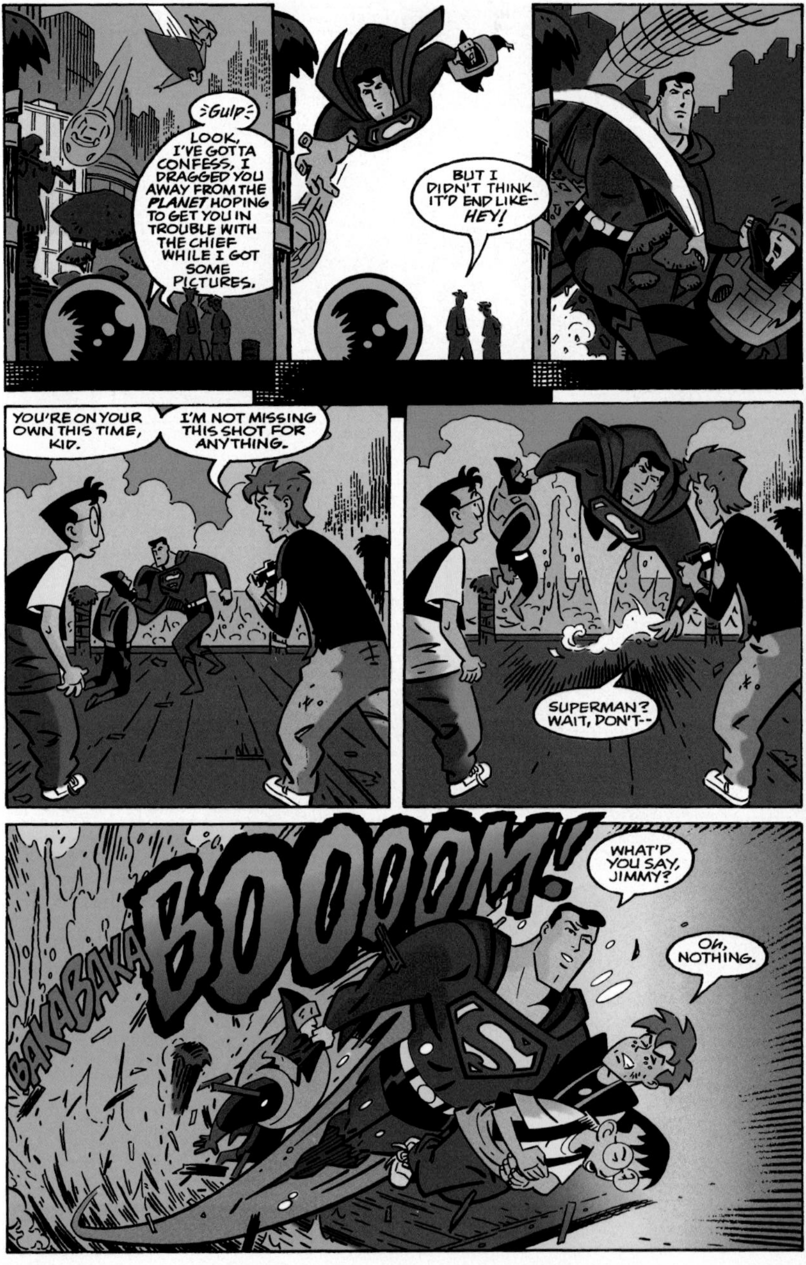
GULP
LOOK, I'VE GOTTA CONFESS, I DRAGGED YOU AWAY FROM THE PLANET HOPING TO GET YOU IN TROUBLE WITH THE CHIEF WHILE I GOT SOME PICTURES.
BUT I DIDN'T THINK IT'D END LIKE-- HEY!
YOU'RE ON YOUR OWN THIS TIME, KID.
I'M NOT MISSING THIS SHOT FOR ANYTHING.
SUPERMAN? WAIT, DON'T--
BAKABAKA BOOOOM!
WHAT'D YOU SAY, JIMMY?
OH, NOTHING.

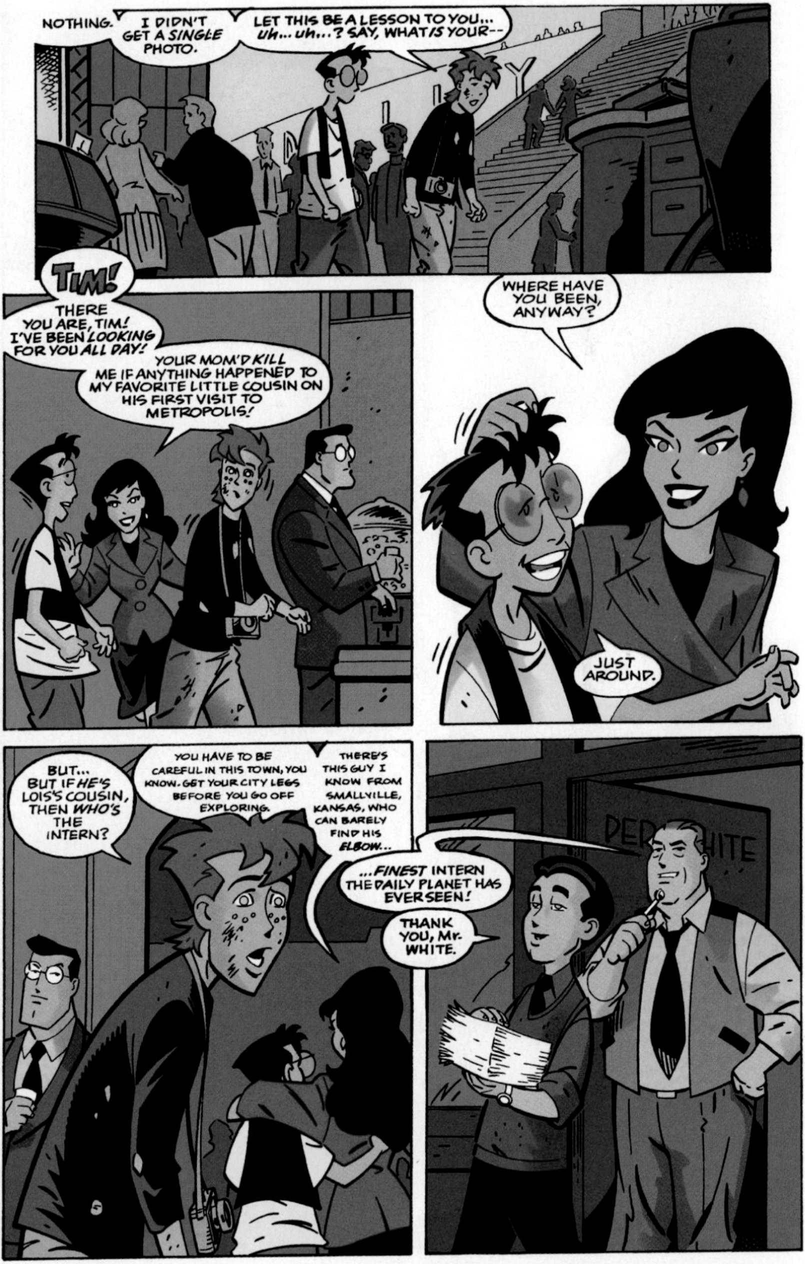
NOTHING.
I DIDN'T GET A *SINGLE* PHOTO.
LET THIS BE A LESSON TO YOU... *uh... uh...?* SAY, WHAT *IS* YOUR--
TIM!
THERE YOU ARE, TIM! I'VE BEEN *LOOKING* FOR YOU *ALL DAY!*
YOUR MOM'D *KILL* ME IF ANYTHING HAPPENED TO MY FAVORITE LITTLE COUSIN ON HIS FIRST VISIT TO METROPOLIS!
WHERE HAVE YOU BEEN, ANYWAY?
JUST AROUND.
BUT... BUT IF *HE'S* LOIS'S COUSIN, THEN *WHO'S* THE INTERN?
YOU HAVE TO BE CAREFUL IN THIS TOWN, YOU KNOW. GET YOUR CITY LEGS BEFORE YOU GO OFF EXPLORING.
THERE'S THIS GUY I KNOW FROM SMALLVILLE, KANSAS, WHO CAN BARELY FIND HIS *ELBOW*...
...*FINEST* INTERN THE DAILY PLANET HAS EVER SEEN!
THANK YOU, Mr. WHITE.

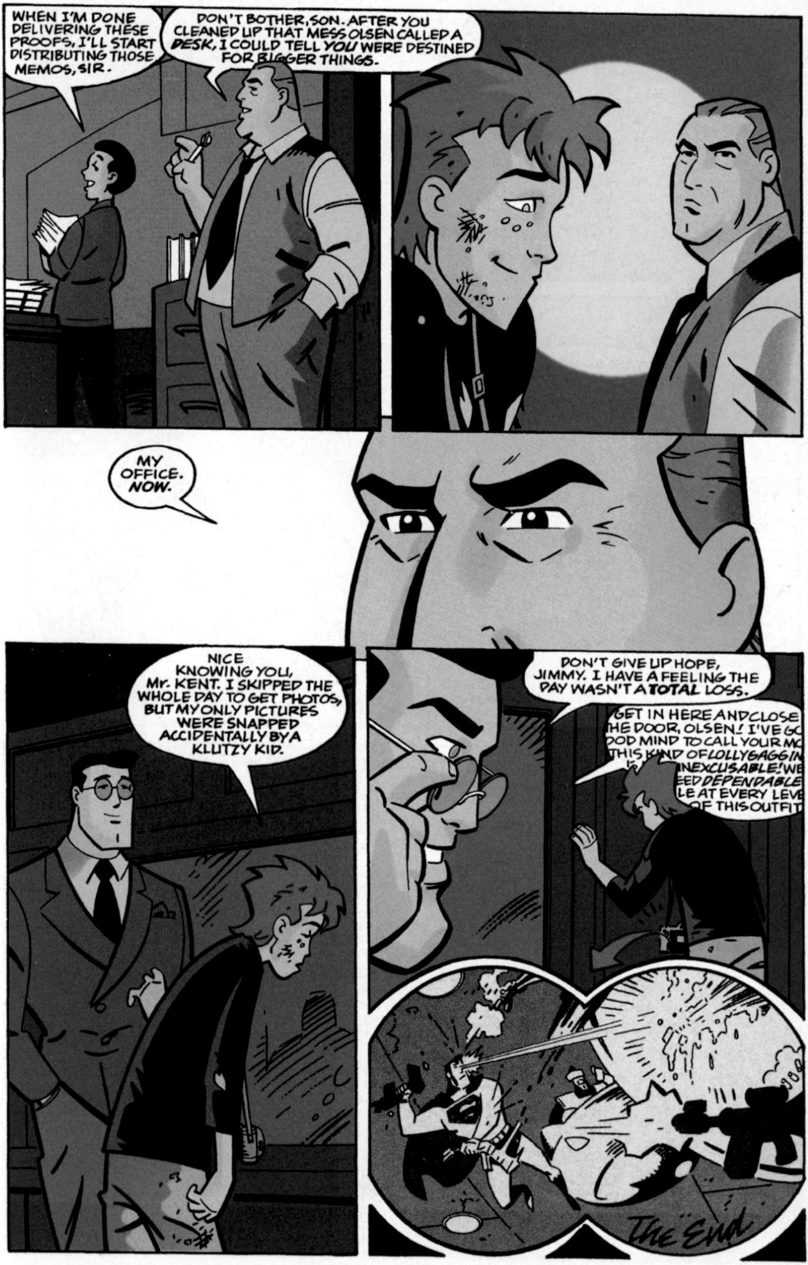

WHEN I'M DONE DELIVERING THESE PROOFS, I'LL START DISTRIBUTING THOSE MEMOS, SIR.
DON'T BOTHER, SON. AFTER YOU CLEANED UP THAT MESS OLSEN CALLED A DESK, I COULD TELL YOU WERE DESTINED FOR BIGGER THINGS.
MY OFFICE. NOW.
NICE KNOWING YOU, Mr. KENT. I SKIPPED THE WHOLE DAY TO GET PHOTOS, BUT MY ONLY PICTURES WERE SNAPPED ACCIDENTALLY BY A KLUTZY KID.
DON'T GIVE UP HOPE, JIMMY. I HAVE A FEELING THE DAY WASN'T A TOTAL LOSS.
GET IN HERE AND CLOSE HE DOOR, OLSEN! I'VE GO OOD MIND TO CALL YOUR MO THIS KIND OF LOLLYGAGGIN INEXCUSABLE! WE EED DEPENDABLE LE AT EVERY LEVE OF THIS OUTFIT
The End

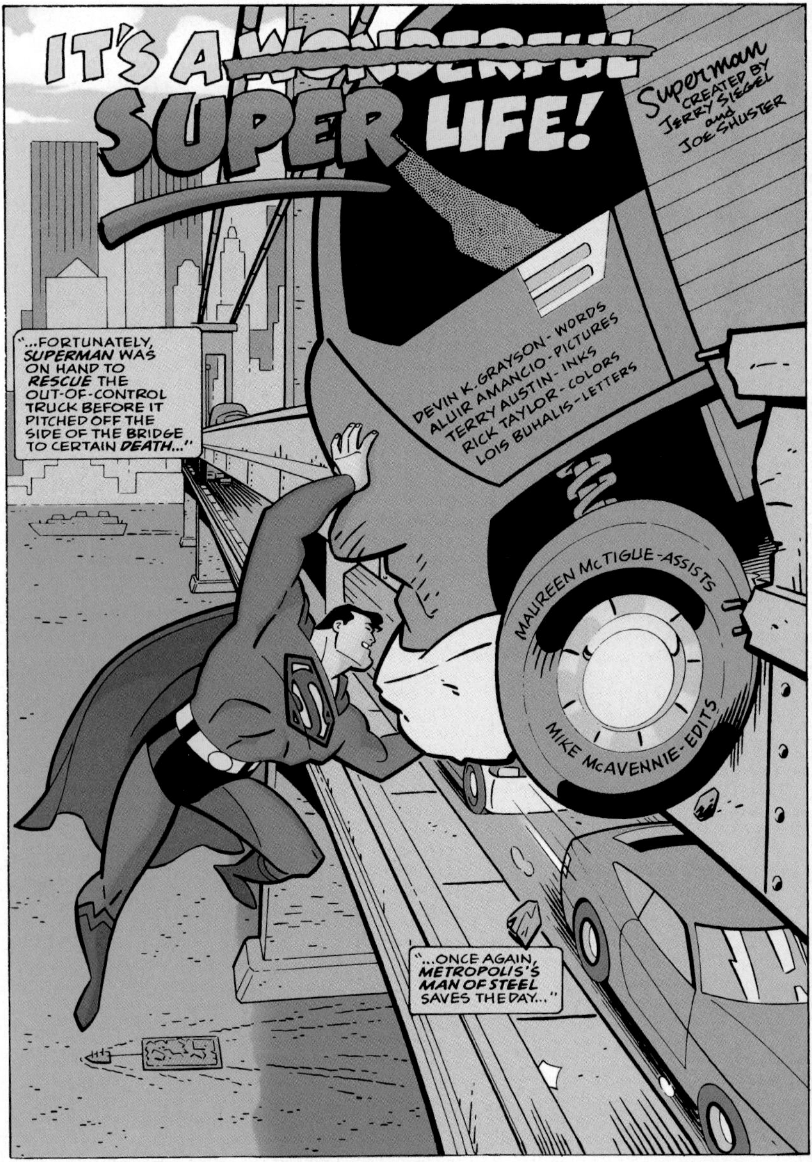
IT'S A WONDERFUL SUPER LIFE!
Superman created by Jerry Siegel and Joe Shuster
"...FORTUNATELY, SUPERMAN WAS ON HAND TO RESCUE THE OUT-OF-CONTROL TRUCK BEFORE IT PITCHED OFF THE SIDE OF THE BRIDGE TO CERTAIN DEATH..."
DEVIN K. GRAYSON - WORDS
ALUIR AMANCIO - PICTURES
TERRY AUSTIN - INKS
RICK TAYLOR - COLORS
LOIS BUHALIS - LETTERS
MAUREEN McTIGUE - ASSISTS
MIKE McAVENNIE - EDITS
"...ONCE AGAIN, METROPOLIS'S MAN OF STEEL SAVES THE DAY..."

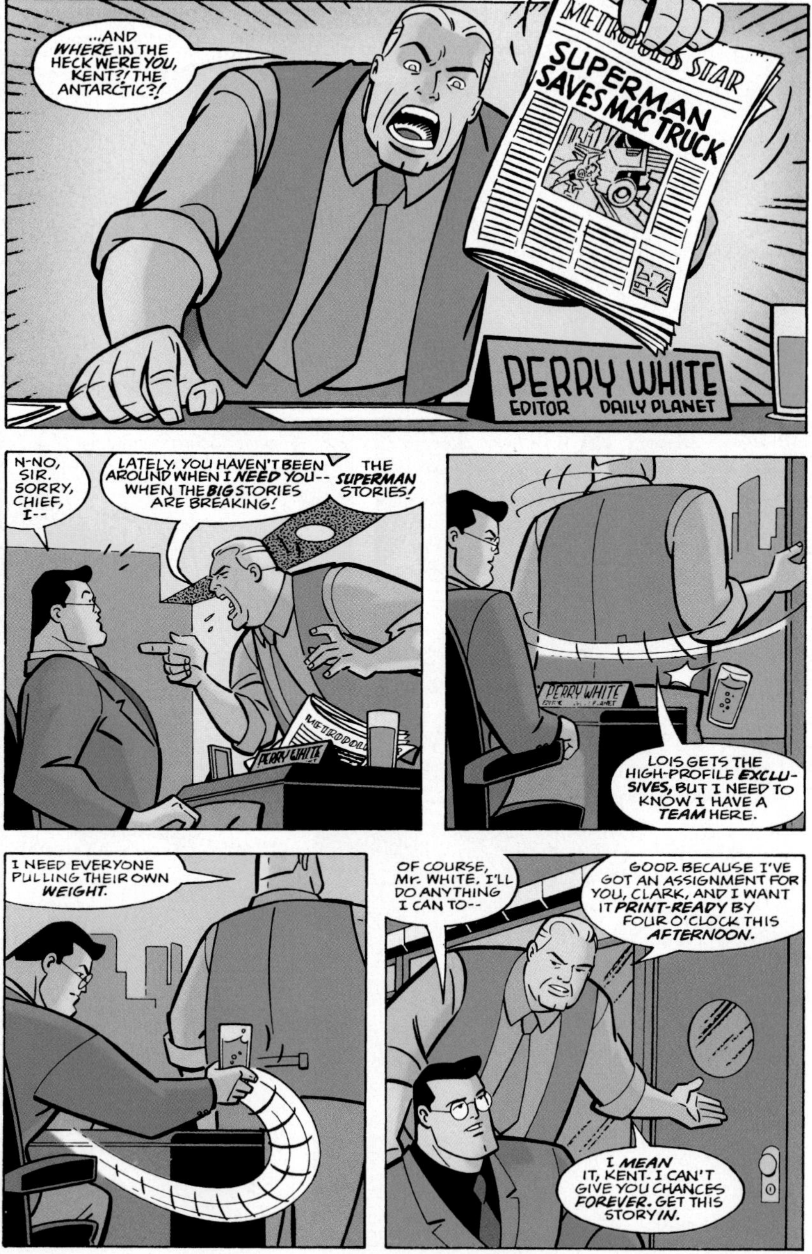
...AND WHERE IN THE HECK WERE YOU, KENT?! THE ANTARCTIC?!
METROPOLIS STAR
SUPERMAN SAVES MAC TRUCK
PERRY WHITE
EDITOR DAILY PLANET
N-NO, SIR. SORRY, CHIEF, I--
LATELY, YOU HAVEN'T BEEN AROUND WHEN I NEED YOU-- WHEN THE BIG STORIES ARE BREAKING!
THE SUPERMAN STORIES!
PERRY WHITE
LOIS GETS THE HIGH-PROFILE EXCLUSIVES, BUT I NEED TO KNOW I HAVE A TEAM HERE.
I NEED EVERYONE PULLING THEIR OWN WEIGHT.
OF COURSE, Mr. WHITE. I'LL DO ANYTHING I CAN TO--
GOOD. BECAUSE I'VE GOT AN ASSIGNMENT FOR YOU, CLARK, AND I WANT IT PRINT-READY BY FOUR O'CLOCK THIS AFTERNOON.
I MEAN IT, KENT. I CAN'T GIVE YOU CHANCES FOREVER. GET THIS STORY IN.

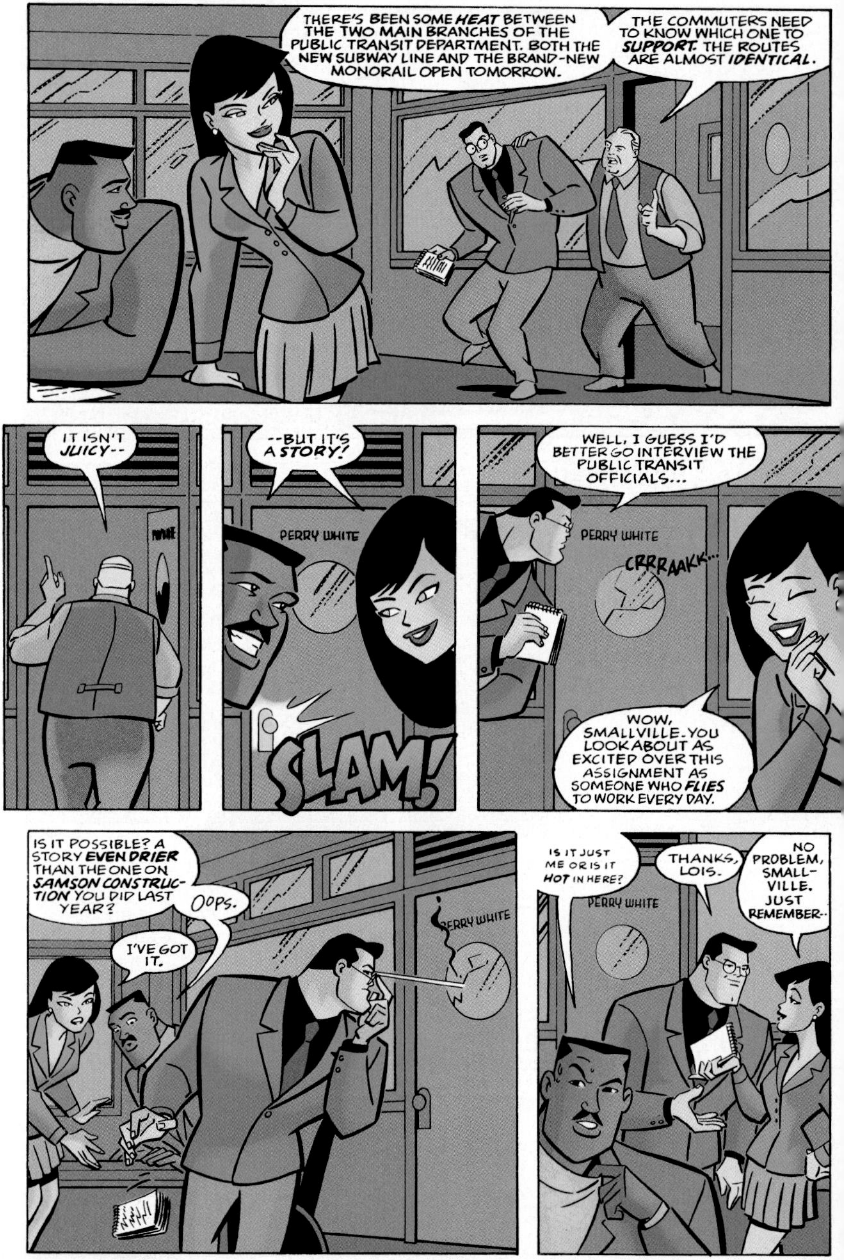
THERE'S BEEN SOME HEAT BETWEEN THE TWO MAIN BRANCHES OF THE PUBLIC TRANSIT DEPARTMENT. BOTH THE NEW SUBWAY LINE AND THE BRAND-NEW MONORAIL OPEN TOMORROW.
THE COMMUTERS NEED TO KNOW WHICH ONE TO SUPPORT. THE ROUTES ARE ALMOST IDENTICAL.
IT ISN'T JUICY--
--BUT IT'S A STORY!
PERRY WHITE
SLAM!
WELL, I GUESS I'D BETTER GO INTERVIEW THE PUBLIC TRANSIT OFFICIALS...
PERRY WHITE
CRRRAAKK...
WOW, SMALLVILLE. YOU LOOK ABOUT AS EXCITED OVER THIS ASSIGNMENT AS SOMEONE WHO FLIES TO WORK EVERY DAY.
IS IT POSSIBLE? A STORY EVEN DRIER THAN THE ONE ON SAMSON CONSTRUCTION YOU DID LAST YEAR?
OOPS.
I'VE GOT IT.
PERRY WHITE
IS IT JUST ME OR IS IT HOT IN HERE?
THANKS, LOIS.
NO PROBLEM, SMALLVILLE. JUST REMEMBER--
PERRY WHITE

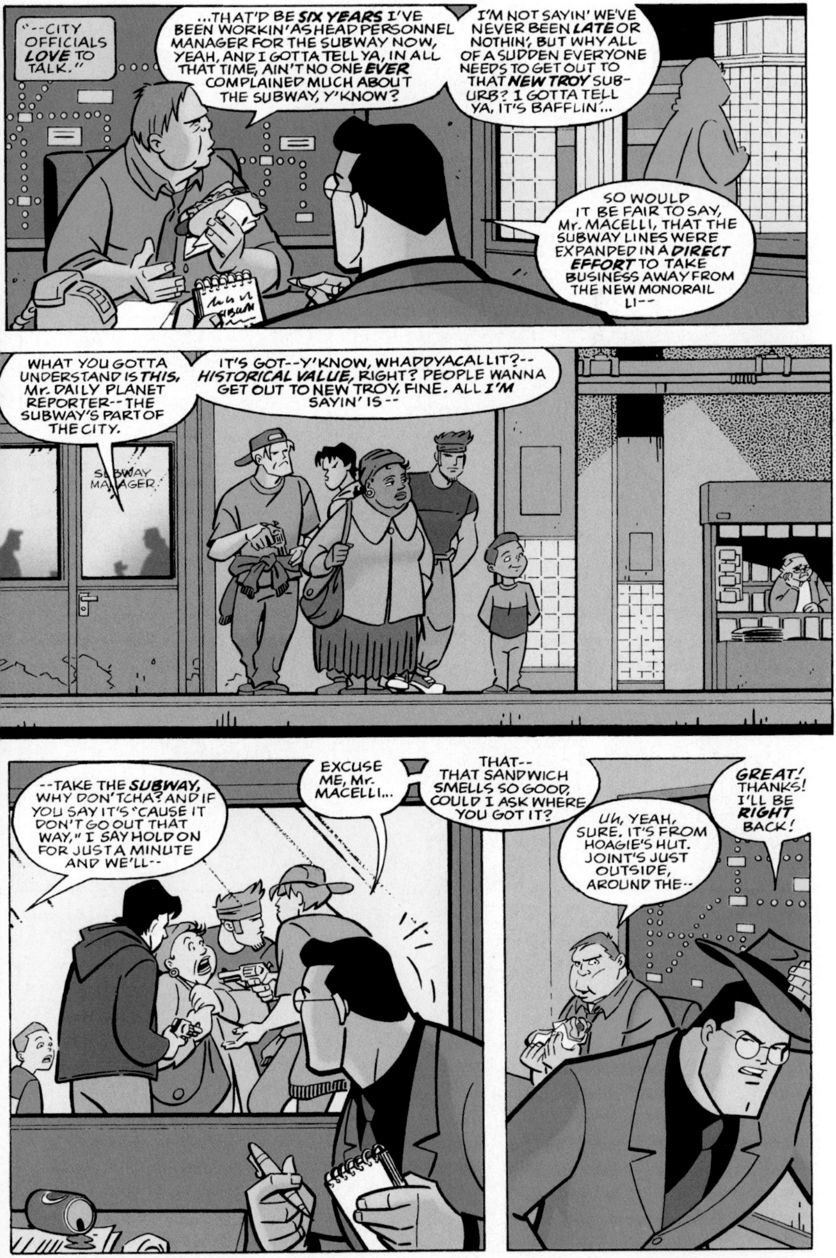
"--CITY OFFICIALS LOVE TO TALK."
...THAT'D BE SIX YEARS I'VE BEEN WORKIN' AS HEAD PERSONNEL MANAGER FOR THE SUBWAY NOW, YEAH, AND I GOTTA TELL YA, IN ALL THAT TIME, AIN'T NO ONE EVER COMPLAINED MUCH ABOUT THE SUBWAY, Y'KNOW?
I'M NOT SAYIN' WE'VE NEVER BEEN LATE OR NOTHIN', BUT WHY ALL OF A SUDDEN EVERYONE NEEDS TO GET OUT TO THAT NEW TROY SUB-URB? I GOTTA TELL YA, IT'S BAFFLIN'...
SO WOULD IT BE FAIR TO SAY, Mr. MACELLI, THAT THE SUBWAY LINES WERE EXPANDED IN A DIRECT EFFORT TO TAKE BUSINESS AWAY FROM THE NEW MONORAIL LI--
WHAT YOU GOTTA UNDERSTAND IS THIS, Mr. DAILY PLANET REPORTER--THE SUBWAY'S PART OF THE CITY.
IT'S GOT--Y'KNOW, WHADDYACALLIT?--HISTORICAL VALUE, RIGHT? PEOPLE WANNA GET OUT TO NEW TROY, FINE. ALL I'M SAYIN' IS--
SUBWAY MANAGER
--TAKE THE SUBWAY, WHY DON'TCHA? AND IF YOU SAY IT'S "CAUSE IT DON'T GO OUT THAT WAY," I SAY HOLD ON FOR JUST A MINUTE AND WE'LL--
EXCUSE ME, Mr. MACELLI...
THAT--THAT SANDWICH SMELLS SO GOOD, COULD I ASK WHERE YOU GOT IT?
UH, YEAH, SURE. IT'S FROM HOAGIE'S HUT. JOINT'S JUST OUTSIDE, AROUND THE--
GREAT! THANKS! I'LL BE RIGHT BACK!

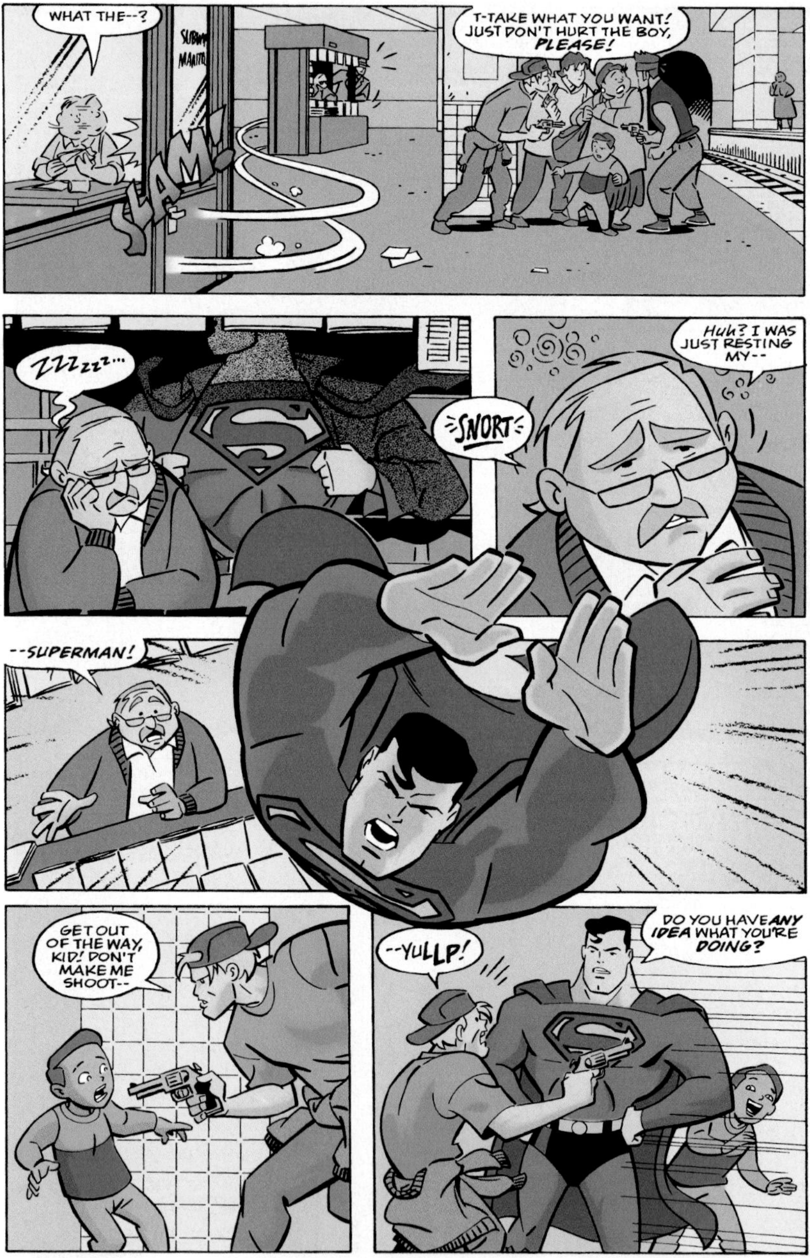
WHAT THE--?
SLAM!
T-TAKE WHAT YOU WANT! JUST DON'T HURT THE BOY, PLEASE!
ZZZzzz...
SNORT
Huh? I WAS JUST RESTING MY--
--SUPERMAN!
GET OUT OF THE WAY, KID! DON'T MAKE ME SHOOT--
--YULLP!
DO YOU HAVE ANY IDEA WHAT YOU'RE DOING?

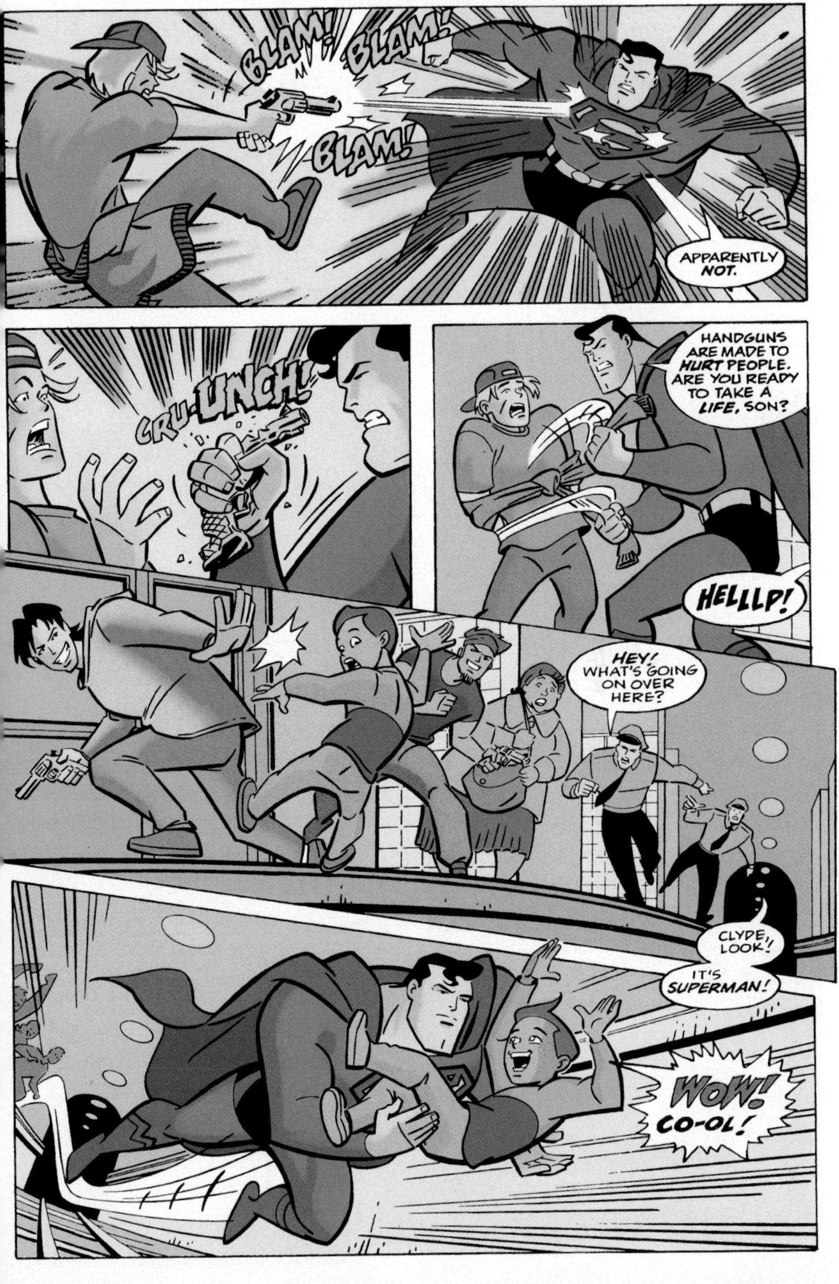
BLAM! BLAM!
BLAM!
APPARENTLY NOT.
CRU-UNCH!
HANDGUNS ARE MADE TO HURT PEOPLE. ARE YOU READY TO TAKE A LIFE, SON?
HELLLP!
HEY! WHAT'S GOING ON OVER HERE?
CLYDE, LOOK!
IT'S SUPERMAN!
WOW! CO-OL!

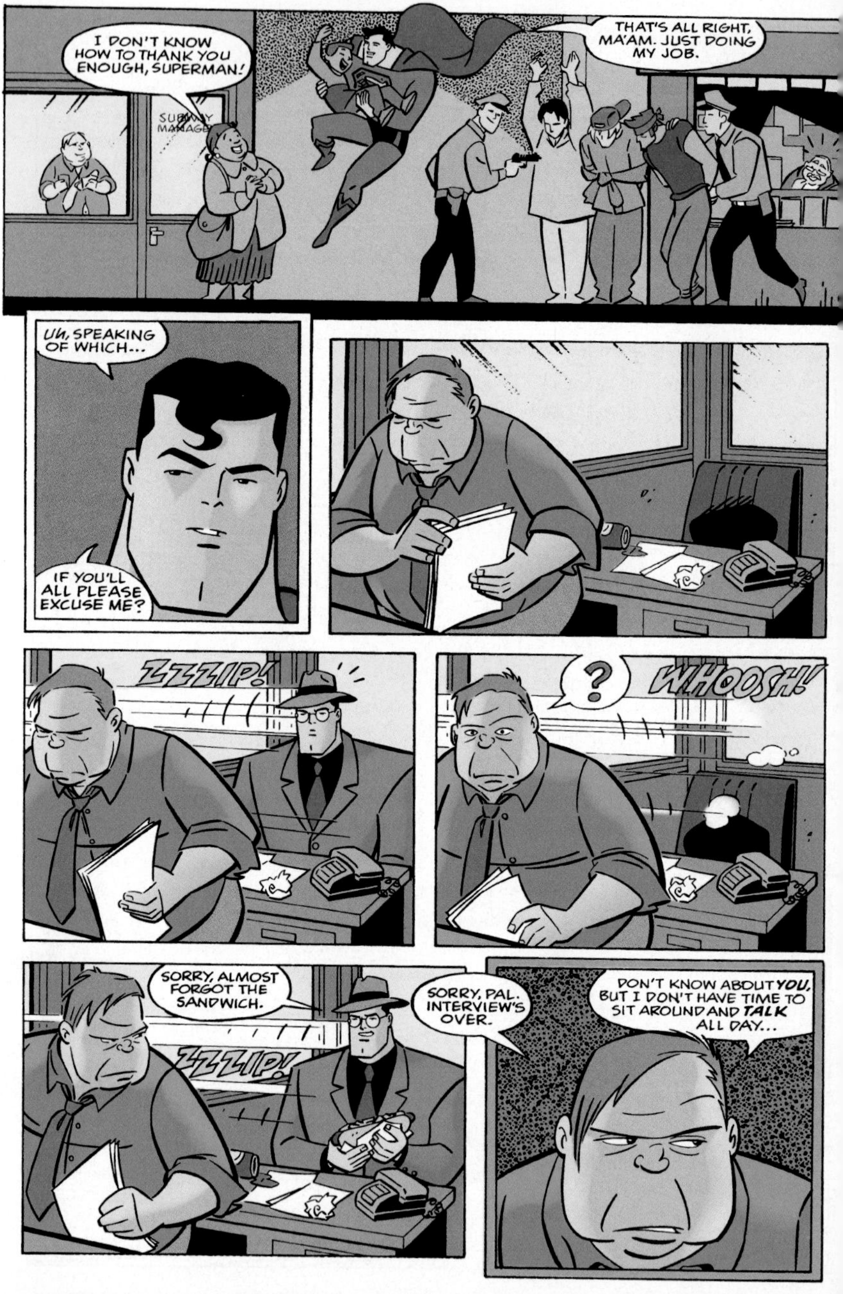
I DON'T KNOW HOW TO THANK YOU ENOUGH, SUPERMAN!
THAT'S ALL RIGHT, MA'AM. JUST DOING MY JOB.
UH, SPEAKING OF WHICH...
IF YOU'LL ALL PLEASE EXCUSE ME?
ZZZIP!
?
WHOOSH!
SORRY, ALMOST FORGOT THE SANDWICH.
ZZZIP!
SORRY, PAL. INTERVIEW'S OVER.
DON'T KNOW ABOUT YOU, BUT I DON'T HAVE TIME TO SIT AROUND AND TALK ALL DAY...

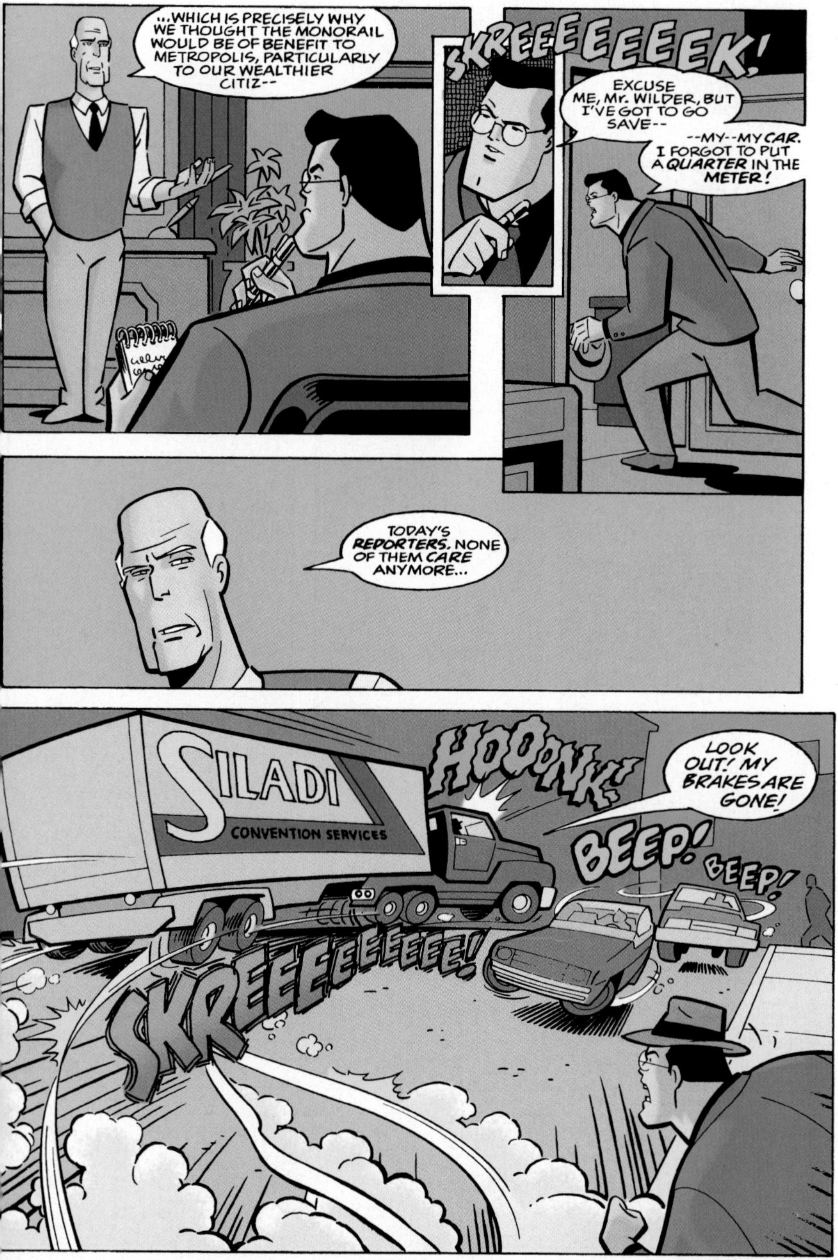
...WHICH IS PRECISELY WHY WE THOUGHT THE MONORAIL WOULD BE OF BENEFIT TO METROPOLIS, PARTICULARLY TO OUR WEALTHIER CITIZ--
SKREEEEEEEK!
EXCUSE ME, Mr. WILDER, BUT I'VE GOT TO GO SAVE--
--MY--MY CAR. I FORGOT TO PUT A QUARTER IN THE METER!
TODAY'S REPORTERS. NONE OF THEM CARE ANYMORE...
SILADI
CONVENTION SERVICES
HOOONK!
LOOK OUT! MY BRAKES ARE GONE!
BEEP! BEEP!
SKREEEEEEEEE!

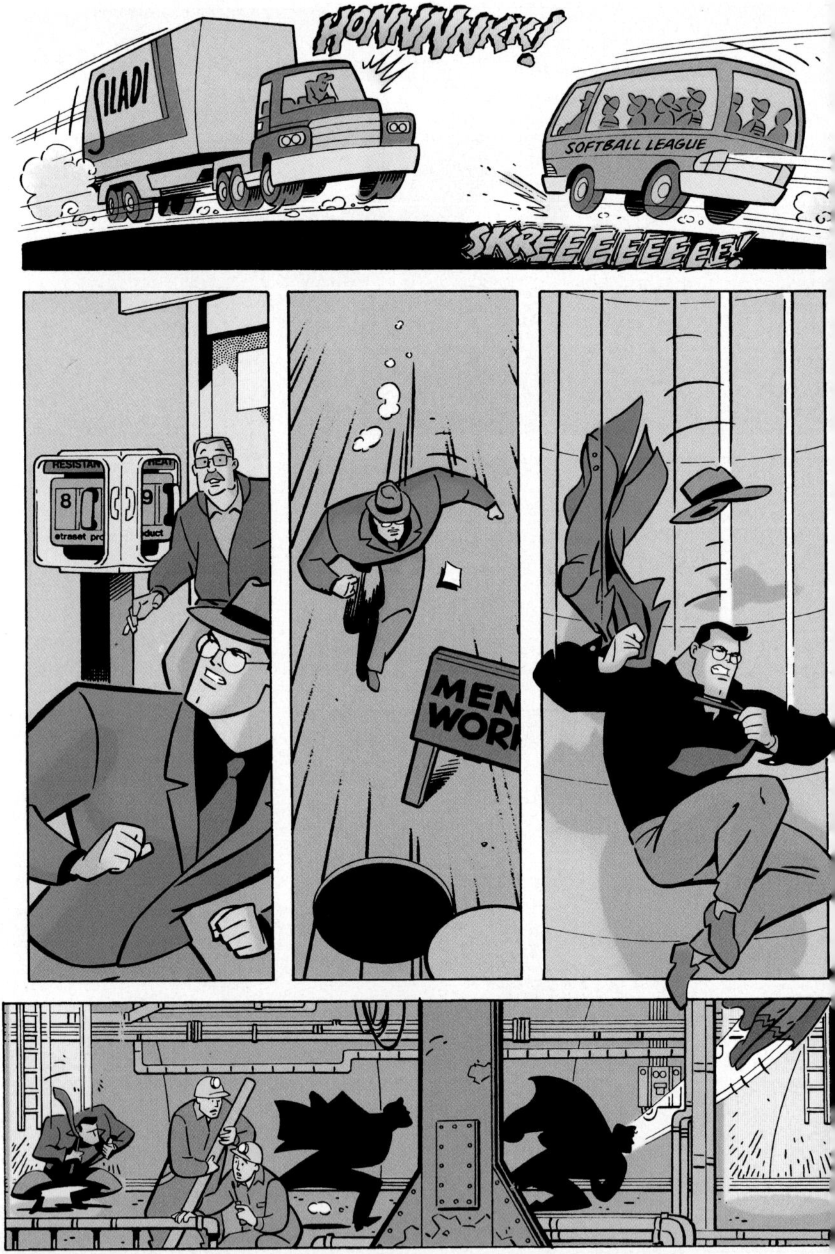
HONNNNKK!
SILADI
SOFTBALL LEAGUE
SKREEEEEEEEE!
MEN
WORK

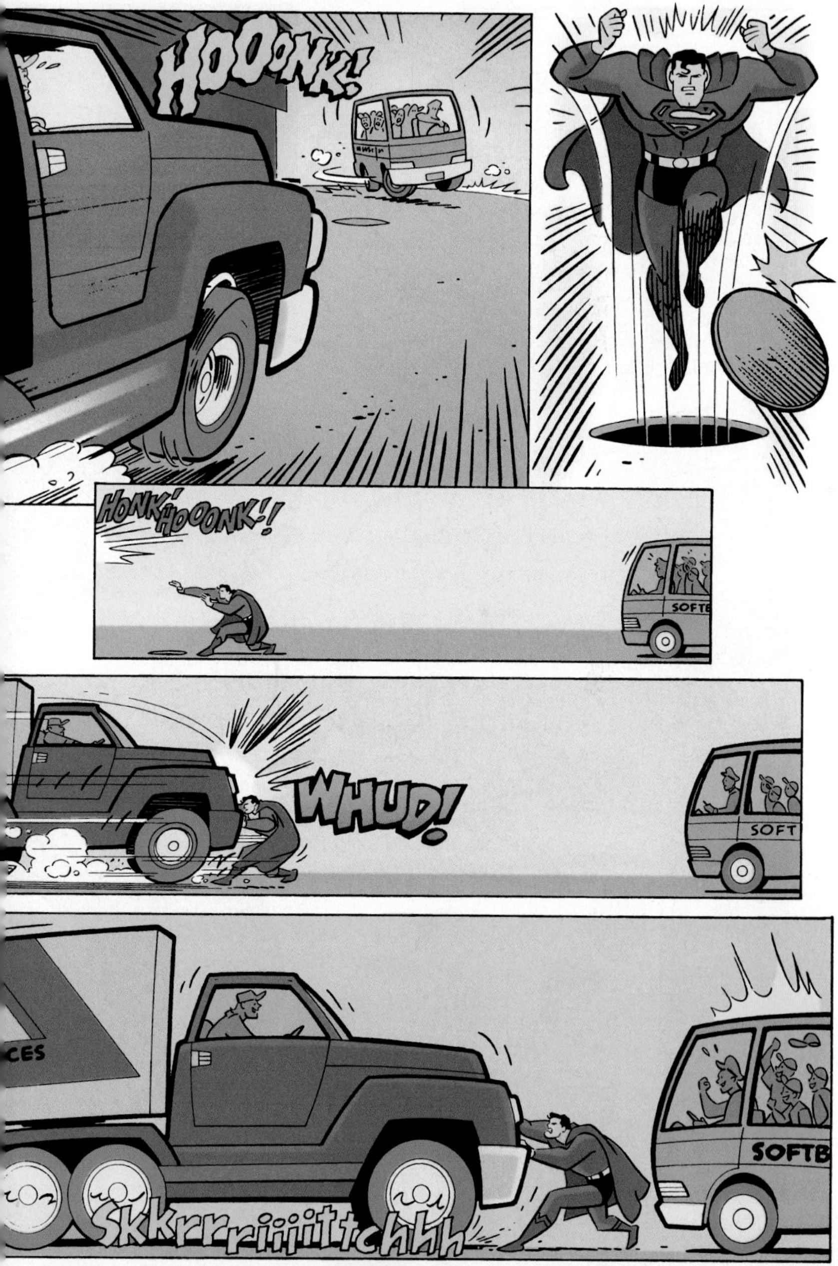

HOOoONK!
HONK! HOOONK!!
SOFTB
WHUD!
SOFT
CES
SOFTB
Skkrrrriiiiittchhh

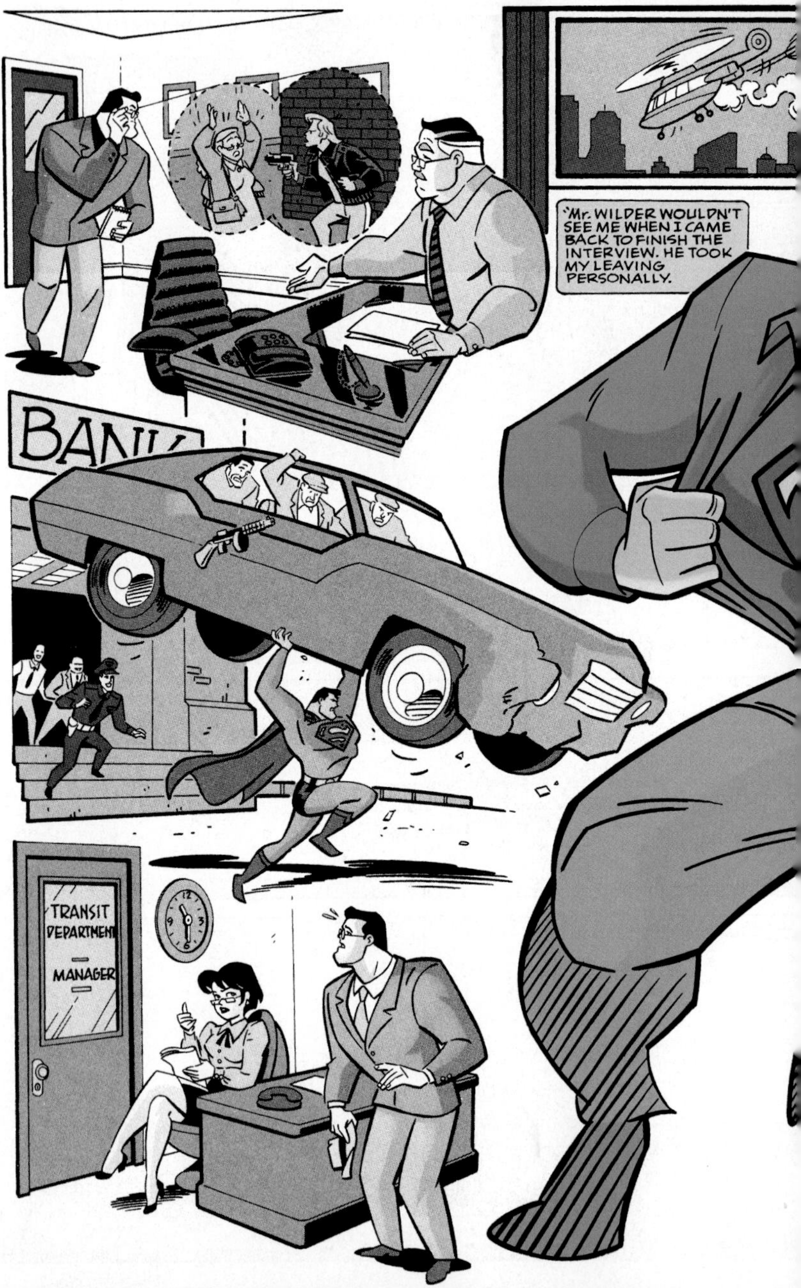
"Mr. WILDER WOULDN'T SEE ME WHEN I CAME BACK TO FINISH THE INTERVIEW. HE TOOK MY LEAVING PERSONALLY.
BANK
TRANSIT DEPARTMENT
MANAGER

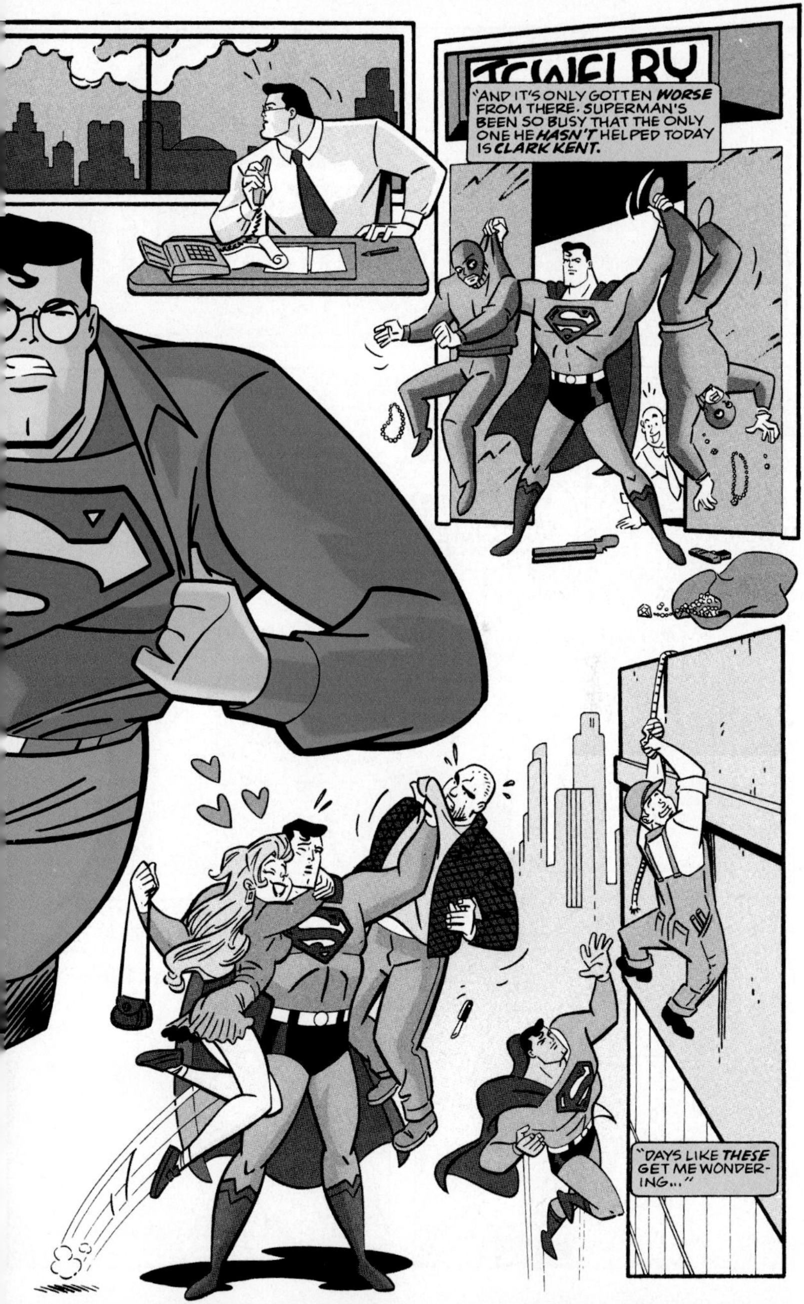

JEWELRY
"AND IT'S ONLY GOTTEN WORSE FROM THERE. SUPERMAN'S BEEN SO BUSY THAT THE ONLY ONE HE HASN'T HELPED TODAY IS CLARK KENT.
"DAYS LIKE THESE GET ME WONDERING..."

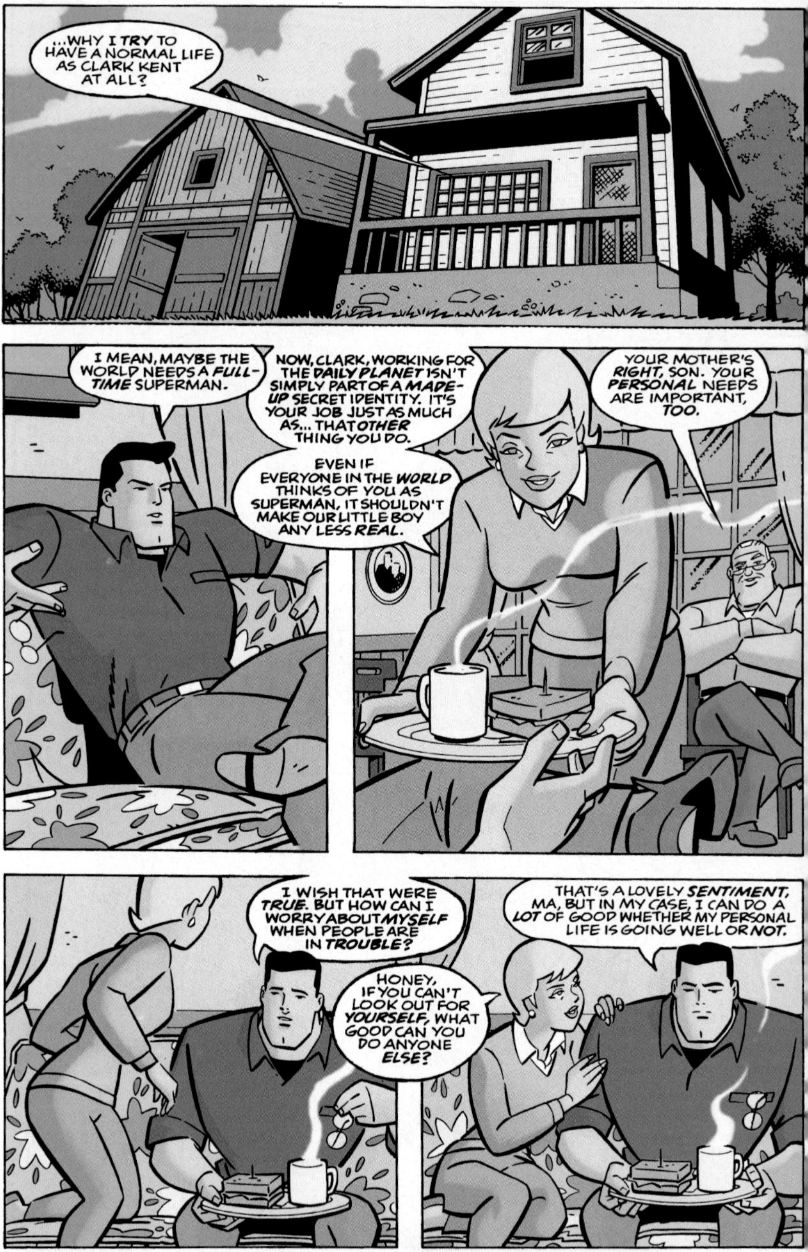
...WHY I TRY TO HAVE A NORMAL LIFE AS CLARK KENT AT ALL?
I MEAN, MAYBE THE WORLD NEEDS A FULL-TIME SUPERMAN.
NOW, CLARK, WORKING FOR THE DAILY PLANET ISN'T SIMPLY PART OF A MADE-UP SECRET IDENTITY. IT'S YOUR JOB JUST AS MUCH AS... THAT OTHER THING YOU DO.
EVEN IF EVERYONE IN THE WORLD THINKS OF YOU AS SUPERMAN, IT SHOULDN'T MAKE OUR LITTLE BOY ANY LESS REAL.
YOUR MOTHER'S RIGHT, SON. YOUR PERSONAL NEEDS ARE IMPORTANT, TOO.
I WISH THAT WERE TRUE. BUT HOW CAN I WORRY ABOUT MYSELF WHEN PEOPLE ARE IN TROUBLE?
HONEY, IF YOU CAN'T LOOK OUT FOR YOURSELF, WHAT GOOD CAN YOU DO ANYONE ELSE?
THAT'S A LOVELY SENTIMENT, MA, BUT IN MY CASE, I CAN DO A LOT OF GOOD WHETHER MY PERSONAL LIFE IS GOING WELL OR NOT.

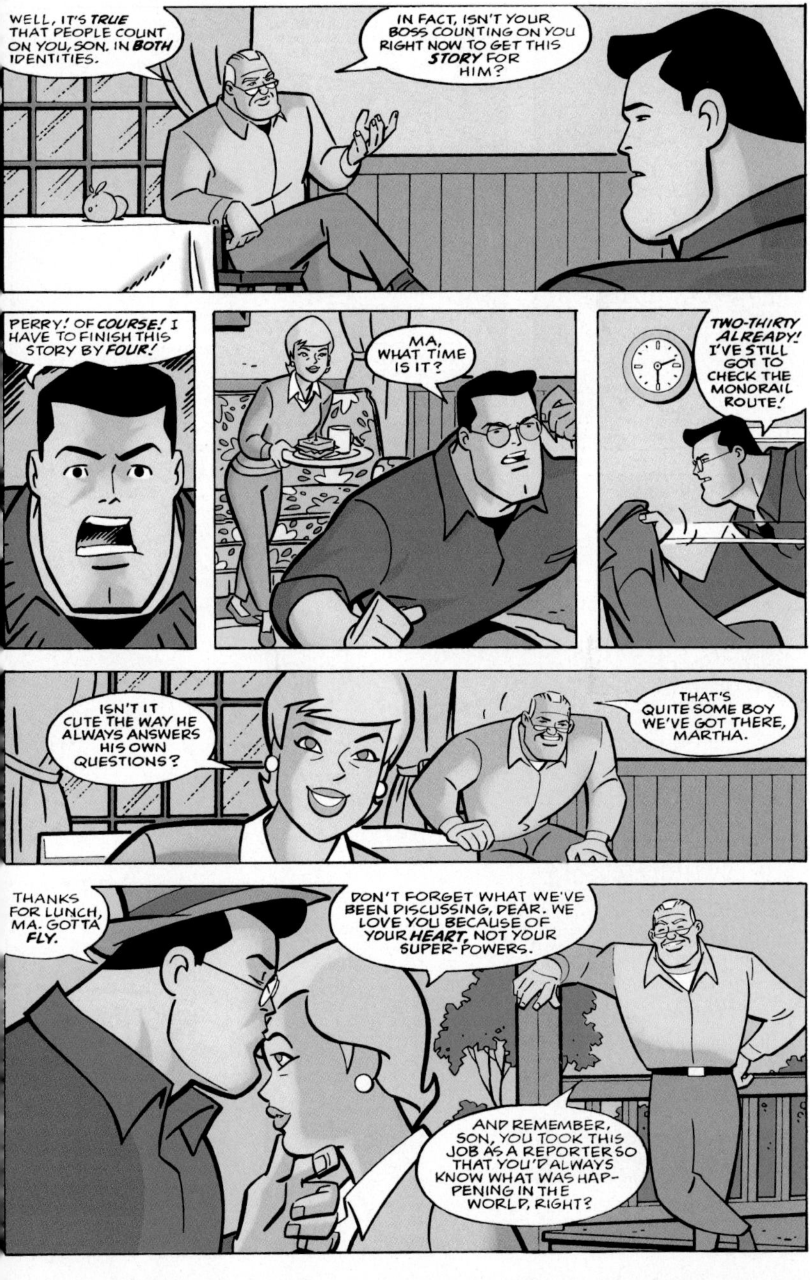
WELL, IT'S TRUE THAT PEOPLE COUNT ON YOU, SON. IN BOTH IDENTITIES.
IN FACT, ISN'T YOUR BOSS COUNTING ON YOU RIGHT NOW TO GET THIS STORY FOR HIM?
PERRY! OF COURSE! I HAVE TO FINISH THIS STORY BY FOUR!
MA, WHAT TIME IS IT?
TWO-THIRTY ALREADY! I'VE STILL GOT TO CHECK THE MONORAIL ROUTE!
ISN'T IT CUTE THE WAY HE ALWAYS ANSWERS HIS OWN QUESTIONS?
THAT'S QUITE SOME BOY WE'VE GOT THERE, MARTHA.
THANKS FOR LUNCH, MA. GOTTA FLY.
DON'T FORGET WHAT WE'VE BEEN DISCUSSING, DEAR. WE LOVE YOU BECAUSE OF YOUR HEART, NOT YOUR SUPER-POWERS.
AND REMEMBER, SON, YOU TOOK THIS JOB AS A REPORTER SO THAT YOU'D ALWAYS KNOW WHAT WAS HAP-PENING IN THE WORLD, RIGHT?

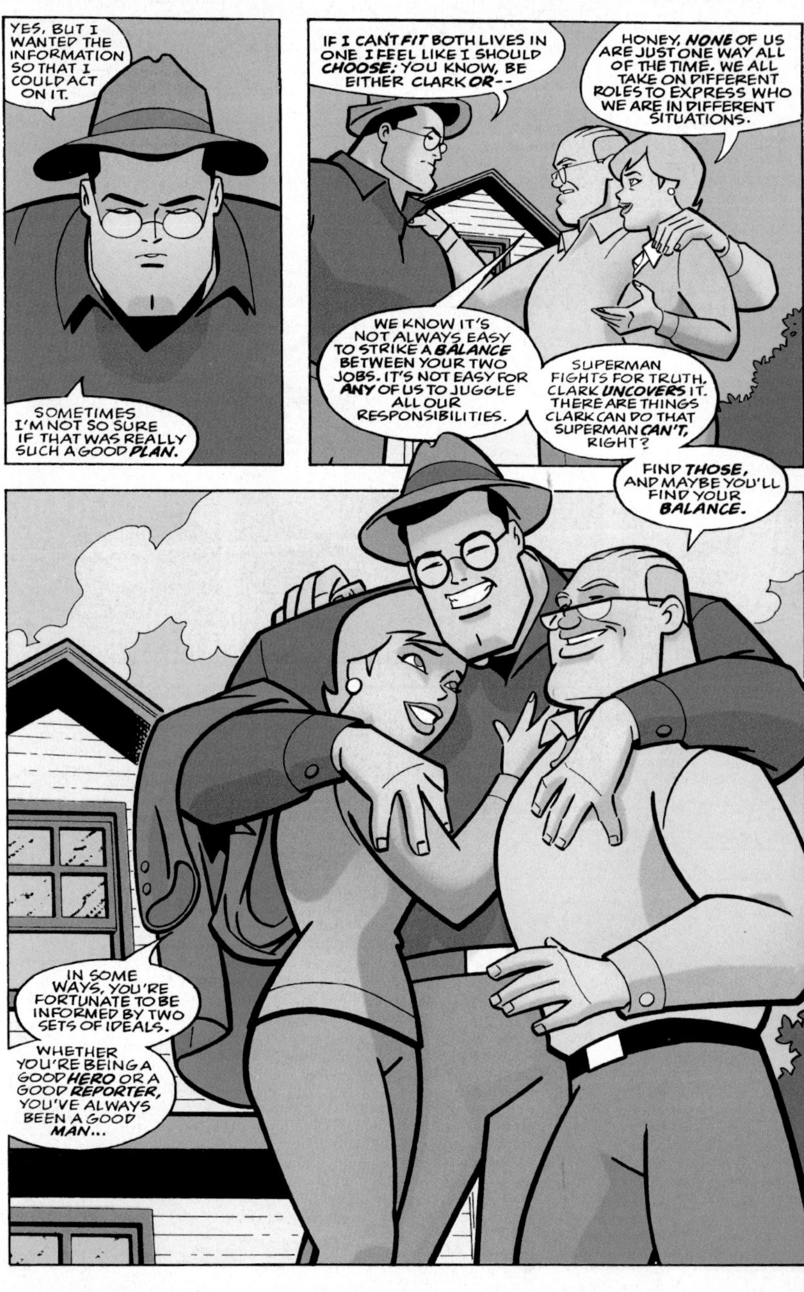
YES, BUT I WANTED THE INFORMATION SO THAT I COULD ACT ON IT.
SOMETIMES I'M NOT SO SURE IF THAT WAS REALLY SUCH A GOOD PLAN.
IF I CAN'T FIT BOTH LIVES IN ONE I FEEL LIKE I SHOULD CHOOSE: YOU KNOW, BE EITHER CLARK OR--
HONEY, NONE OF US ARE JUST ONE WAY ALL OF THE TIME. WE ALL TAKE ON DIFFERENT ROLES TO EXPRESS WHO WE ARE IN DIFFERENT SITUATIONS.
WE KNOW IT'S NOT ALWAYS EASY TO STRIKE A BALANCE BETWEEN YOUR TWO JOBS. IT'S NOT EASY FOR ANY OF US TO JUGGLE ALL OUR RESPONSIBILITIES.
SUPERMAN FIGHTS FOR TRUTH. CLARK UNCOVERS IT. THERE ARE THINGS CLARK CAN DO THAT SUPERMAN CAN'T, RIGHT?
FIND THOSE, AND MAYBE YOU'LL FIND YOUR BALANCE.
IN SOME WAYS, YOU'RE FORTUNATE TO BE INFORMED BY TWO SETS OF IDEALS.
WHETHER YOU'RE BEING A GOOD HERO OR A GOOD REPORTER, YOU'VE ALWAYS BEEN A GOOD MAN...

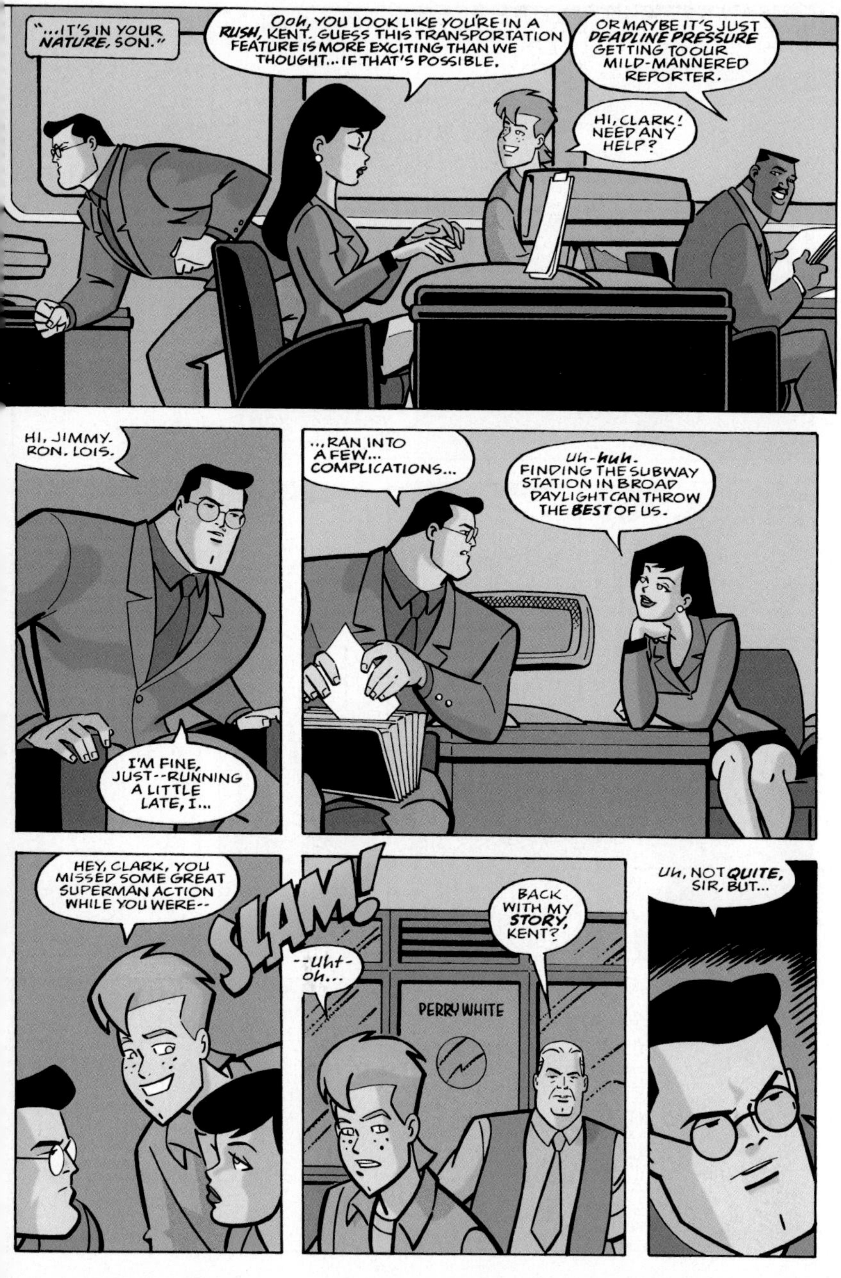
"...IT'S IN YOUR NATURE, SON."
Ooh, YOU LOOK LIKE YOU'RE IN A RUSH, KENT. GUESS THIS TRANSPORTATION FEATURE IS MORE EXCITING THAN WE THOUGHT... IF THAT'S POSSIBLE.
OR MAYBE IT'S JUST DEADLINE PRESSURE GETTING TO OUR MILD-MANNERED REPORTER.
HI, CLARK! NEED ANY HELP?
HI, JIMMY. RON. LOIS.
I'M FINE, JUST--RUNNING A LITTLE LATE, I...
...RAN INTO A FEW... COMPLICATIONS...
Uh-huh. FINDING THE SUBWAY STATION IN BROAD DAYLIGHT CAN THROW THE BEST OF US.
HEY, CLARK, YOU MISSED SOME GREAT SUPERMAN ACTION WHILE YOU WERE--
SLAM!
--uht-oh...
PERRY WHITE
BACK WITH MY STORY, KENT?
Uh, NOT QUITE, SIR, BUT...

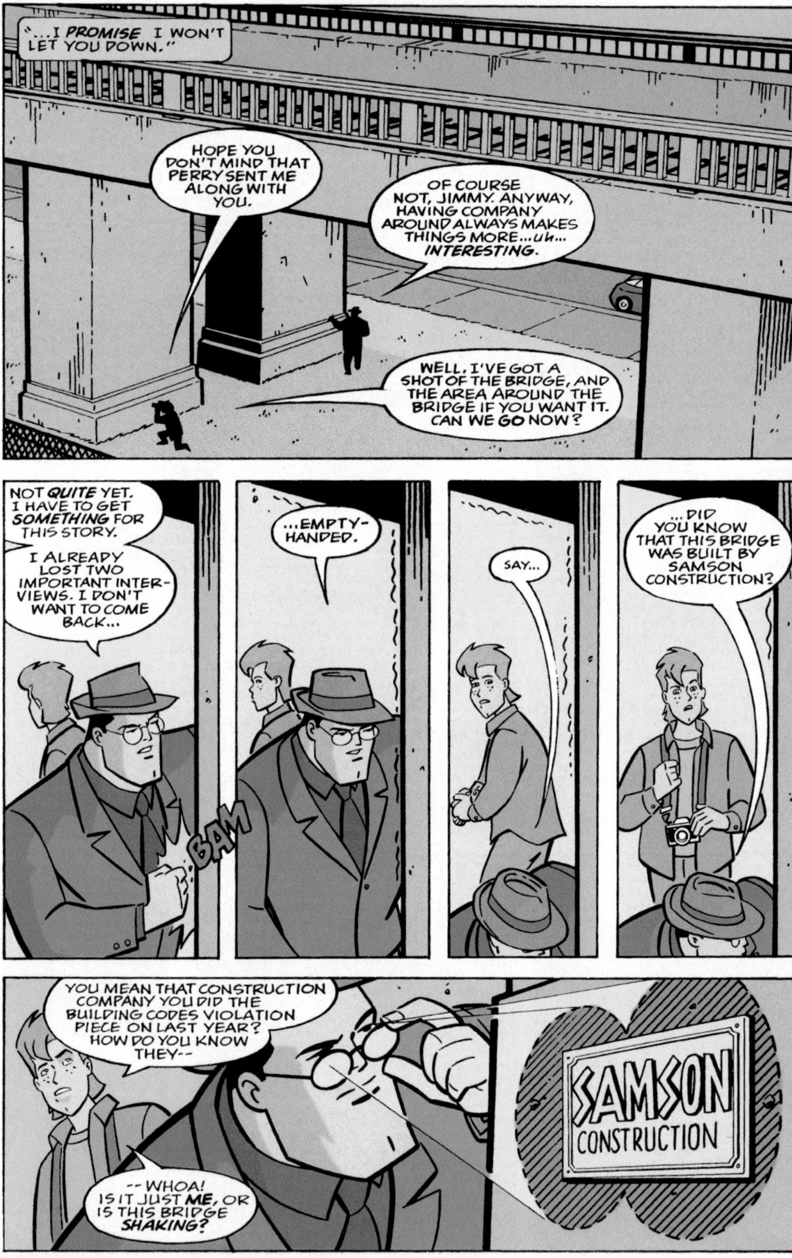
"...I PROMISE I WON'T LET YOU DOWN."
HOPE YOU DON'T MIND THAT PERRY SENT ME ALONG WITH YOU.
OF COURSE NOT, JIMMY. ANYWAY, HAVING COMPANY AROUND ALWAYS MAKES THINGS MORE...uh... INTERESTING.
WELL, I'VE GOT A SHOT OF THE BRIDGE, AND THE AREA AROUND THE BRIDGE IF YOU WANT IT. CAN WE GO NOW?
NOT QUITE YET. I HAVE TO GET SOMETHING FOR THIS STORY.
I ALREADY LOST TWO IMPORTANT INTER-VIEWS. I DON'T WANT TO COME BACK...
BAM
...EMPTY-HANDED.
SAY...
...DID YOU KNOW THAT THIS BRIDGE WAS BUILT BY SAMSON CONSTRUCTION?
YOU MEAN THAT CONSTRUCTION COMPANY YOU DID THE BUILDING CODES VIOLATION PIECE ON LAST YEAR? HOW DO YOU KNOW THEY--
SAMSON CONSTRUCTION
--WHOA! IS IT JUST ME, OR IS THIS BRIDGE SHAKING?

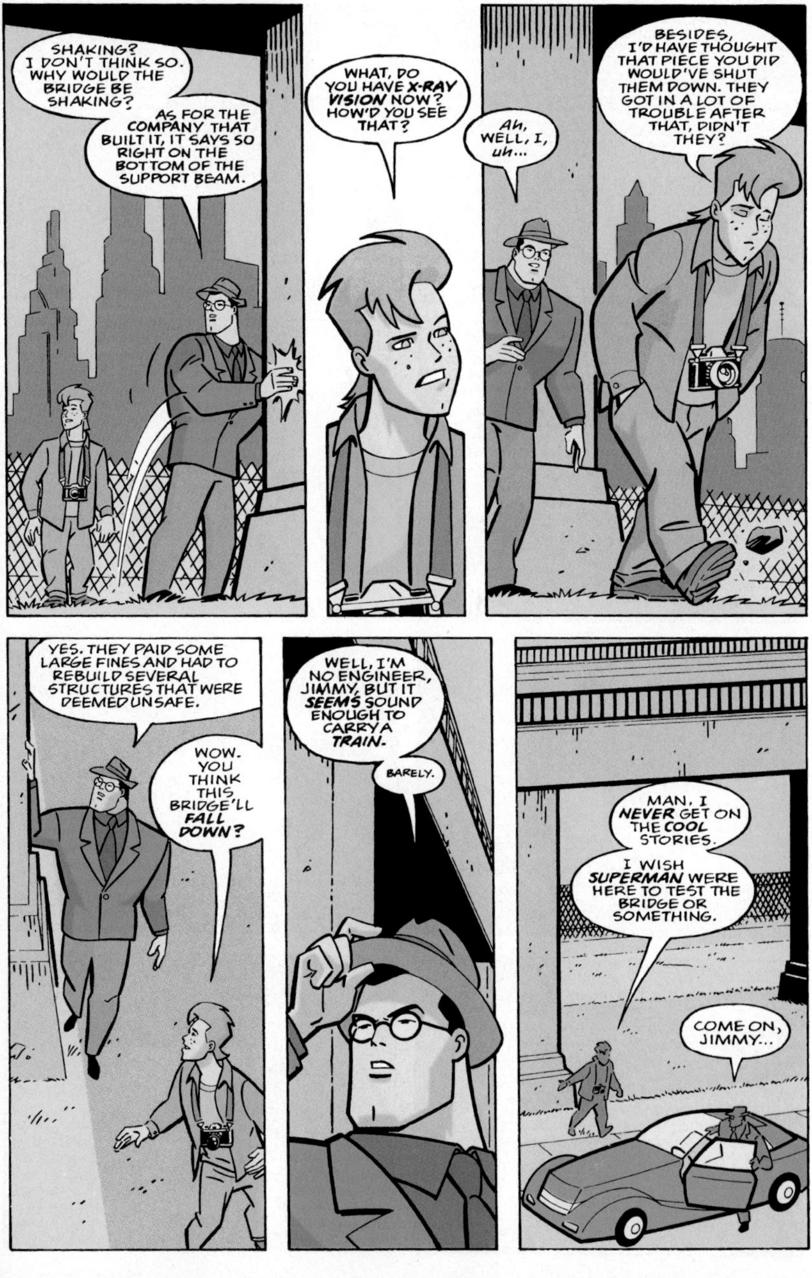
SHAKING? I DON'T THINK SO. WHY WOULD THE BRIDGE BE SHAKING?
AS FOR THE COMPANY THAT BUILT IT, IT SAYS SO RIGHT ON THE BOTTOM OF THE SUPPORT BEAM.
WHAT, DO YOU HAVE X-RAY VISION NOW? HOW'D YOU SEE THAT?
Ah, WELL, I, uh...
BESIDES, I'D HAVE THOUGHT THAT PIECE YOU DID WOULD'VE SHUT THEM DOWN. THEY GOT IN A LOT OF TROUBLE AFTER THAT, DIDN'T THEY?
YES. THEY PAID SOME LARGE FINES AND HAD TO REBUILD SEVERAL STRUCTURES THAT WERE DEEMED UNSAFE.
WOW. YOU THINK THIS BRIDGE'LL FALL DOWN?
WELL, I'M NO ENGINEER, JIMMY, BUT IT SEEMS SOUND ENOUGH TO CARRY A TRAIN.
BARELY.
MAN, I NEVER GET ON THE COOL STORIES.
I WISH SUPERMAN WERE HERE TO TEST THE BRIDGE OR SOMETHING.
COME ON, JIMMY...

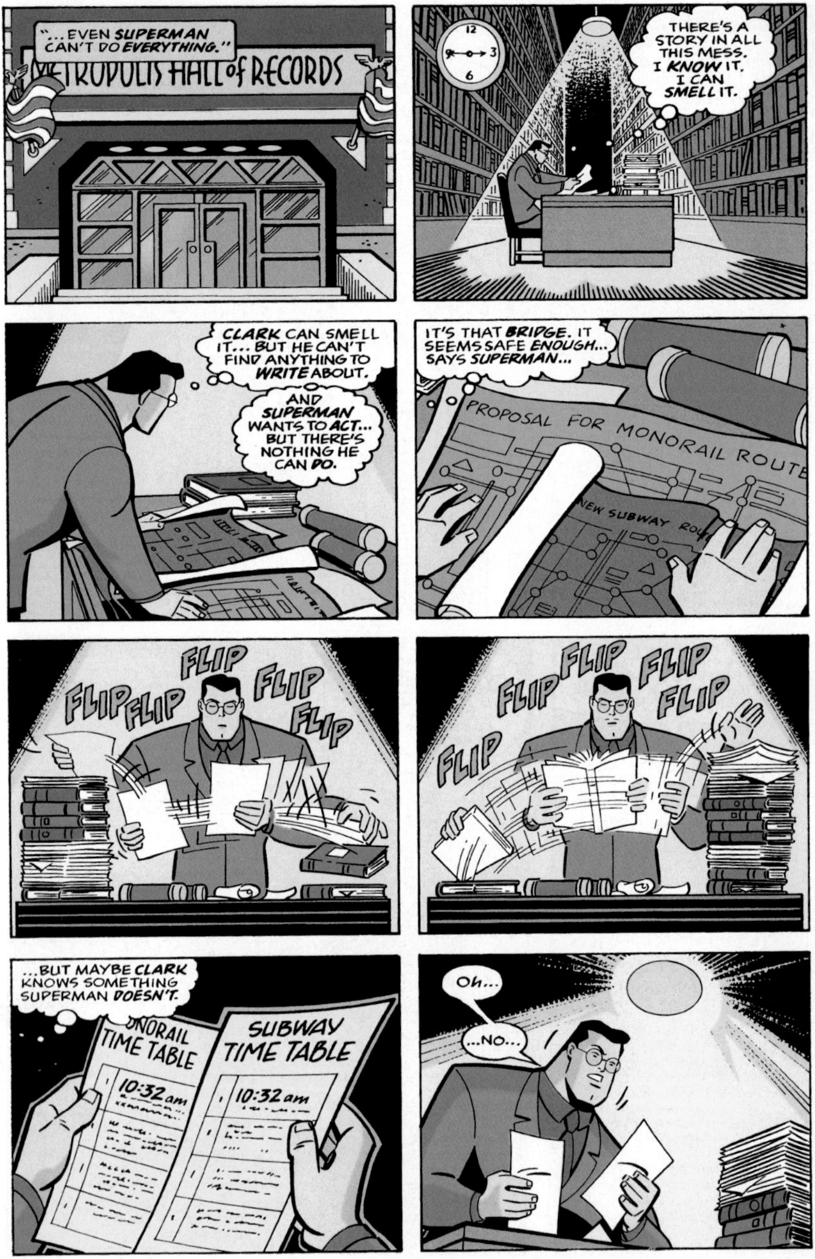
"...EVEN SUPERMAN CAN'T DO EVERYTHING."
METROPOLIS HALL of RECORDS
THERE'S A STORY IN ALL THIS MESS. I KNOW IT. I CAN SMELL IT.
CLARK CAN SMELL IT... BUT HE CAN'T FIND ANYTHING TO WRITE ABOUT.
AND SUPERMAN WANTS TO ACT... BUT THERE'S NOTHING HE CAN DO.
IT'S THAT BRIDGE. IT SEEMS SAFE ENOUGH... SAYS SUPERMAN...
PROPOSAL FOR MONORAIL ROUTE
NEW SUBWAY ROUTE
FLIP FLIP FLIP FLIP FLIP
FLIP FLIP FLIP FLIP FLIP
...BUT MAYBE CLARK KNOWS SOMETHING SUPERMAN DOESN'T.
TIME TABLE
10:32 am
SUBWAY TIME TABLE
10:32 am
Oh...
...NO...

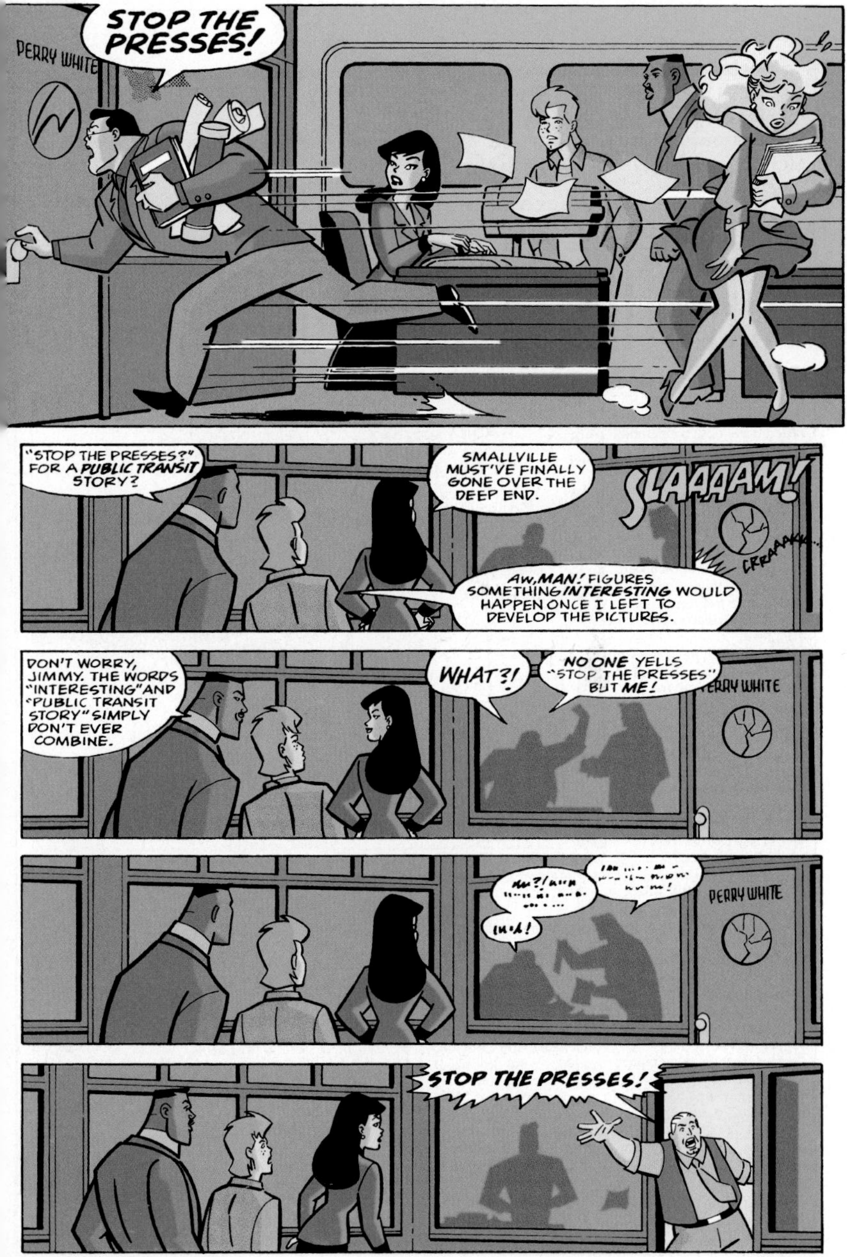
STOP THE PRESSES!
PERRY WHITE
"STOP THE PRESSES?" FOR A PUBLIC TRANSIT STORY?
SMALLVILLE MUST'VE FINALLY GONE OVER THE DEEP END.
SLAAAAM!
CRRAAAKK...
AW, MAN! FIGURES SOMETHING INTERESTING WOULD HAPPEN ONCE I LEFT TO DEVELOP THE PICTURES.
DON'T WORRY, JIMMY. THE WORDS "INTERESTING" AND "PUBLIC TRANSIT STORY" SIMPLY DON'T EVER COMBINE.
WHAT?!
NO ONE YELLS "STOP THE PRESSES" BUT ME!
PERRY WHITE
PERRY WHITE
STOP THE PRESSES!

# DAILY ★ PLANET

Early Edition     "A GREAT METROPOLITAN NEWSPAPER"     50 Cents

# POTENTIAL TRAIN TRAGEDY AVOIDED

By Clark Kent

After months of competitive feuding, city officials are now cooperating to avert what could have become a potentially fatal disaster for Metropolis mass transit commuters today.

The DAILY PLANET learned yesterday that had Metropolis's new monorail and subway lines proceeded on schedule today, the two would have run through the New Troy Bridge at precisely 10:32 a.m.

Although the trains would not have collided, last-minute research proved the bridge to be incapable of supporting the weight of both trains at the same time, due to defective erection by a construction company previously cited for building code violations.

"The bridge literally would have broken apart under the weight of both trains," said engineering expert Dr. Richard Kasden. "Hundreds, if not thousands, could have been injured, or worse, killed."

The construction company that built the bridge, Samson Construction, was cited for seven separate infractions of building code regulations last year. According to Samson representative Charles Rihga, the New Troy Bridge passed all tests, but they are never the less glad that the city officials have decided to "make certain" the trains can run on the bridge.

"We aren't responsible for their poor scheduling," Rihga added. "Our

**The New Troy Bridge, which could have been the site for tragedy had Metropolis's new monorail and subway lines met at 10:32 today as scheduled.**

work on that bridge passed all of the minimum construction requirements. These trains weren't even in concept stages when we built the bridge, so if it can't handle the combined weight, it's not because of 'faulty construction.'"

Regardless of Mr. Rihga's comments, city officials fully intend to investigate Samson's records, and are considering what action, legal or otherwise, to take against the company.

*Continued on pg.3*

# SUPERMAN FOILS BANK ROBBERS-p.4

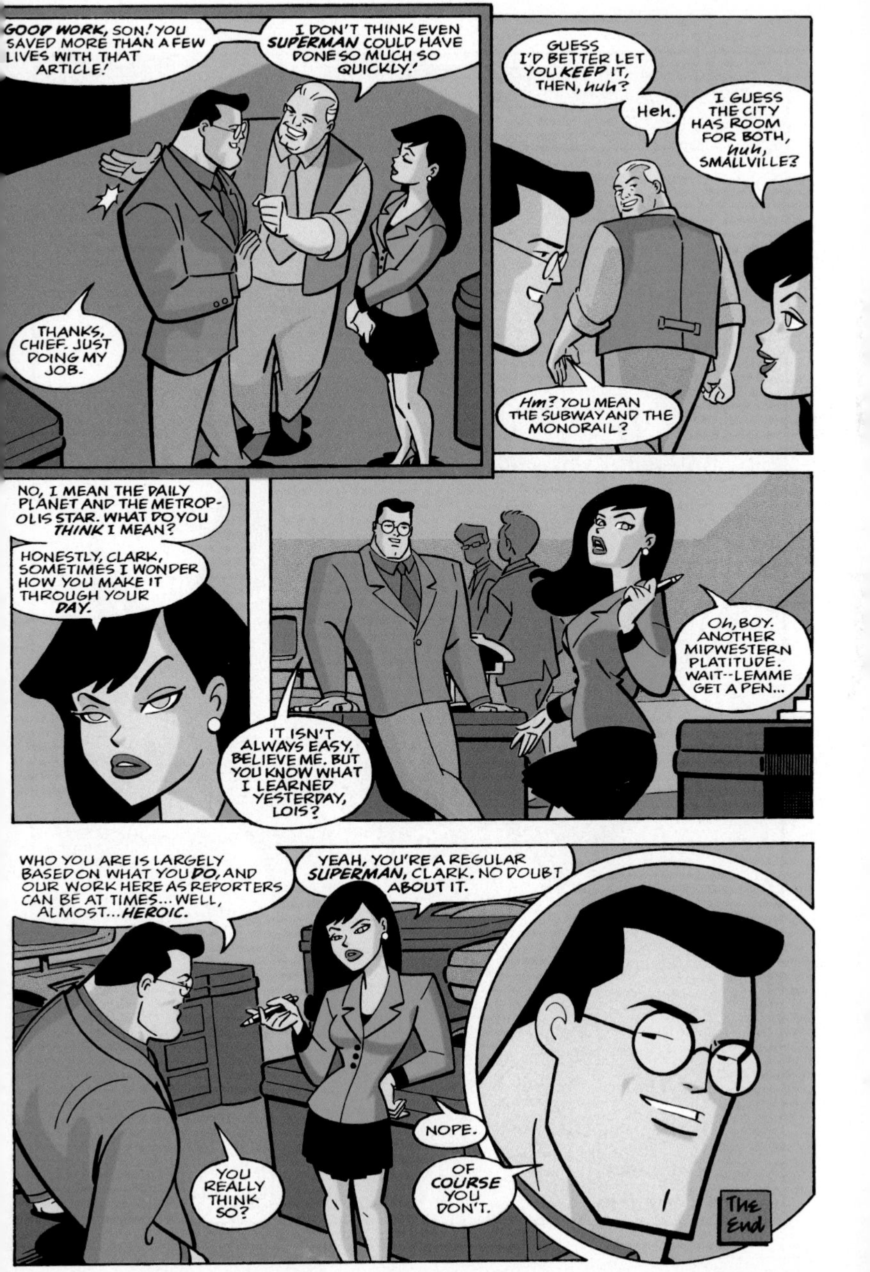
GOOD WORK, SON! YOU SAVED MORE THAN A FEW LIVES WITH THAT ARTICLE!
I DON'T THINK EVEN SUPERMAN COULD HAVE DONE SO MUCH SO QUICKLY!
THANKS, CHIEF. JUST DOING MY JOB.
GUESS I'D BETTER LET YOU KEEP IT, THEN, huh?
Heh.
I GUESS THE CITY HAS ROOM FOR BOTH, huh, SMALLVILLE?
Hm? YOU MEAN THE SUBWAY AND THE MONORAIL?
NO, I MEAN THE DAILY PLANET AND THE METROPOLIS STAR. WHAT DO YOU THINK I MEAN?
HONESTLY, CLARK, SOMETIMES I WONDER HOW YOU MAKE IT THROUGH YOUR DAY.
IT ISN'T ALWAYS EASY, BELIEVE ME. BUT YOU KNOW WHAT I LEARNED YESTERDAY, LOIS?
Oh, BOY. ANOTHER MIDWESTERN PLATITUDE. WAIT--LEMME GET A PEN...
WHO YOU ARE IS LARGELY BASED ON WHAT YOU DO, AND OUR WORK HERE AS REPORTERS CAN BE AT TIMES... WELL, ALMOST... HEROIC.
YOU REALLY THINK SO?
YEAH, YOU'RE A REGULAR SUPERMAN, CLARK. NO DOUBT ABOUT IT.
NOPE.
OF COURSE YOU DON'T.
The End

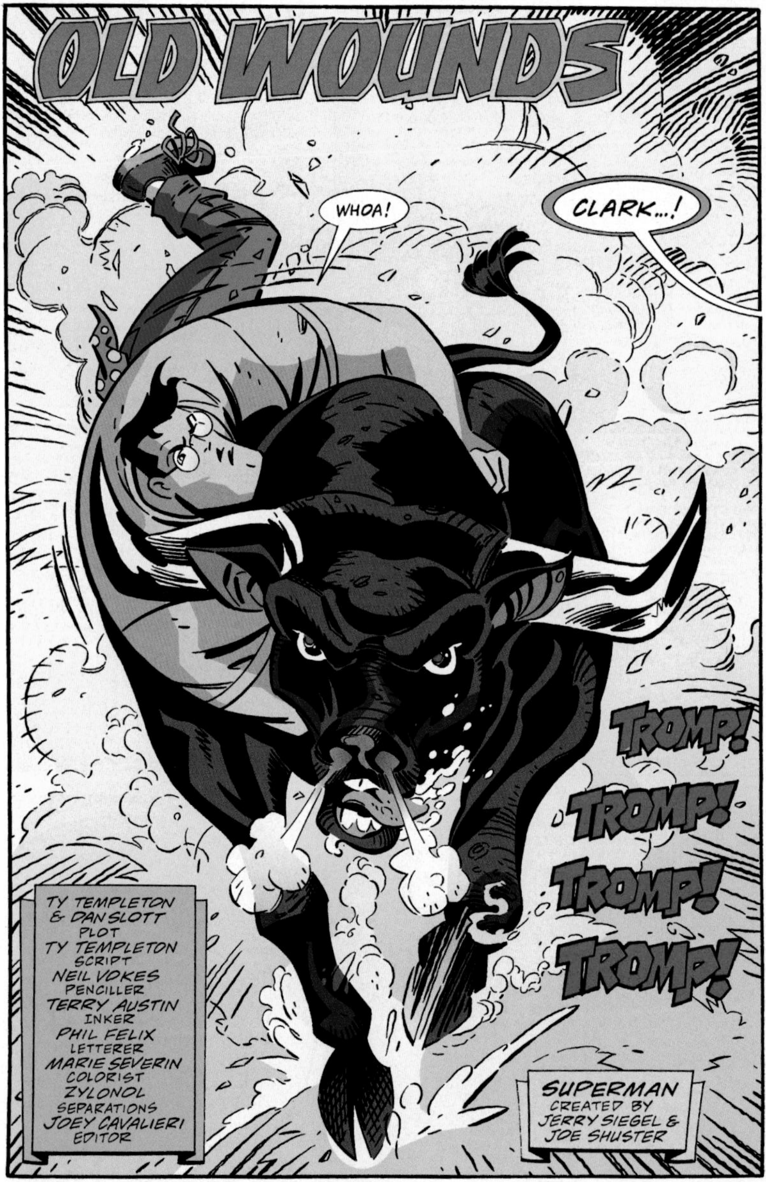
OLD WOUNDS
WHOA!
CLARK...!
TROMP!
TROMP!
TROMP!
TROMP!
TY TEMPLETON & DAN SLOTT PLOT
TY TEMPLETON SCRIPT
NEIL VOKES PENCILLER
TERRY AUSTIN INKER
PHIL FELIX LETTERER
MARIE SEVERIN COLORIST
ZYLONOL SEPARATIONS
JOEY CAVALIERI EDITOR
SUPERMAN CREATED BY JERRY SIEGEL & JOE SHUSTER

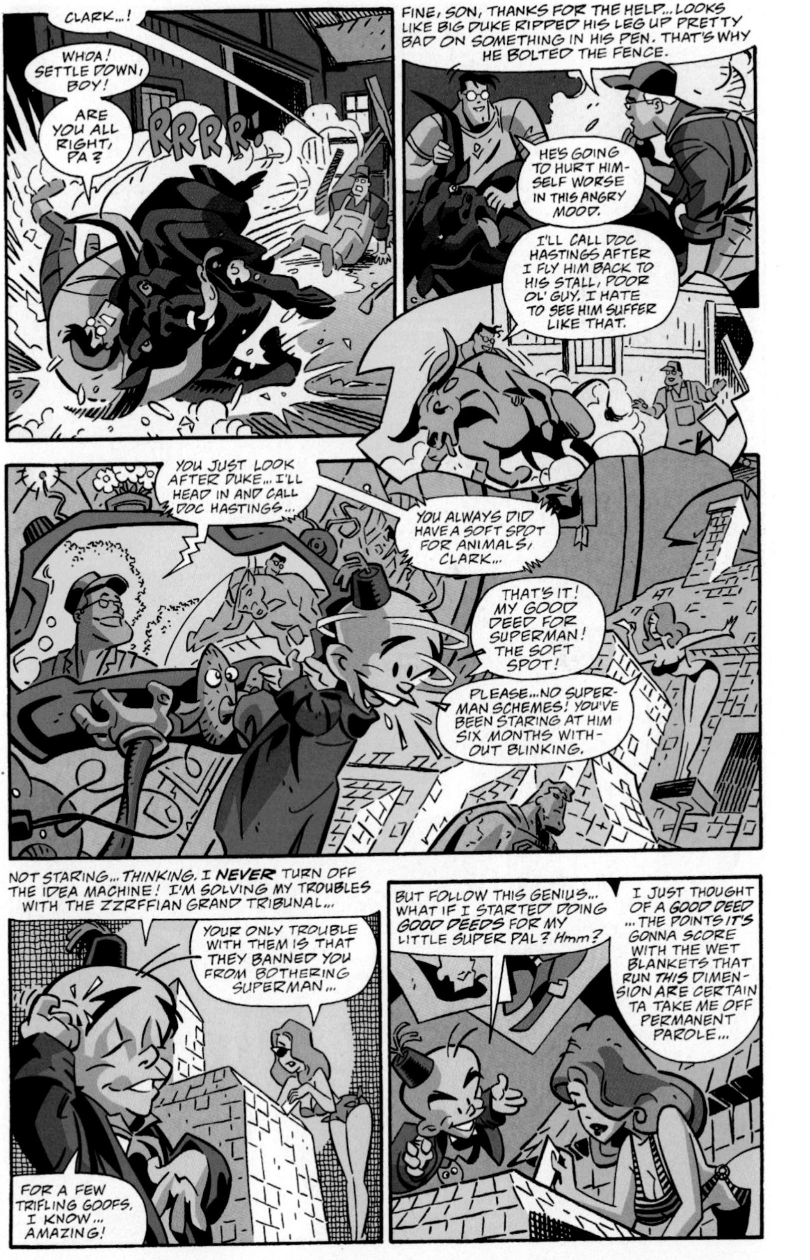

CLARK...!
WHOA! SETTLE DOWN, BOY!
ARE YOU ALL RIGHT, PA?
RRRR!
FINE, SON, THANKS FOR THE HELP... LOOKS LIKE BIG DUKE RIPPED HIS LEG UP PRETTY BAD ON SOMETHING IN HIS PEN. THAT'S WHY HE BOLTED THE FENCE.
HE'S GOING TO HURT HIMSELF WORSE IN THIS ANGRY MOOD.
I'LL CALL DOC HASTINGS AFTER I FLY HIM BACK TO HIS STALL, POOR OL' GUY. I HATE TO SEE HIM SUFFER LIKE THAT.
YOU JUST LOOK AFTER DUKE... I'LL HEAD IN AND CALL DOC HASTINGS...
YOU ALWAYS DID HAVE A SOFT SPOT FOR ANIMALS, CLARK...
THAT'S IT! MY GOOD DEED FOR SUPERMAN! THE SOFT SPOT!
PLEASE...NO SUPERMAN SCHEMES! YOU'VE BEEN STARING AT HIM SIX MONTHS WITHOUT BLINKING.
NOT STARING... THINKING. I NEVER TURN OFF THE IDEA MACHINE! I'M SOLVING MY TROUBLES WITH THE ZZRFFIAN GRAND TRIBUNAL...
YOUR ONLY TROUBLE WITH THEM IS THAT THEY BANNED YOU FROM BOTHERING SUPERMAN...
FOR A FEW TRIFLING GOOFS, I KNOW... AMAZING!
BUT FOLLOW THIS GENIUS... WHAT IF I STARTED DOING GOOD DEEDS FOR MY LITTLE SUPER PAL? Hmm?
I JUST THOUGHT OF A GOOD DEED ...THE POINTS IT'S GONNA SCORE WITH THE WET BLANKETS THAT RUN THIS DIMENSION ARE CERTAIN TA TAKE ME OFF PERMANENT PAROLE...

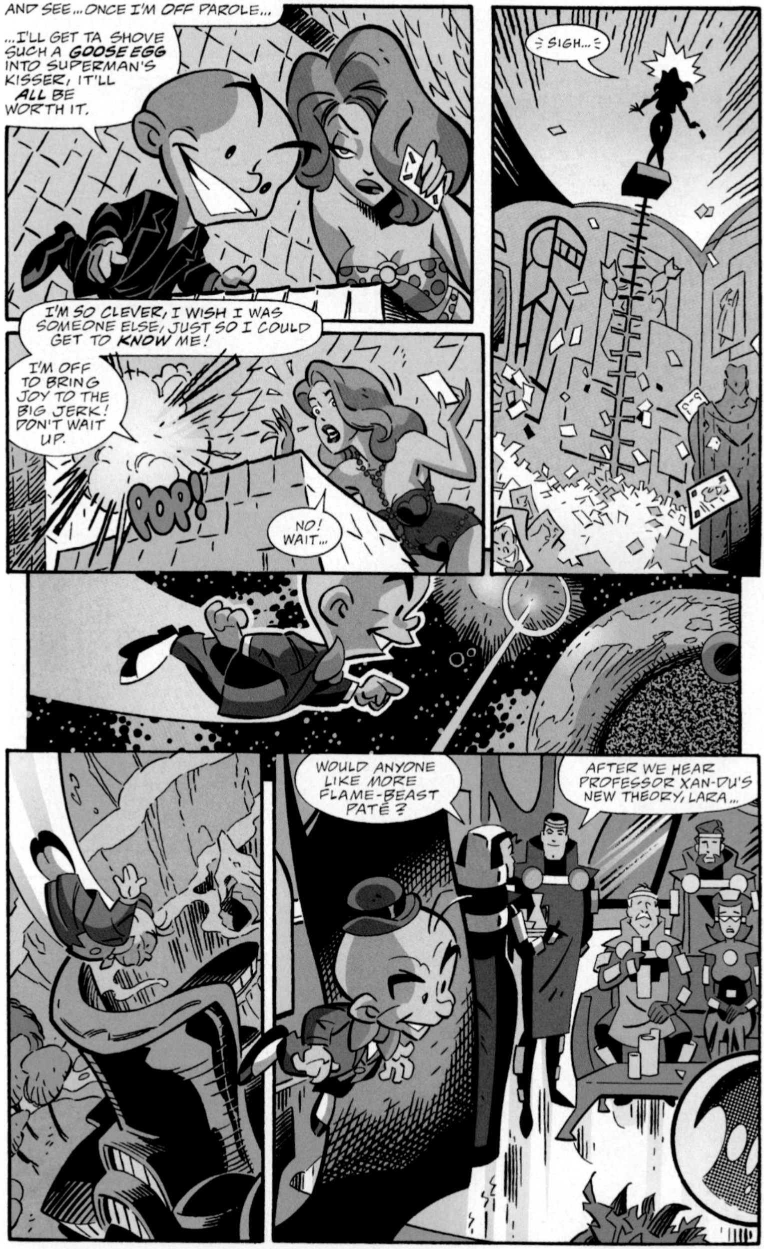

AND SEE... ONCE I'M OFF PAROLE...
...I'LL GET TA SHOVE SUCH A GOOSE EGG INTO SUPERMAN'S KISSER, IT'LL ALL BE WORTH IT.
SIGH...
I'M SO CLEVER, I WISH I WAS SOMEONE ELSE, JUST SO I COULD GET TO KNOW ME!
I'M OFF TO BRING JOY TO THE BIG JERK! DON'T WAIT UP.
POP!
NO! WAIT...
WOULD ANYONE LIKE MORE FLAME-BEAST PATÉ?
AFTER WE HEAR PROFESSOR XAN-DU'S NEW THEORY, LARA...

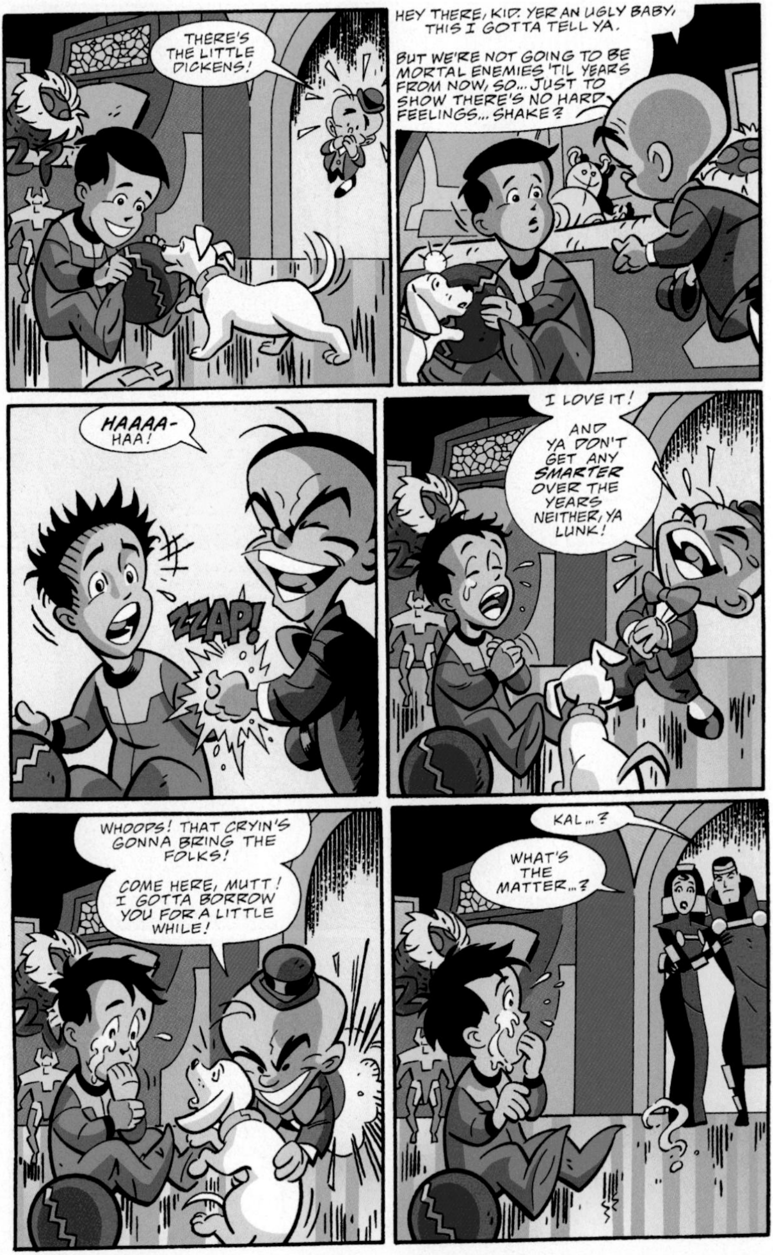
THERE'S THE LITTLE DICKENS!
HEY THERE, KID. YER AN UGLY BABY, THIS I GOTTA TELL YA.
BUT WE'RE NOT GOING TO BE MORTAL ENEMIES 'TIL YEARS FROM NOW, SO... JUST TO SHOW THERE'S NO HARD FEELINGS... SHAKE?
HAAAA-HAA!
ZZAP!
I LOVE IT!
AND YA DON'T GET ANY SMARTER OVER THE YEARS NEITHER, YA LUNK!
WHOOPS! THAT CRYIN'S GONNA BRING THE FOLKS!
COME HERE, MUTT! I GOTTA BORROW YOU FOR A LITTLE WHILE!
KAL...?
WHAT'S THE MATTER...?

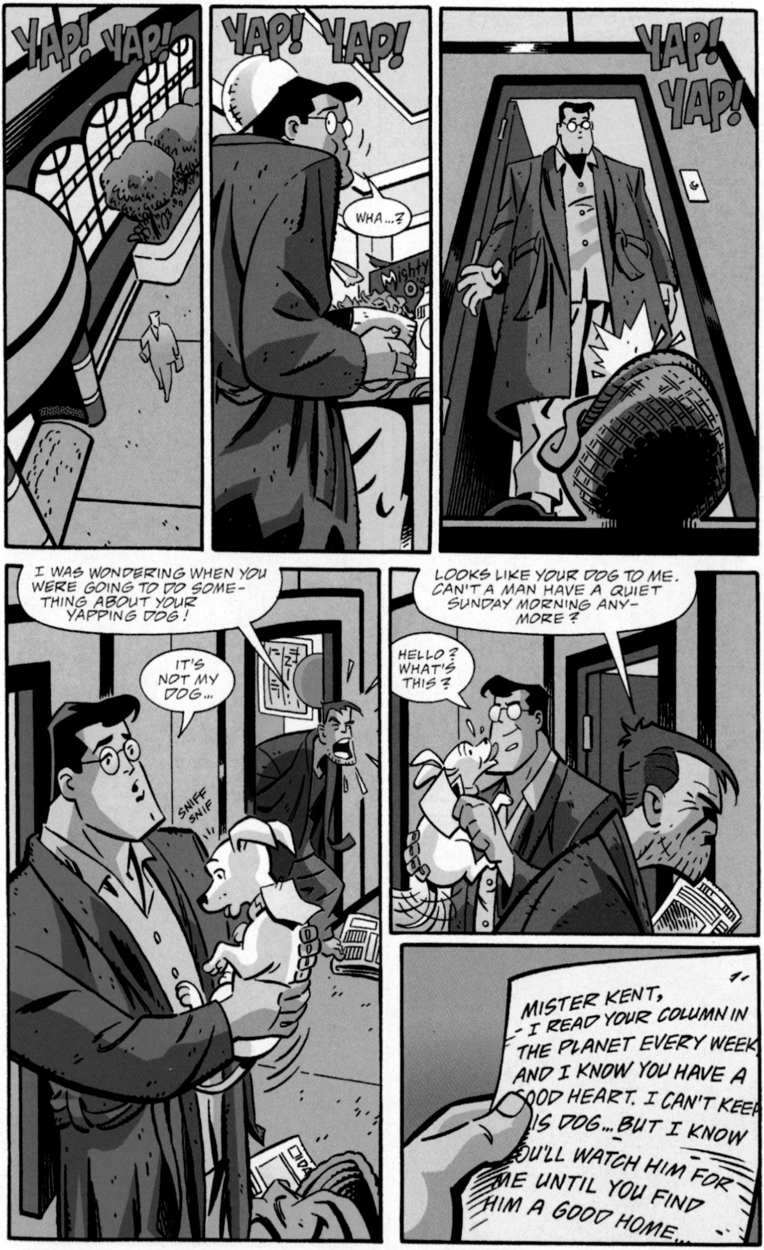

YAP! YAP!
YAP! YAP!
WHA...?
Mighty O's
YAP! YAP!
I WAS WONDERING WHEN YOU WERE GOING TO DO SOMETHING ABOUT YOUR YAPPING DOG!
IT'S NOT MY DOG...
SNIFF SNIF
LOOKS LIKE YOUR DOG TO ME. CAN'T A MAN HAVE A QUIET SUNDAY MORNING ANYMORE?
HELLO? WHAT'S THIS?
MISTER KENT,
I READ YOUR COLUMN IN THE PLANET EVERY WEEK AND I KNOW YOU HAVE A
OOD HEART. I CAN'T KEE
IS DOG... BUT I KNOW
OU'LL WATCH HIM FOR ME UNTIL YOU FIND HIM A GOOD HOME...

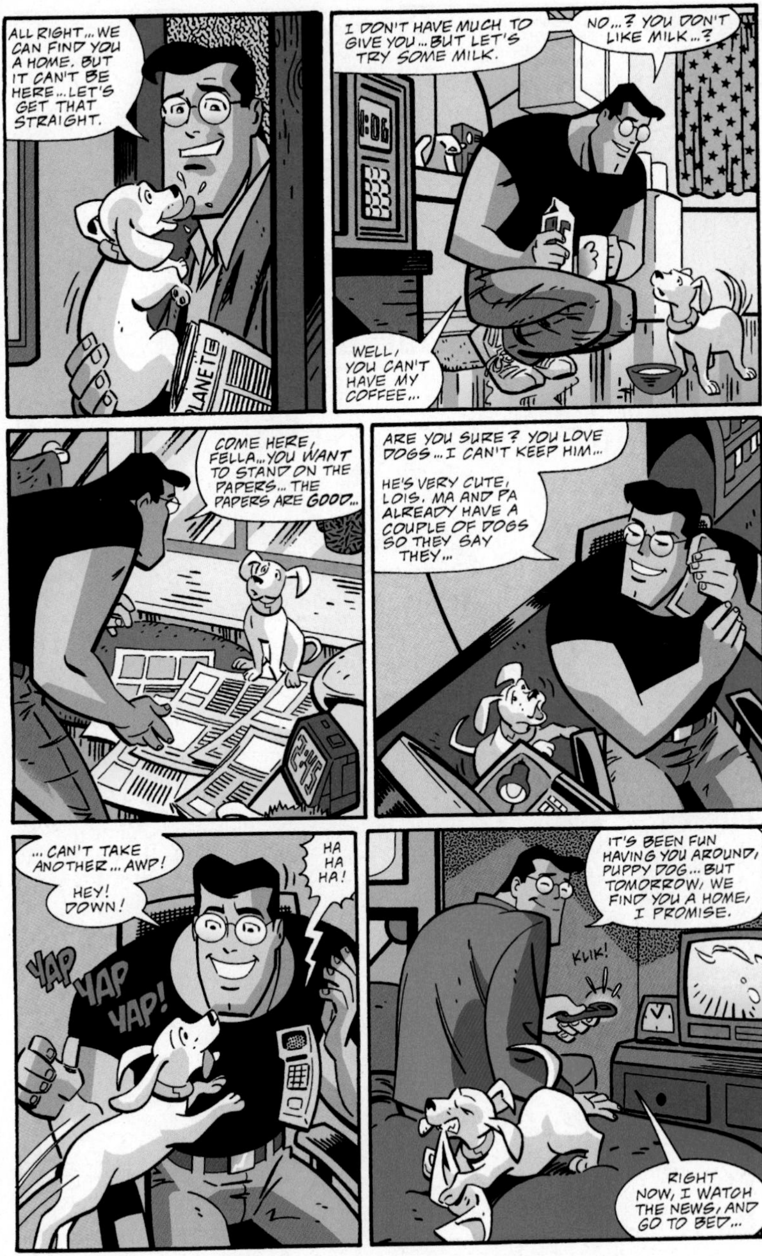
ALL RIGHT... WE CAN FIND YOU A HOME. BUT IT CAN'T BE HERE... LET'S GET THAT STRAIGHT.
PLANET
I DON'T HAVE MUCH TO GIVE YOU... BUT LET'S TRY SOME MILK.
NO...? YOU DON'T LIKE MILK...?
WELL, YOU CAN'T HAVE MY COFFEE...
COME HERE, FELLA... YOU WANT TO STAND ON THE PAPERS... THE PAPERS ARE GOOD...
ARE YOU SURE? YOU LOVE DOGS... I CAN'T KEEP HIM...
HE'S VERY CUTE, LOIS. MA AND PA ALREADY HAVE A COUPLE OF DOGS SO THEY SAY THEY...
...CAN'T TAKE ANOTHER... AWP!
HEY! DOWN!
HA HA HA!
YAP YAP YAP!
IT'S BEEN FUN HAVING YOU AROUND, PUPPY DOG... BUT TOMORROW, WE FIND YOU A HOME, I PROMISE.
KLIK!
RIGHT NOW, I WATCH THE NEWS, AND GO TO BED...

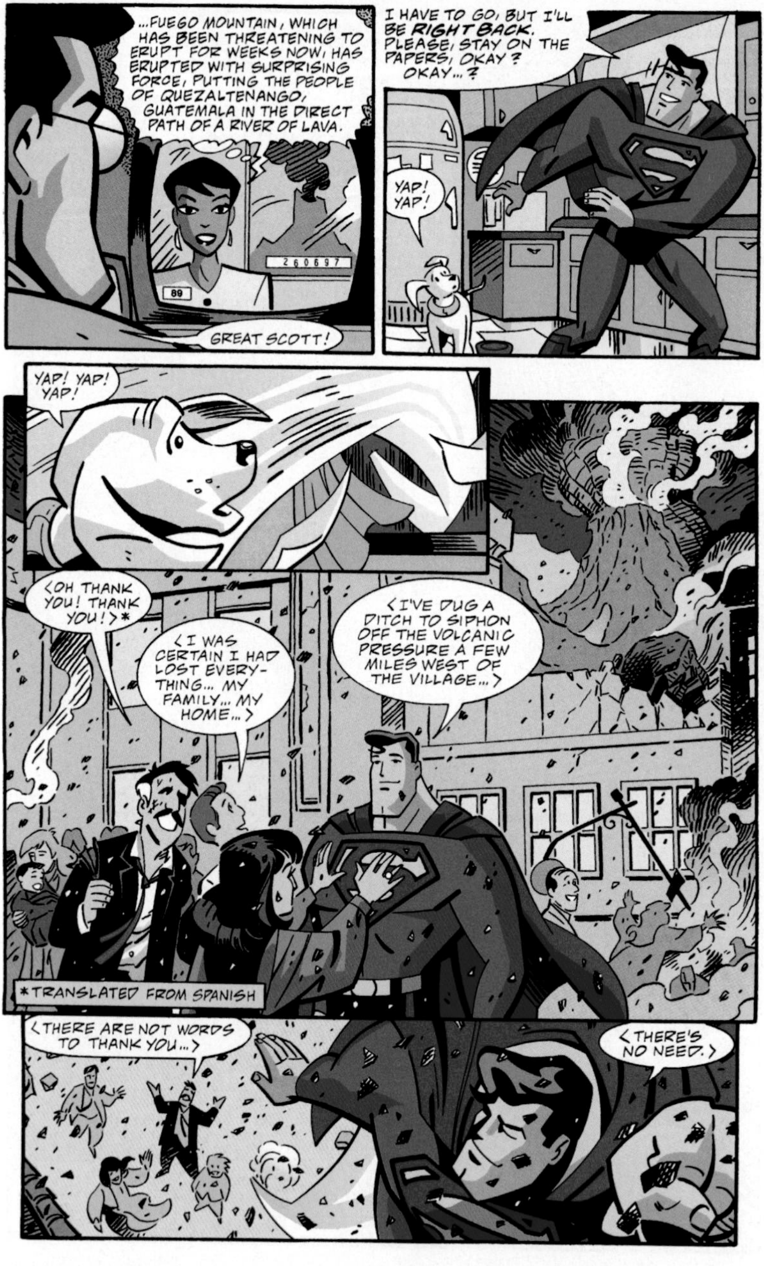
...FUEGO MOUNTAIN, WHICH HAS BEEN THREATENING TO ERUPT FOR WEEKS NOW, HAS ERUPTED WITH SURPRISING FORCE, PUTTING THE PEOPLE OF QUEZALTENANGO, GUATEMALA IN THE DIRECT PATH OF A RIVER OF LAVA.
260697
89
GREAT SCOTT!
I HAVE TO GO, BUT I'LL BE RIGHT BACK. PLEASE, STAY ON THE PAPERS, OKAY? OKAY...?
YAP! YAP!
YAP! YAP! YAP!
<OH THANK YOU! THANK YOU!>*
<I WAS CERTAIN I HAD LOST EVERYTHING... MY FAMILY... MY HOME...>
<I'VE DUG A DITCH TO SIPHON OFF THE VOLCANIC PRESSURE A FEW MILES WEST OF THE VILLAGE...>
*TRANSLATED FROM SPANISH
<THERE ARE NOT WORDS TO THANK YOU...>
<THERE'S NO NEED.>

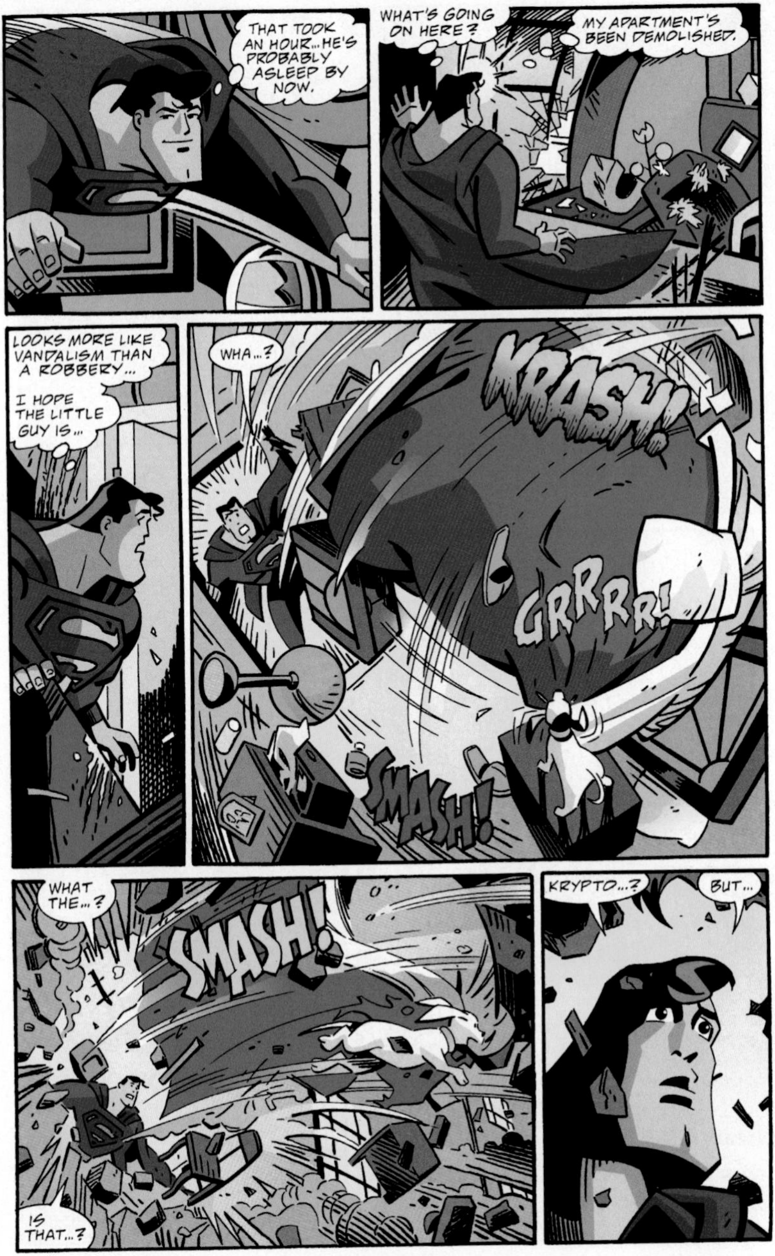
THAT TOOK AN HOUR... HE'S PROBABLY ASLEEP BY NOW.
WHAT'S GOING ON HERE?
MY APARTMENT'S BEEN DEMOLISHED.
LOOKS MORE LIKE VANDALISM THAN A ROBBERY...
I HOPE THE LITTLE GUY IS...
WHA...?
KRASH!
GRRRR!
SMASH!
WHAT THE...?
SMASH!
IS THAT...?
KRYPTO...?
BUT...

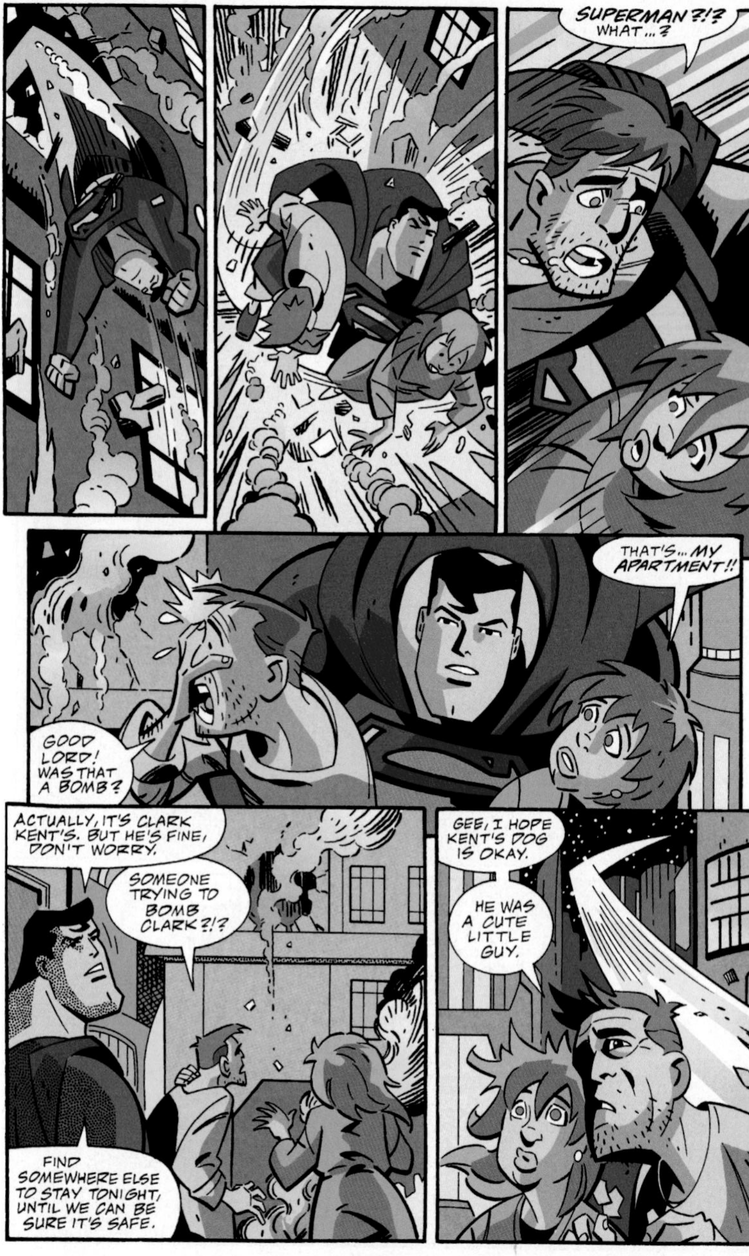
SUPERMAN?!? WHAT...?
THAT'S... MY APARTMENT!!
GOOD LORD! WAS THAT A BOMB?
ACTUALLY, IT'S CLARK KENT'S. BUT HE'S FINE, DON'T WORRY.
SOMEONE TRYING TO BOMB CLARK?!?
FIND SOMEWHERE ELSE TO STAY TONIGHT, UNTIL WE CAN BE SURE IT'S SAFE.
GEE, I HOPE KENT'S DOG IS OKAY.
HE WAS A CUTE LITTLE GUY.

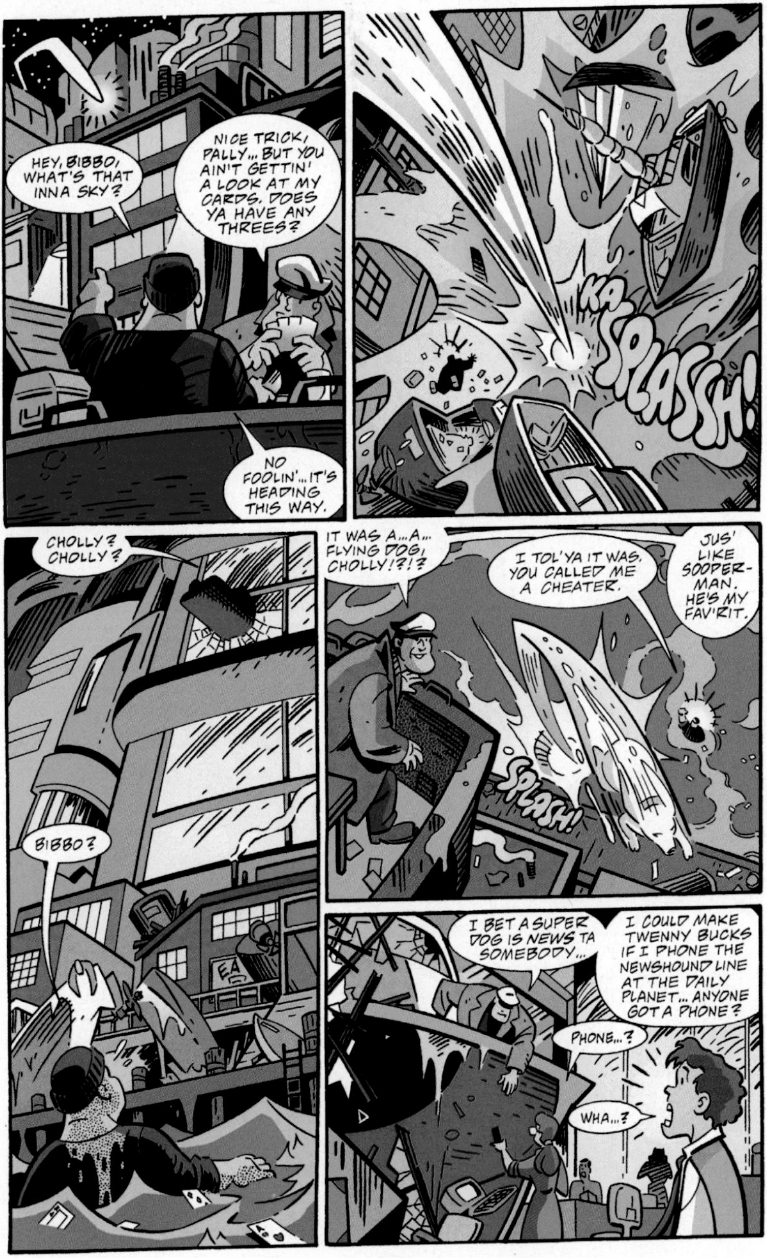
HEY, BIBBO, WHAT'S THAT INNA SKY?
NICE TRICK, PALLY... BUT YOU AIN'T GETTIN' A LOOK AT MY CARDS. DOES YA HAVE ANY THREES?
NO FOOLIN'... IT'S HEADING THIS WAY.
KA-SPLASSH!
CHOLLY? CHOLLY?
BIBBO?
IT WAS A... A... FLYING DOG, CHOLLY!?!?
I TOL'YA IT WAS. YOU CALLED ME A CHEATER.
JUS' LIKE SOOPER-MAN. HE'S MY FAV'RIT.
SPLASH!
I BET A SUPER DOG IS NEWS TA SOMEBODY...
I COULD MAKE TWENNY BUCKS IF I PHONE THE NEWSHOUND LINE AT THE DAILY PLANET... ANYONE GOT A PHONE?
PHONE...?
WHA...?

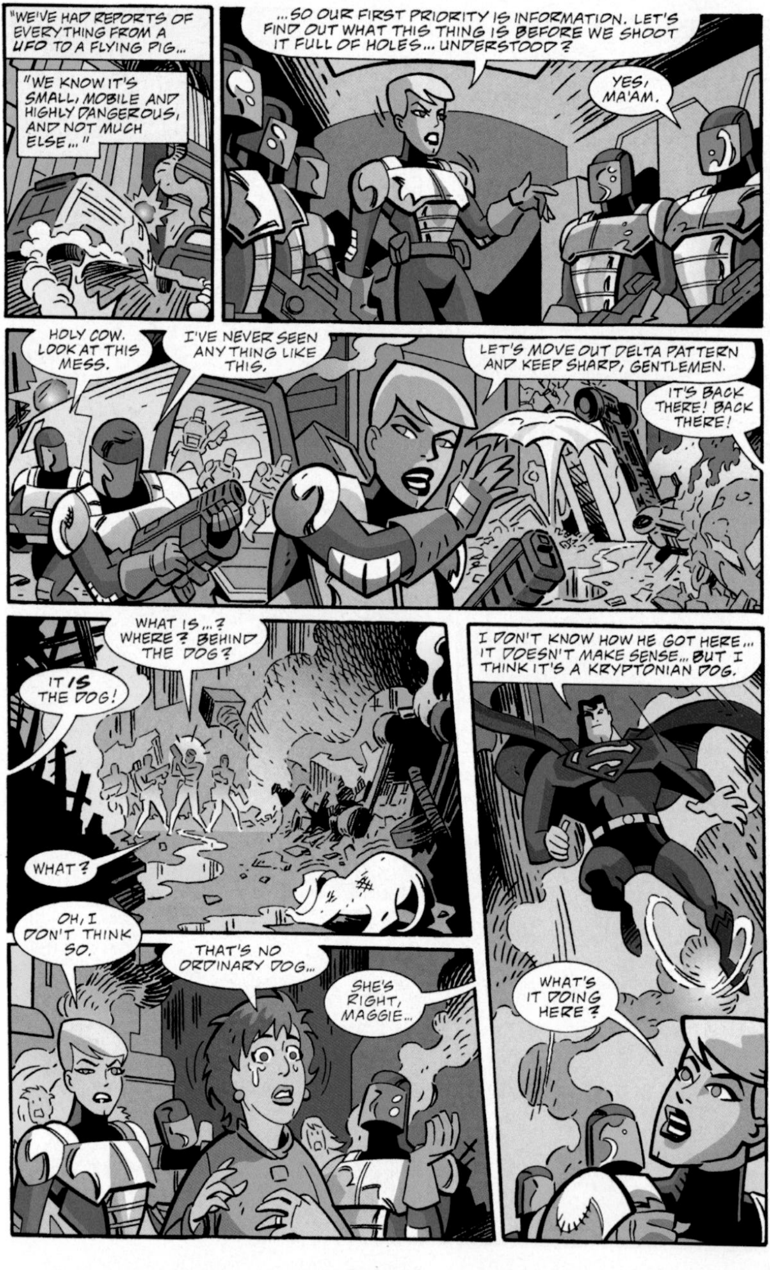
"WE'VE HAD REPORTS OF EVERYTHING FROM A UFO TO A FLYING PIG...
"WE KNOW IT'S SMALL, MOBILE AND HIGHLY DANGEROUS, AND NOT MUCH ELSE..."
...SO OUR FIRST PRIORITY IS INFORMATION. LET'S FIND OUT WHAT THIS THING IS BEFORE WE SHOOT IT FULL OF HOLES... UNDERSTOOD?
YES, MA'AM.
HOLY COW. LOOK AT THIS MESS.
I'VE NEVER SEEN ANY THING LIKE THIS.
LET'S MOVE OUT DELTA PATTERN AND KEEP SHARP, GENTLEMEN.
IT'S BACK THERE! BACK THERE!
WHAT IS...? WHERE? BEHIND THE DOG?
IT IS THE DOG!
WHAT?
I DON'T KNOW HOW HE GOT HERE... IT DOESN'T MAKE SENSE... BUT I THINK IT'S A KRYPTONIAN DOG.
OH, I DON'T THINK SO.
THAT'S NO ORDINARY DOG...
SHE'S RIGHT, MAGGIE...
WHAT'S IT DOING HERE?

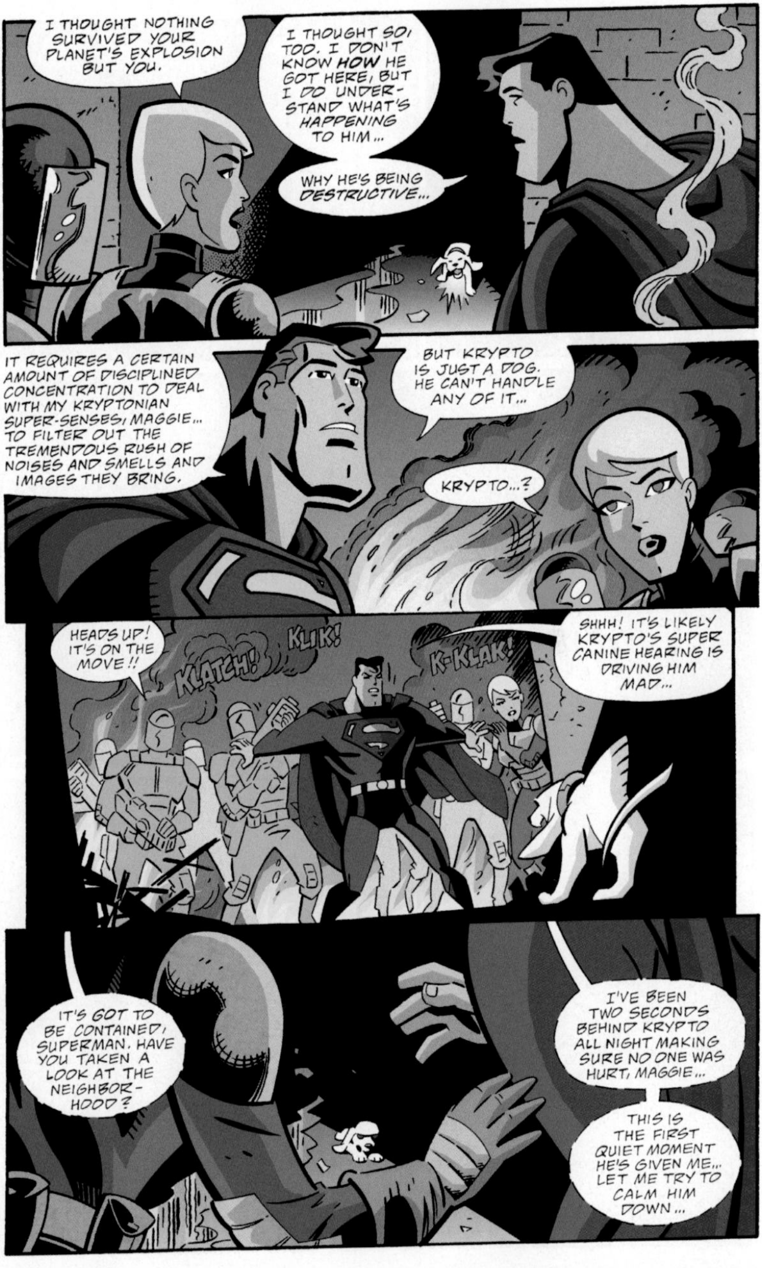
I THOUGHT NOTHING SURVIVED YOUR PLANET'S EXPLOSION BUT YOU.
I THOUGHT SO, TOO. I DON'T KNOW **HOW** HE GOT HERE, BUT I DO UNDER-STAND WHAT'S *HAPPENING* TO HIM...
WHY HE'S BEING *DESTRUCTIVE*...
IT REQUIRES A CERTAIN AMOUNT OF DISCIPLINED CONCENTRATION TO DEAL WITH MY KRYPTONIAN SUPER-SENSES, MAGGIE... TO FILTER OUT THE TREMENDOUS RUSH OF NOISES AND SMELLS AND IMAGES THEY BRING.
BUT KRYPTO IS JUST A DOG. HE CAN'T HANDLE ANY OF IT...
KRYPTO...?
HEADS UP! IT'S ON THE MOVE!!
KLATCH!
KLIK!
K-KLAK!
SHHH! IT'S LIKELY KRYPTO'S SUPER CANINE HEARING IS DRIVING HIM MAD...
IT'S GOT TO BE CONTAINED, SUPERMAN. HAVE YOU TAKEN A LOOK AT THE NEIGHBOR-HOOD?
I'VE BEEN TWO SECONDS BEHIND KRYPTO ALL NIGHT MAKING SURE NO ONE WAS HURT, MAGGIE...
THIS IS THE FIRST QUIET MOMENT HE'S GIVEN ME... LET ME TRY TO CALM HIM DOWN...

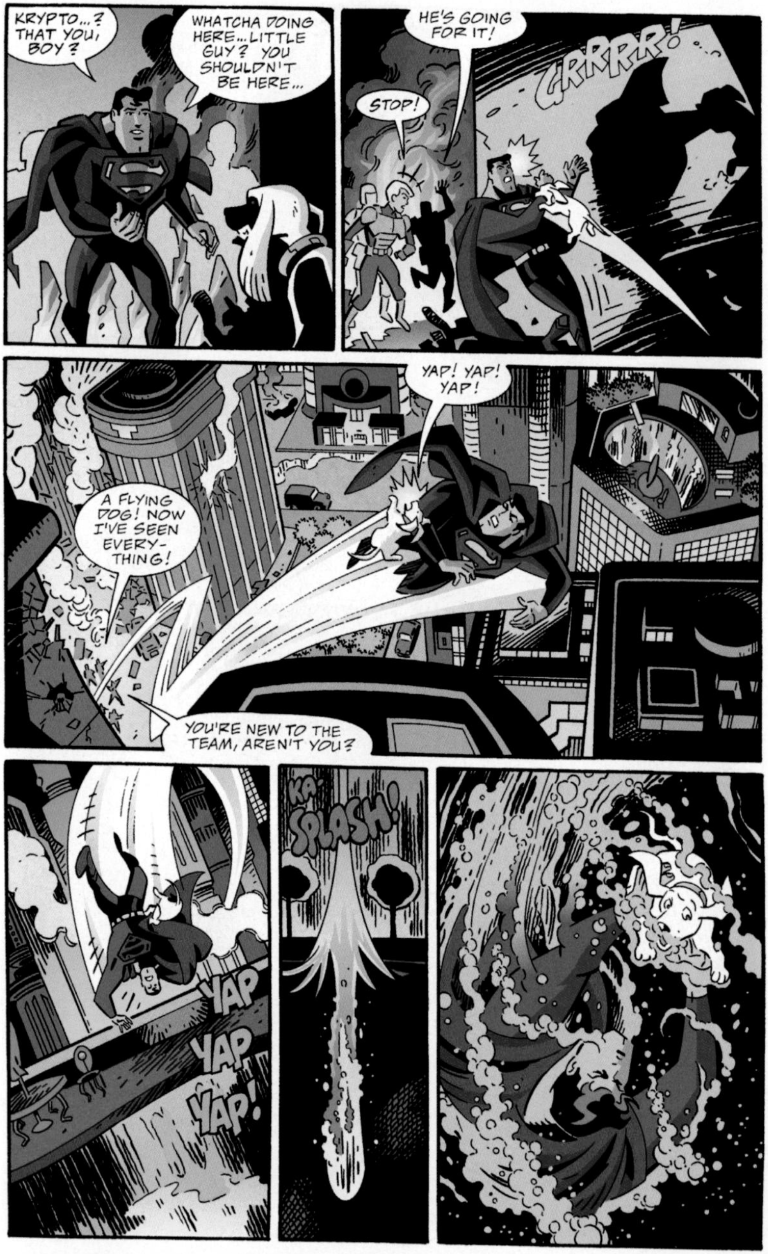
KRYPTO...? THAT YOU, BOY?
WHATCHA DOING HERE...LITTLE GUY? YOU SHOULDN'T BE HERE...
HE'S GOING FOR IT!
STOP!
GRRRR!
YAP! YAP! YAP!
A FLYING DOG! NOW I'VE SEEN EVERYTHING!
YOU'RE NEW TO THE TEAM, AREN'T YOU?
YAP
YAP
YAP!
KA-SPLASH!

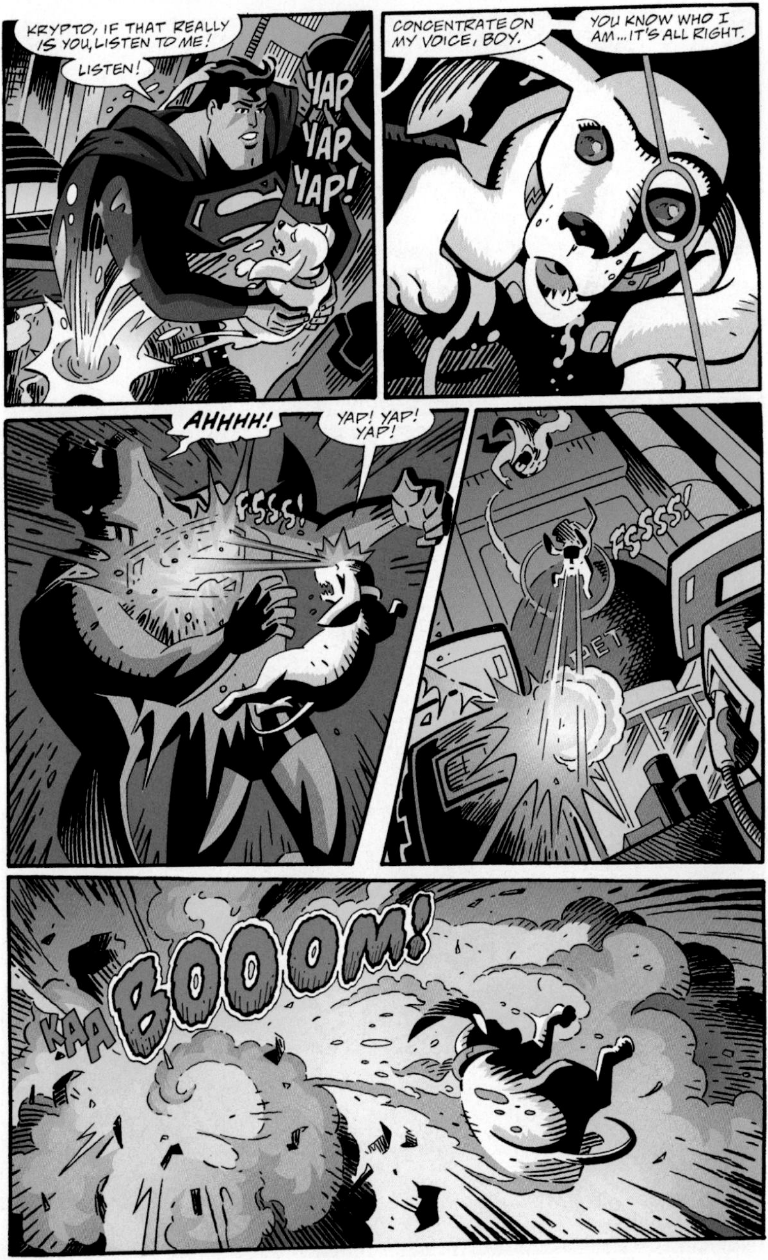

KRYPTO, IF THAT REALLY IS YOU, LISTEN TO ME!
LISTEN!
YAP YAP YAP!
CONCENTRATE ON MY VOICE, BOY.
YOU KNOW WHO I AM... IT'S ALL RIGHT.
AHHHH!
YAP! YAP! YAP!
FSSSS!
FSSSS!
KAA BOOOM!

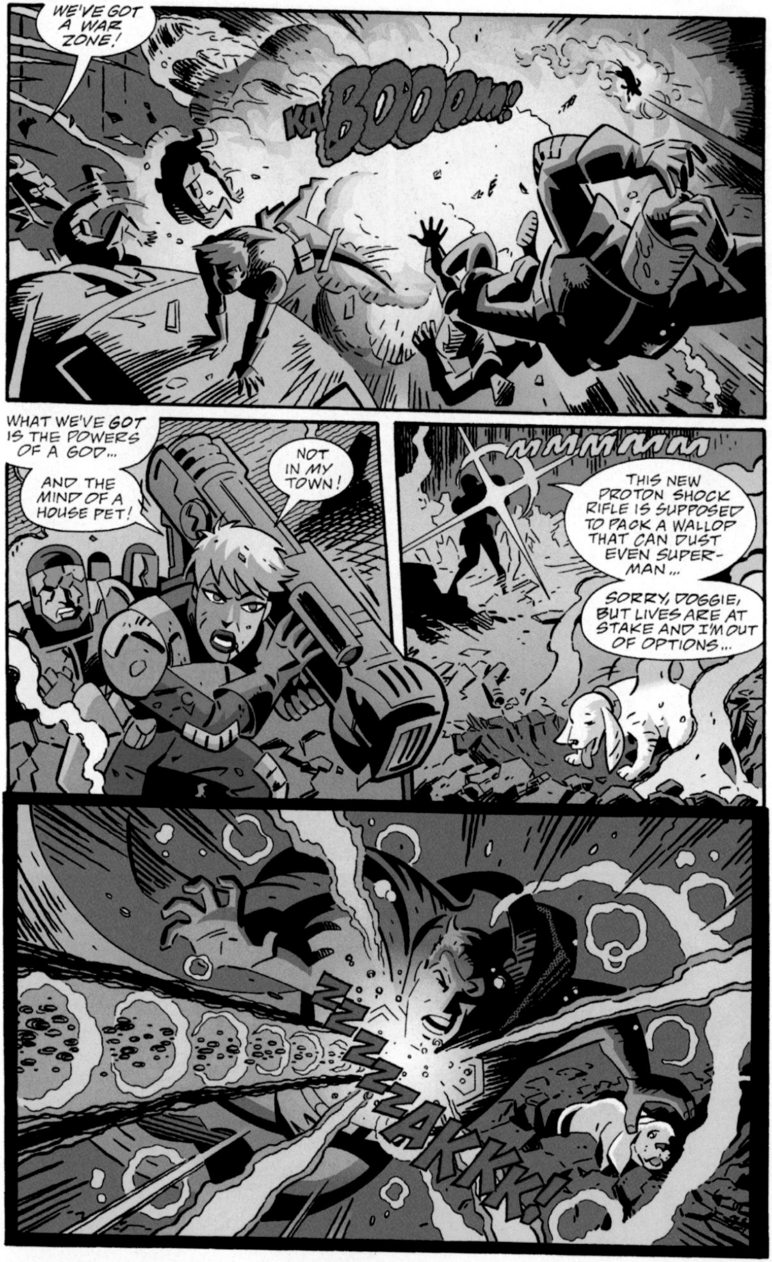
WE'VE GOT A WAR ZONE!
KABOOOM!
WHAT WE'VE GOT IS THE POWERS OF A GOD...
AND THE MIND OF A HOUSE PET!
NOT IN MY TOWN!
MMMMMMM
THIS NEW PROTON SHOCK RIFLE IS SUPPOSED TO PACK A WALLOP THAT CAN DUST EVEN SUPER-MAN...
SORRY, DOGGIE, BUT LIVES ARE AT STAKE AND I'M OUT OF OPTIONS...
ZZZZZAKKK!

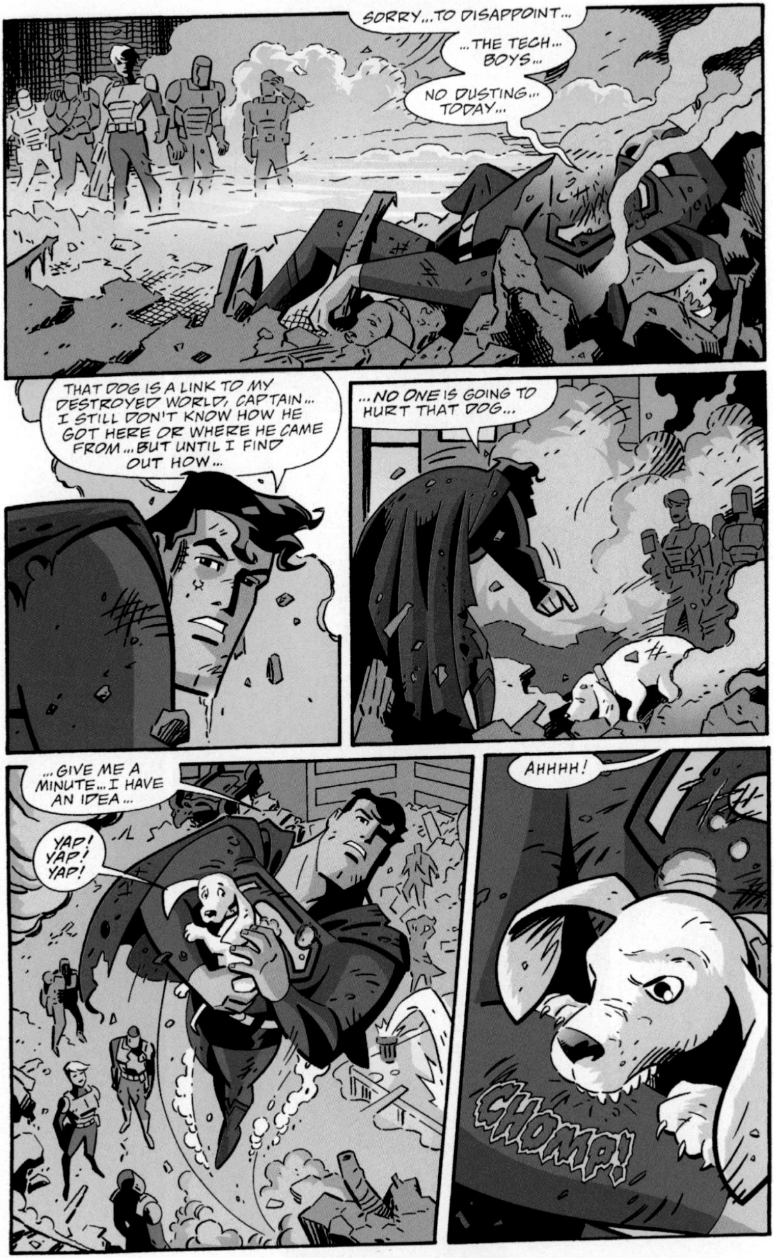
SORRY... TO DISAPPOINT...
...THE TECH... BOYS...
NO DUSTING... TODAY...
THAT DOG IS A LINK TO MY DESTROYED WORLD, CAPTAIN... I STILL DON'T KNOW HOW HE GOT HERE OR WHERE HE CAME FROM... BUT UNTIL I FIND OUT HOW...
...NO ONE IS GOING TO HURT THAT DOG...
...GIVE ME A MINUTE... I HAVE AN IDEA...
YAP! YAP! YAP!
AHHHH!
CHOMP!

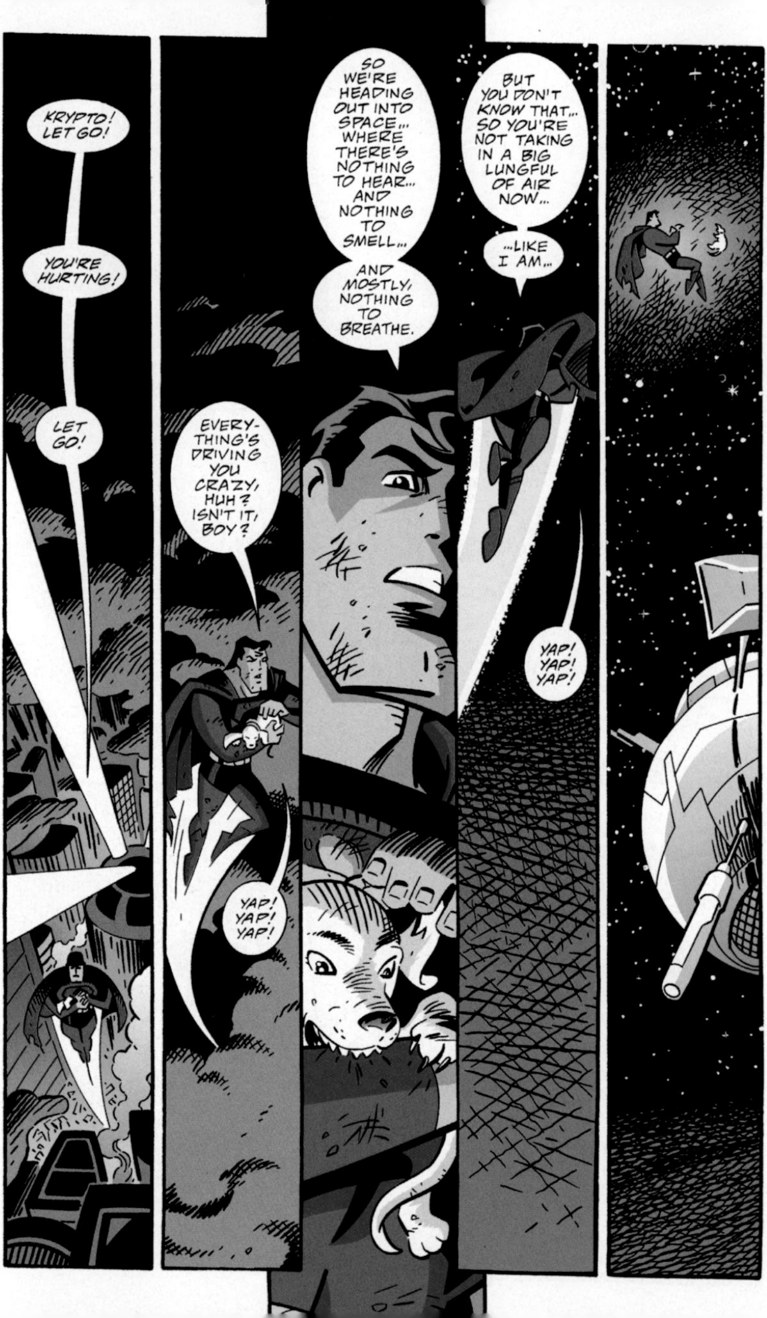
KRYPTO! LET GO!
YOU'RE HURTING!
LET GO!
EVERY-THING'S DRIVING YOU CRAZY, HUH? ISN'T IT, BOY?
YAP! YAP! YAP!
SO WE'RE HEADING OUT INTO SPACE... WHERE THERE'S NOTHING TO HEAR... AND NOTHING TO SMELL...
AND MOSTLY, NOTHING TO BREATHE.
BUT YOU DON'T KNOW THAT... SO YOU'RE NOT TAKING IN A BIG LUNGFUL OF AIR NOW...
...LIKE I AM...
YAP! YAP! YAP!

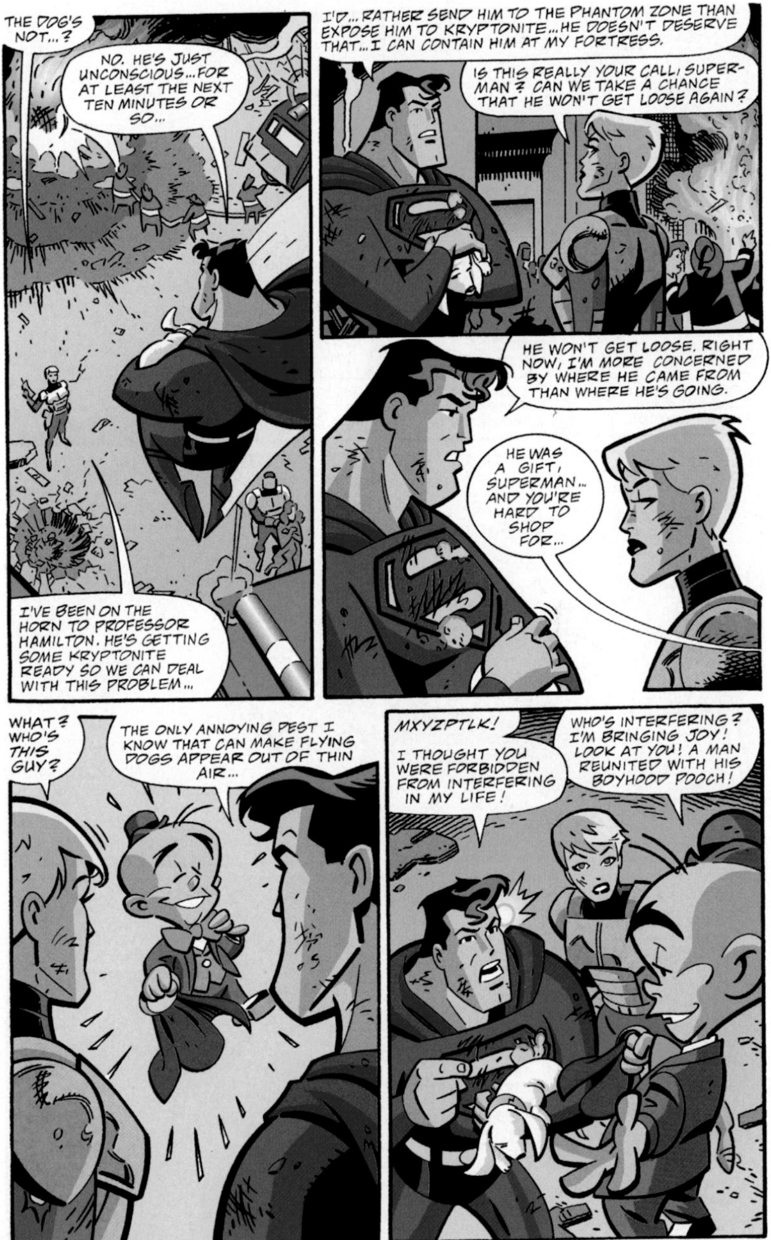

THE DOG'S NOT...?
NO. HE'S JUST UNCONSCIOUS...FOR AT LEAST THE NEXT TEN MINUTES OR SO...
I'VE BEEN ON THE HORN TO PROFESSOR HAMILTON. HE'S GETTING SOME KRYPTONITE READY SO WE CAN DEAL WITH THIS PROBLEM...
I'D... RATHER SEND HIM TO THE PHANTOM ZONE THAN EXPOSE HIM TO KRYPTONITE... HE DOESN'T DESERVE THAT... I CAN CONTAIN HIM AT MY FORTRESS.
IS THIS REALLY YOUR CALL, SUPER-MAN? CAN WE TAKE A CHANCE THAT HE WON'T GET LOOSE AGAIN?
HE WON'T GET LOOSE. RIGHT NOW, I'M MORE CONCERNED BY WHERE HE CAME FROM THAN WHERE HE'S GOING.
HE WAS A GIFT, SUPERMAN... AND YOU'RE HARD TO SHOP FOR...
WHAT? WHO'S THIS GUY?
THE ONLY ANNOYING PEST I KNOW THAT CAN MAKE FLYING DOGS APPEAR OUT OF THIN AIR...
MXYZPTLK!
I THOUGHT YOU WERE FORBIDDEN FROM INTERFERING IN MY LIFE!
WHO'S INTERFERING? I'M BRINGING JOY! LOOK AT YOU! A MAN REUNITED WITH HIS BOYHOOD POOCH!

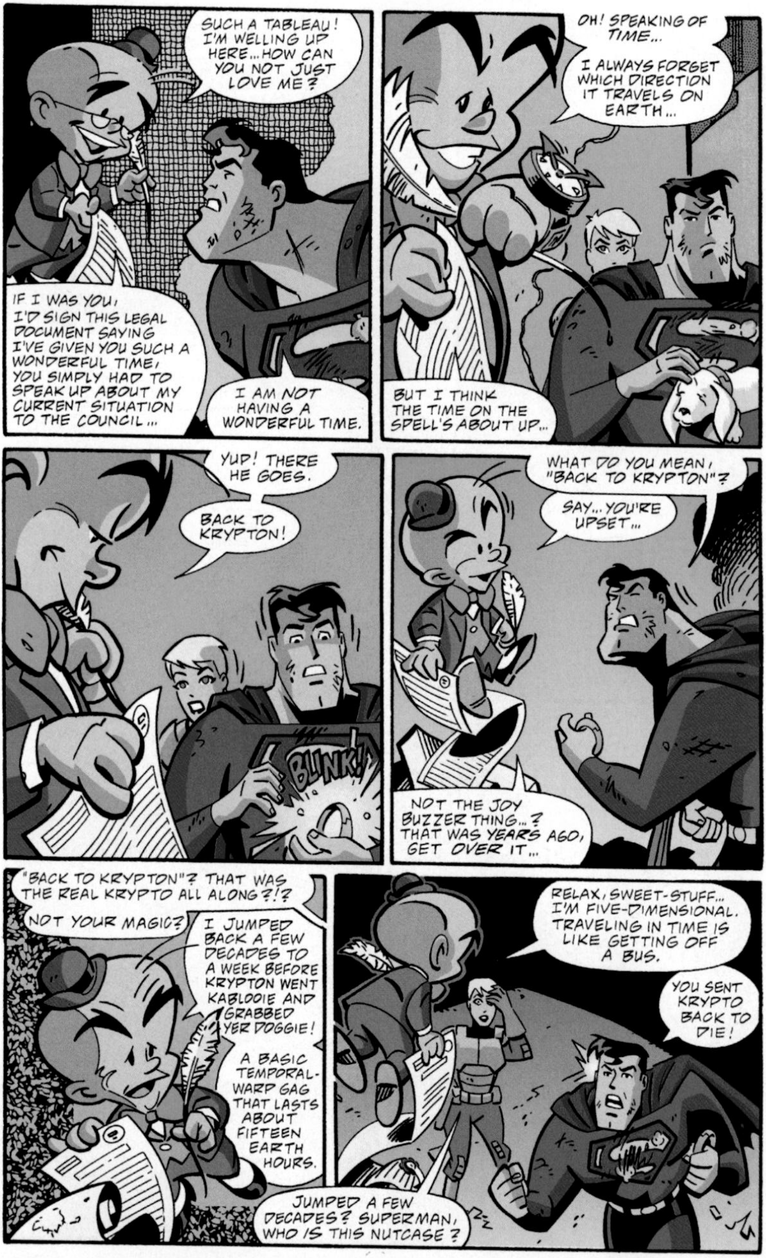

SUCH A TABLEAU! I'M WELLING UP HERE... HOW CAN YOU NOT JUST LOVE ME?
IF I WAS YOU, I'D SIGN THIS LEGAL DOCUMENT SAYING I'VE GIVEN YOU SUCH A WONDERFUL TIME, YOU SIMPLY HAD TO SPEAK UP ABOUT MY CURRENT SITUATION TO THE COUNCIL...
I AM NOT HAVING A WONDERFUL TIME.
OH! SPEAKING OF TIME...
I ALWAYS FORGET WHICH DIRECTION IT TRAVELS ON EARTH...
BUT I THINK THE TIME ON THE SPELL'S ABOUT UP...
YUP! THERE HE GOES.
BACK TO KRYPTON!
BLINK!
WHAT DO YOU MEAN, "BACK TO KRYPTON"?
SAY... YOU'RE UPSET...
NOT THE JOY BUZZER THING...? THAT WAS YEARS AGO, GET OVER IT...
"BACK TO KRYPTON"? THAT WAS THE REAL KRYPTO ALL ALONG?!?
NOT YOUR MAGIC?
I JUMPED BACK A FEW DECADES TO A WEEK BEFORE KRYPTON WENT KABLOOIE AND GRABBED YER DOGGIE!
A BASIC TEMPORAL-WARP GAG THAT LASTS ABOUT FIFTEEN EARTH HOURS.
RELAX, SWEET-STUFF... I'M FIVE-DIMENSIONAL. TRAVELING IN TIME IS LIKE GETTING OFF A BUS.
YOU SENT KRYPTO BACK TO DIE!
JUMPED A FEW DECADES? SUPERMAN, WHO IS THIS NUTCASE?

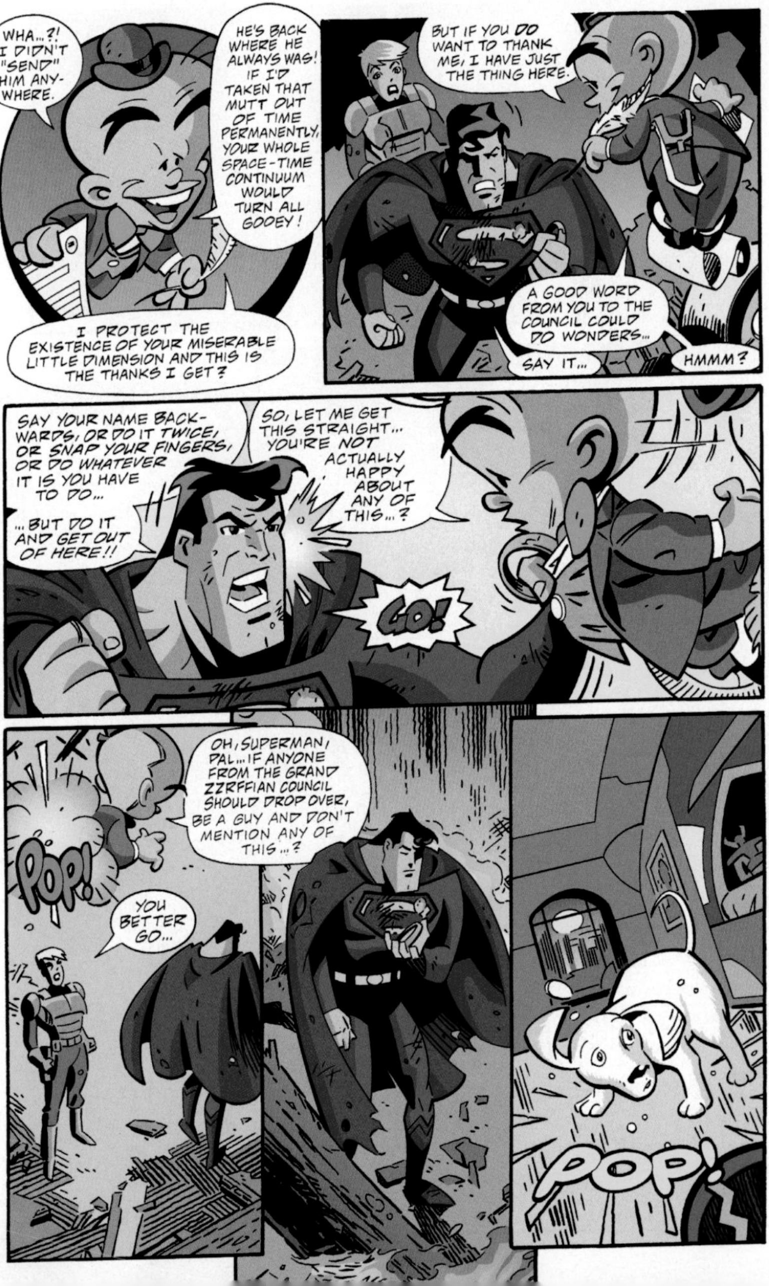
WHA...?! I DIDN'T "SEND" HIM ANYWHERE.
HE'S BACK WHERE HE ALWAYS WAS! IF I'D TAKEN THAT MUTT OUT OF TIME PERMANENTLY, YOUR WHOLE SPACE-TIME CONTINUUM WOULD TURN ALL GOOEY!
I PROTECT THE EXISTENCE OF YOUR MISERABLE LITTLE DIMENSION AND THIS IS THE THANKS I GET?
BUT IF YOU DO WANT TO THANK ME, I HAVE JUST THE THING HERE.
A GOOD WORD FROM YOU TO THE COUNCIL COULD DO WONDERS...
SAY IT...
HMMM?
SO, LET ME GET THIS STRAIGHT... YOU'RE NOT ACTUALLY HAPPY ABOUT ANY OF THIS...?
SAY YOUR NAME BACKWARDS, OR DO IT TWICE, OR SNAP YOUR FINGERS, OR DO WHATEVER IT IS YOU HAVE TO DO...
...BUT DO IT AND GET OUT OF HERE!!
GO!
OH, SUPERMAN, PAL... IF ANYONE FROM THE GRAND ZZRFFIAN COUNCIL SHOULD DROP OVER, BE A GUY AND DON'T MENTION ANY OF THIS...?
POP!
YOU BETTER GO...
POP!

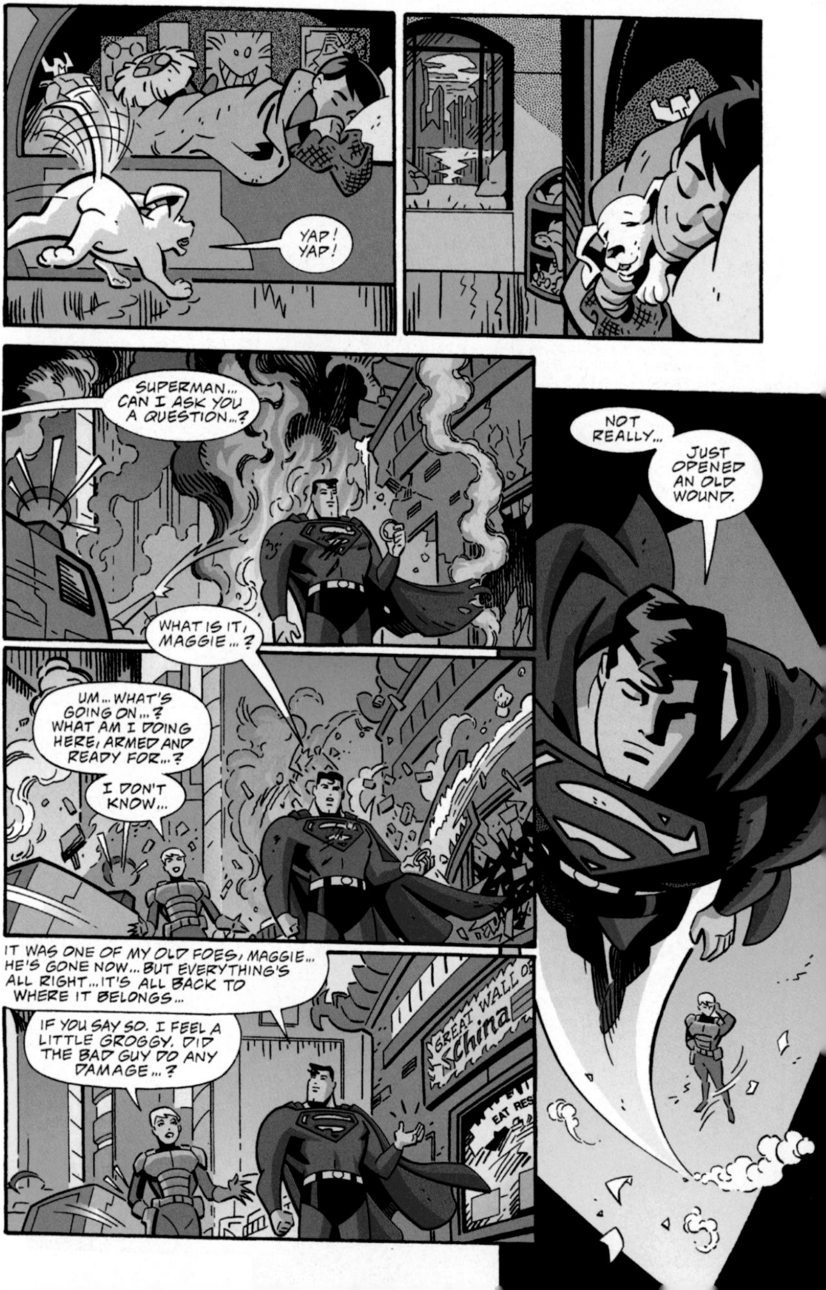
YAP! YAP!
SUPERMAN... CAN I ASK YOU A QUESTION...?
WHAT IS IT, MAGGIE...?
UM... WHAT'S GOING ON...? WHAT AM I DOING HERE, ARMED AND READY FOR...?
I DON'T KNOW...
IT WAS ONE OF MY OLD FOES, MAGGIE... HE'S GONE NOW... BUT EVERYTHING'S ALL RIGHT... IT'S ALL BACK TO WHERE IT BELONGS...
IF YOU SAY SO. I FEEL A LITTLE GROGGY. DID THE BAD GUY DO ANY DAMAGE...?
GREAT WALL OF
China
NOT REALLY...
JUST OPENED AN OLD WOUND.

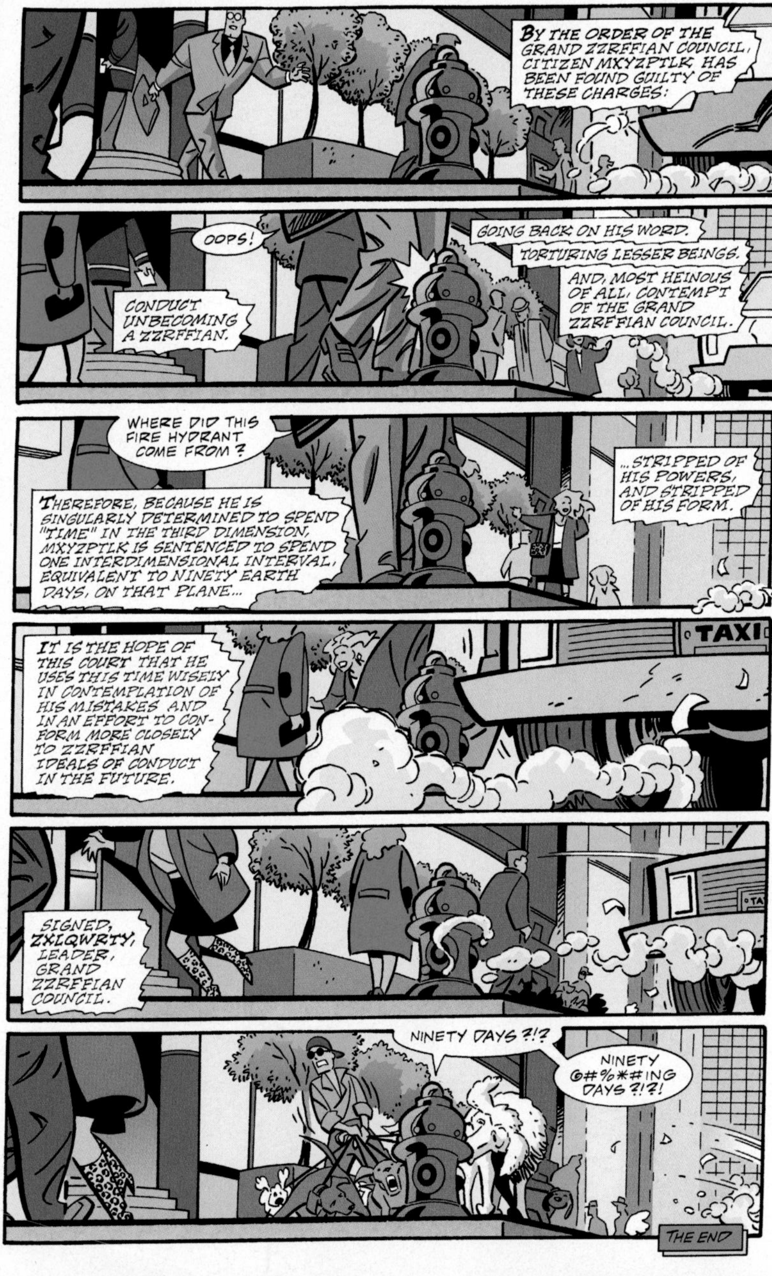
BY THE ORDER OF THE GRAND ZZRFFIAN COUNCIL, CITIZEN MXYZPTLK HAS BEEN FOUND GUILTY OF THESE CHARGES:
OOPS!
CONDUCT UNBECOMING A ZZRFFIAN.
GOING BACK ON HIS WORD.
TORTURING LESSER BEINGS.
AND, MOST HEINOUS OF ALL, CONTEMPT OF THE GRAND ZZRFFIAN COUNCIL.
WHERE DID THIS FIRE HYDRANT COME FROM?
THEREFORE, BECAUSE HE IS SINGULARLY DETERMINED TO SPEND "TIME" IN THE THIRD DIMENSION, MXYZPTLK IS SENTENCED TO SPEND ONE INTERDIMENSIONAL INTERVAL, EQUIVALENT TO NINETY EARTH DAYS, ON THAT PLANE...
...STRIPPED OF HIS POWERS, AND STRIPPED OF HIS FORM.
TAXI
IT IS THE HOPE OF THIS COURT THAT HE USES THIS TIME WISELY IN CONTEMPLATION OF HIS MISTAKES AND IN AN EFFORT TO CONFORM MORE CLOSELY TO ZZRFFIAN IDEALS OF CONDUCT IN THE FUTURE.
SIGNED, ZXLQWRTY, LEADER, GRAND ZZRFFIAN COUNCIL.
NINETY DAYS?!?
NINETY @#%*#ING DAYS?!?!
THE END

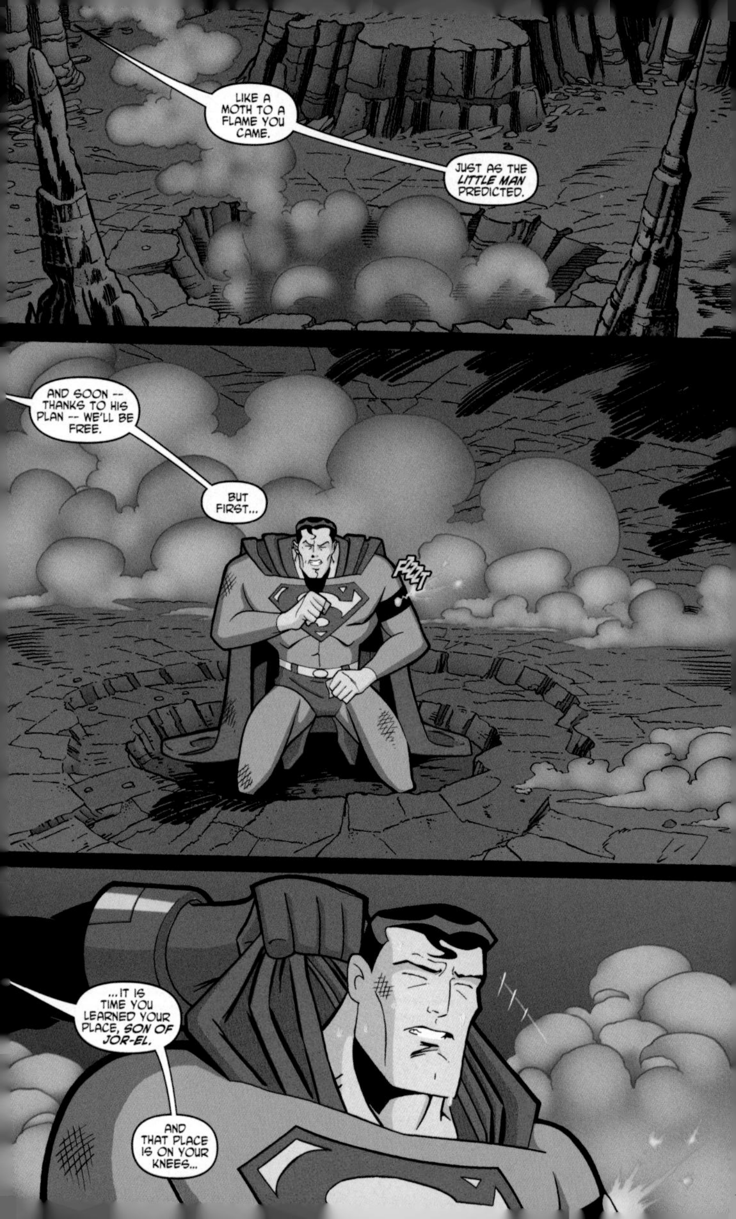

LIKE A MOTH TO A FLAME YOU CAME.
JUST AS THE *LITTLE MAN* PREDICTED.
AND SOON -- THANKS TO HIS PLAN -- WE'LL BE FREE.
BUT FIRST...
FZZZT
...IT IS TIME YOU LEARNED YOUR PLACE, *SON OF JOR-EL.*
AND THAT PLACE IS ON YOUR KNEES...

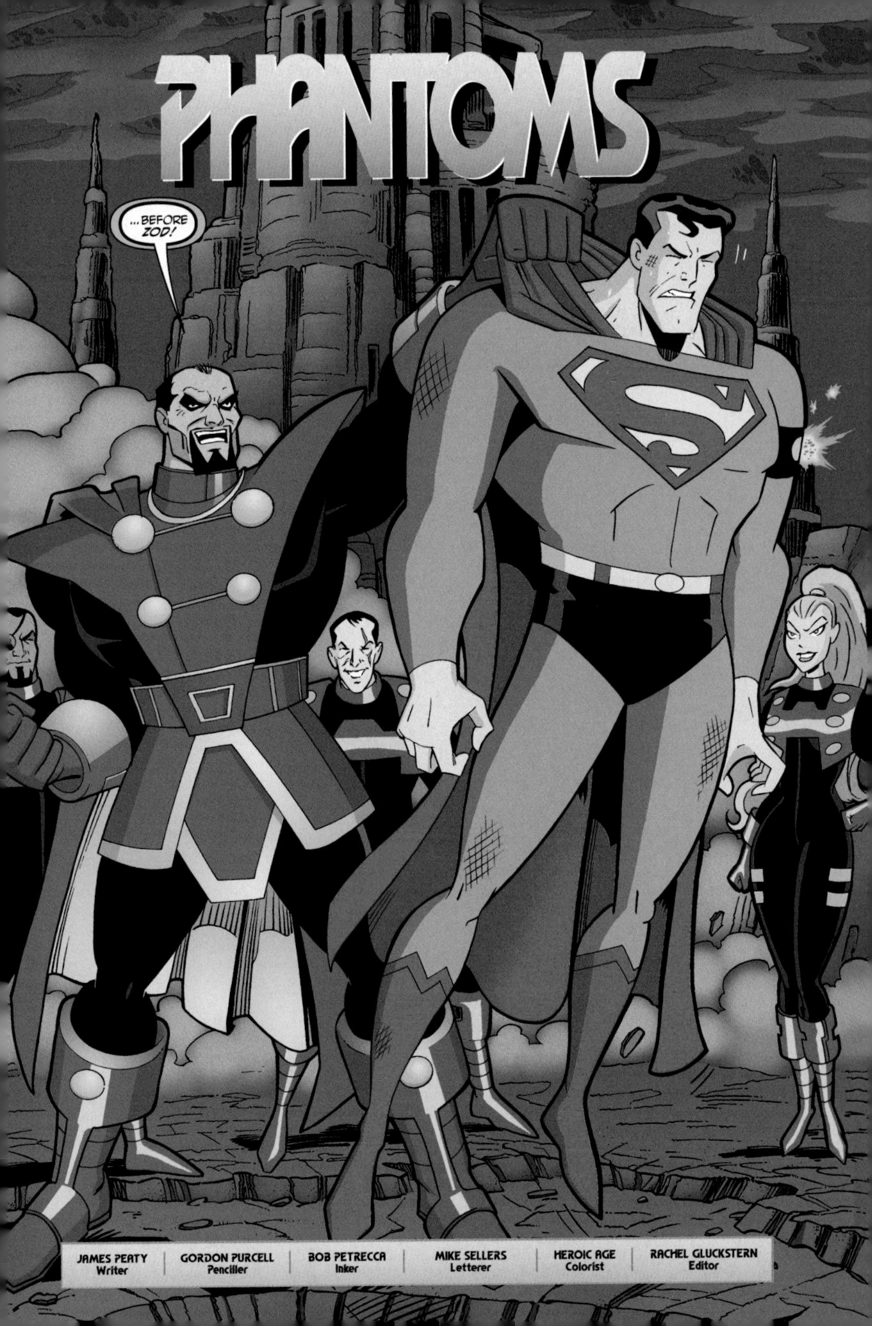
PHANTOMS
...BEFORE ZOD!
JAMES PEATY Writer
GORDON PURCELL Penciller
BOB PETRECCA Inker
MIKE SELLERS Letterer
HEROIC AGE Colorist
RACHEL GLUCKSTERN Editor

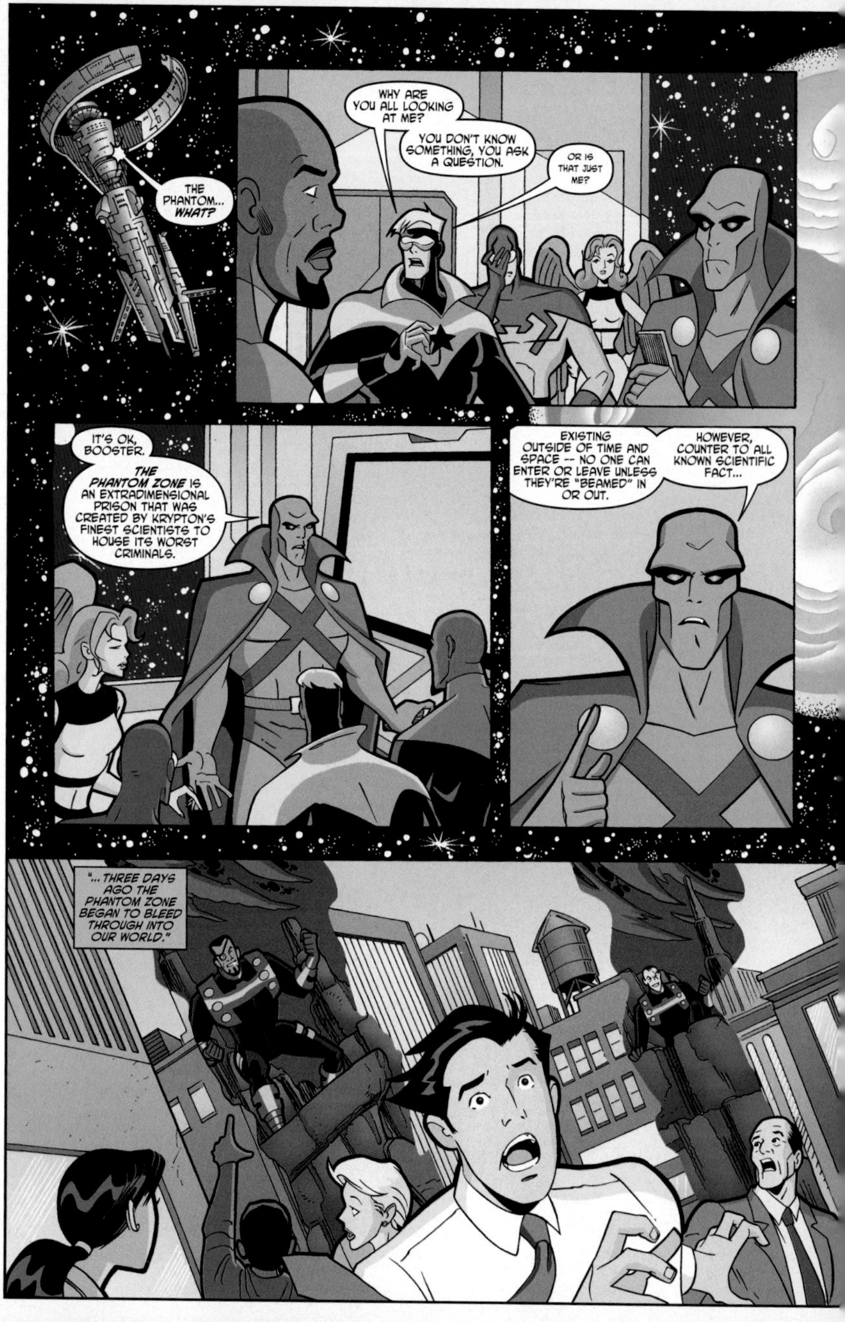
THE PHANTOM... WHAT?
WHY ARE YOU ALL LOOKING AT ME?
YOU DON'T KNOW SOMETHING, YOU ASK A QUESTION.
OR IS THAT JUST ME?
IT'S OK, BOOSTER.
THE PHANTOM ZONE IS AN EXTRADIMENSIONAL PRISON THAT WAS CREATED BY KRYPTON'S FINEST SCIENTISTS TO HOUSE ITS WORST CRIMINALS.
EXISTING OUTSIDE OF TIME AND SPACE -- NO ONE CAN ENTER OR LEAVE UNLESS THEY'RE "BEAMED" IN OR OUT.
HOWEVER, COUNTER TO ALL KNOWN SCIENTIFIC FACT...
"...THREE DAYS AGO THE PHANTOM ZONE BEGAN TO BLEED THROUGH INTO OUR WORLD."

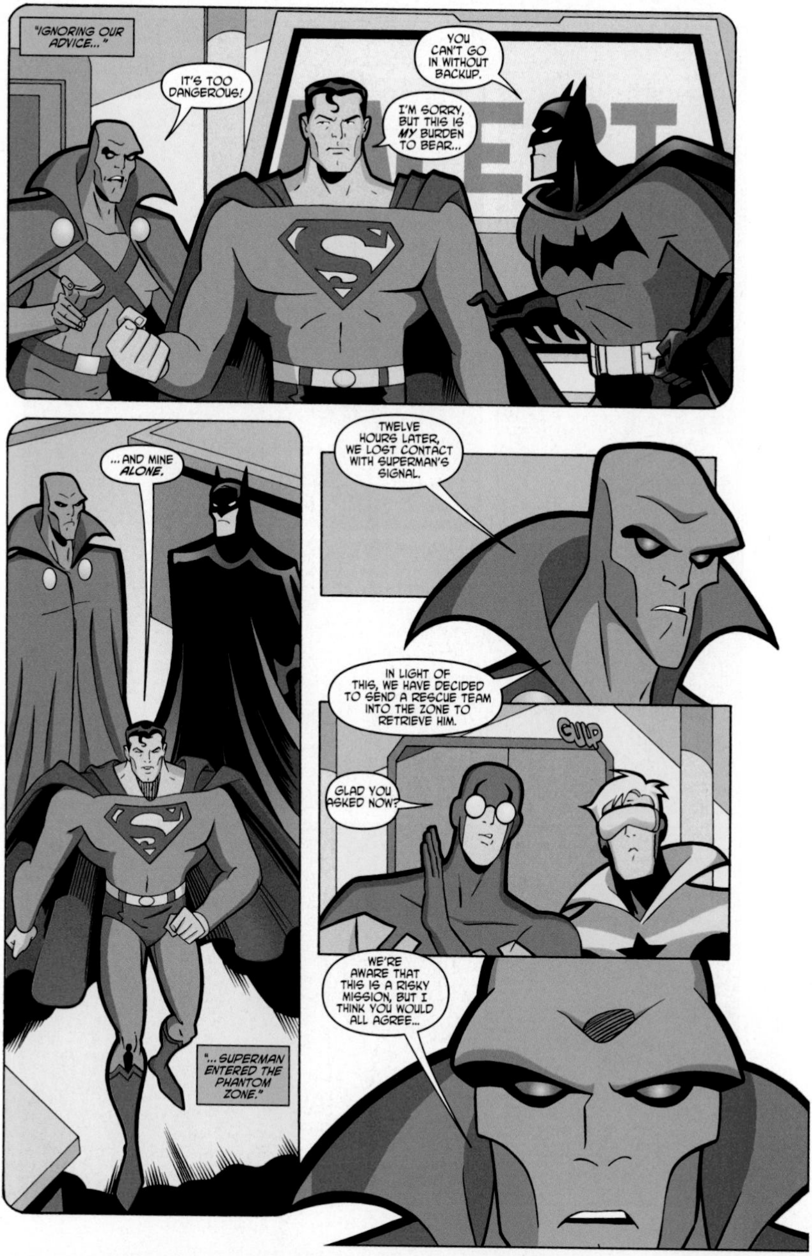
"IGNORING OUR ADVICE..."
IT'S TOO DANGEROUS!
YOU CAN'T GO IN WITHOUT BACKUP.
I'M SORRY, BUT THIS IS MY BURDEN TO BEAR...
...AND MINE ALONE.
"...SUPERMAN ENTERED THE PHANTOM ZONE."
TWELVE HOURS LATER, WE LOST CONTACT WITH SUPERMAN'S SIGNAL.
IN LIGHT OF THIS, WE HAVE DECIDED TO SEND A RESCUE TEAM INTO THE ZONE TO RETRIEVE HIM.
GULP
GLAD YOU ASKED NOW?
WE'RE AWARE THAT THIS IS A RISKY MISSION, BUT I THINK YOU WOULD ALL AGREE...

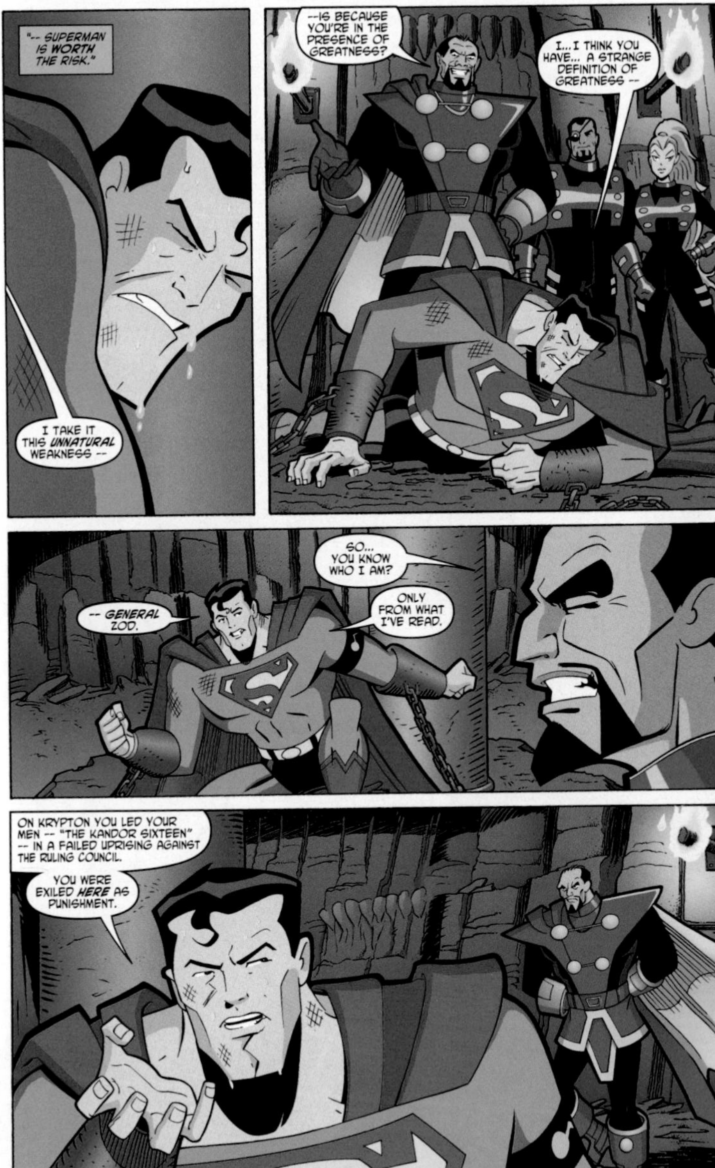
"-- SUPERMAN IS WORTH THE RISK."
I TAKE IT THIS UNNATURAL WEAKNESS --
--IS BECAUSE YOU'RE IN THE PRESENCE OF GREATNESS?
I... I THINK YOU HAVE... A STRANGE DEFINITION OF GREATNESS --
-- GENERAL ZOD.
SO... YOU KNOW WHO I AM?
ONLY FROM WHAT I'VE READ.
ON KRYPTON YOU LED YOUR MEN -- "THE KANDOR SIXTEEN" -- IN A FAILED UPRISING AGAINST THE RULING COUNCIL.
YOU WERE EXILED HERE AS PUNISHMENT.

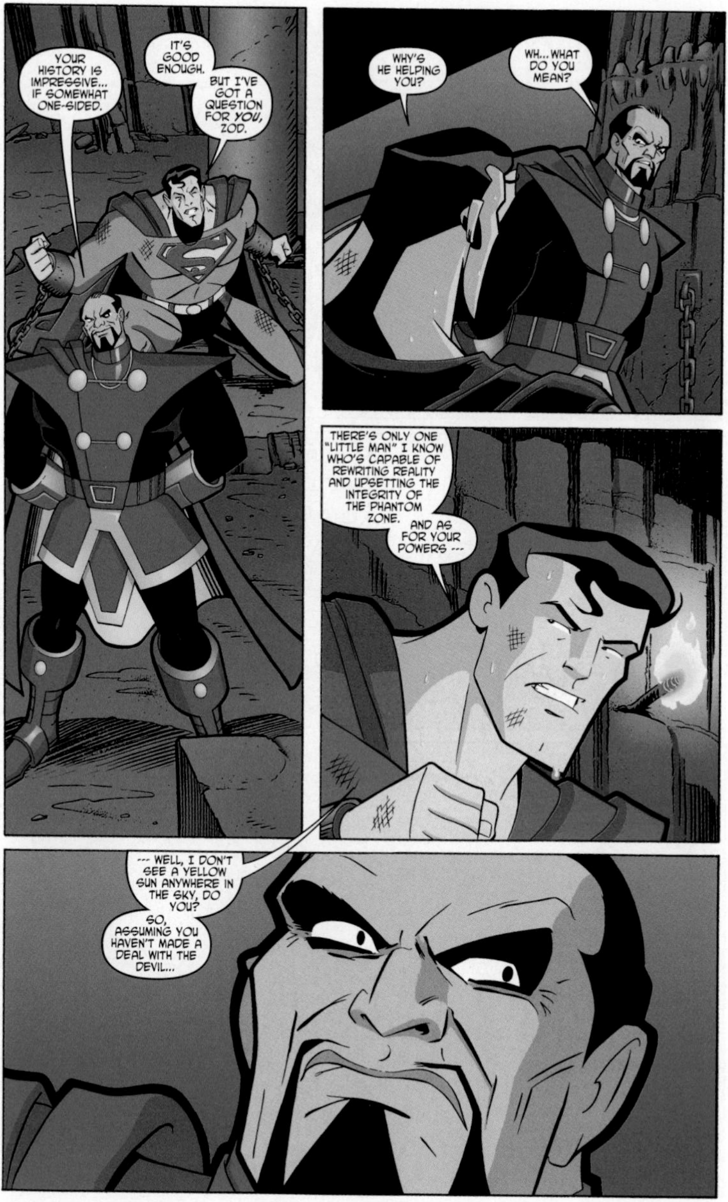
YOUR HISTORY IS IMPRESSIVE... IF SOMEWHAT ONE-SIDED.
IT'S GOOD ENOUGH.
BUT I'VE GOT A QUESTION FOR *YOU*, ZOD.
WHY'S HE HELPING YOU?
WH...WHAT DO YOU MEAN?
THERE'S ONLY ONE "LITTLE MAN" I KNOW WHO'S CAPABLE OF REWRITING REALITY AND UPSETTING THE INTEGRITY OF THE PHANTOM ZONE.
AND AS FOR YOUR POWERS ---
--- WELL, I DON'T SEE A YELLOW SUN ANYWHERE IN THE SKY, DO YOU?
SO, ASSUMING YOU HAVEN'T MADE A DEAL WITH THE DEVIL...

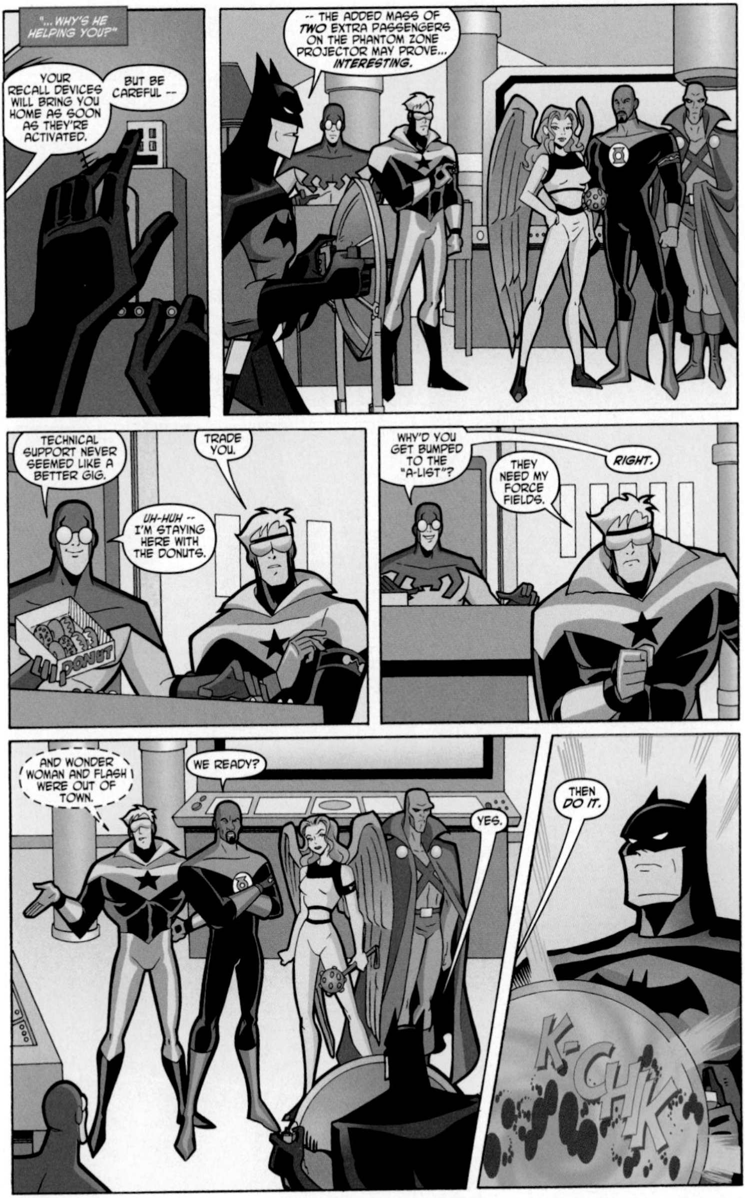
"...WHY'S HE HELPING YOU?"
YOUR RECALL DEVICES WILL BRING YOU HOME AS SOON AS THEY'RE ACTIVATED.
BUT BE CAREFUL --
-- THE ADDED MASS OF TWO EXTRA PASSENGERS ON THE PHANTOM ZONE PROJECTOR MAY PROVE... INTERESTING.
TECHNICAL SUPPORT NEVER SEEMED LIKE A BETTER GIG.
TRADE YOU.
UH-HUH -- I'M STAYING HERE WITH THE DONUTS.
DONUT
WHY'D YOU GET BUMPED TO THE "A-LIST"?
THEY NEED MY FORCE FIELDS.
RIGHT.
AND WONDER WOMAN AND FLASH WERE OUT OF TOWN.
WE READY?
YES.
THEN DO IT.
K-CHK

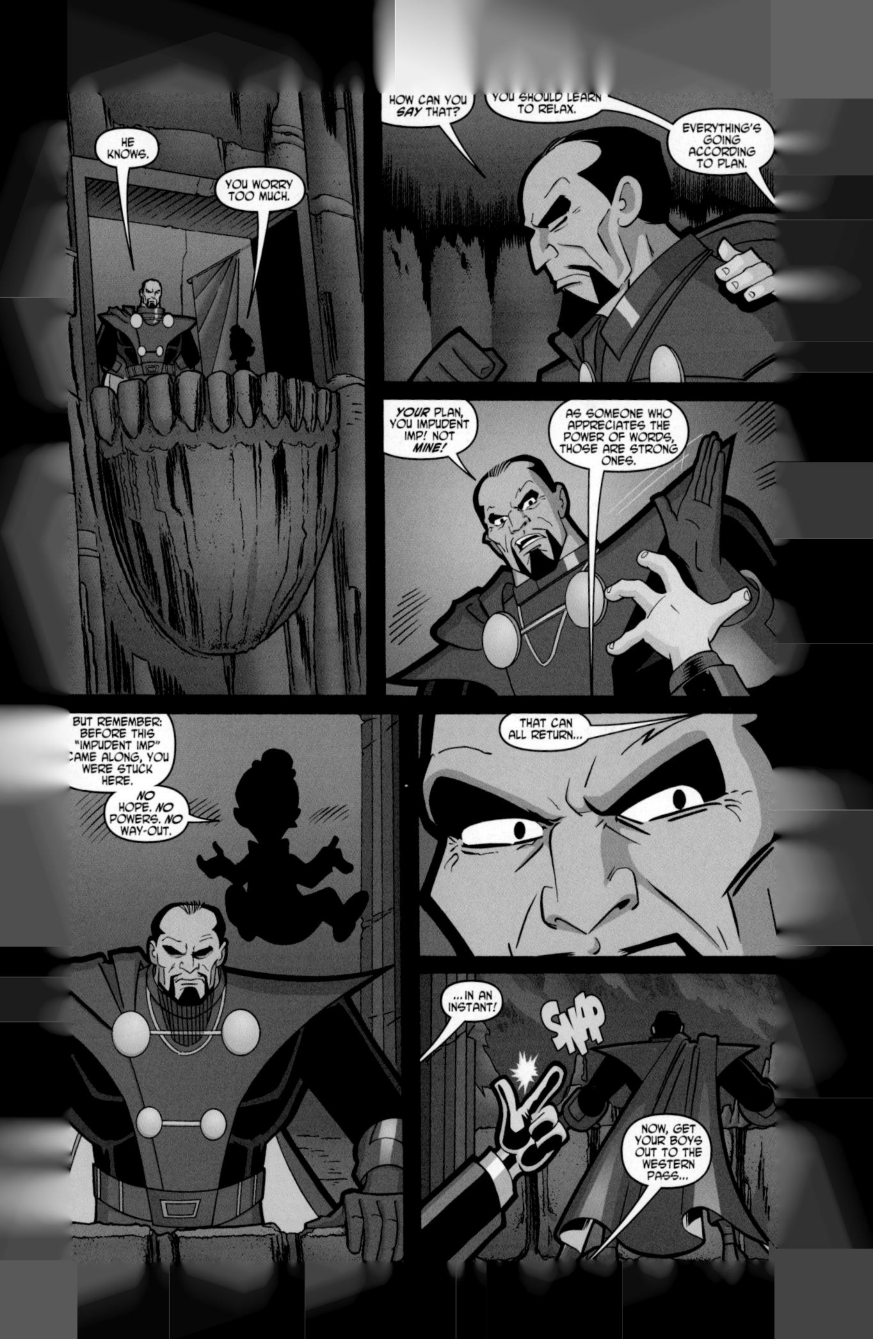

HE KNOWS.
YOU WORRY TOO MUCH.
HOW CAN YOU SAY THAT?
YOU SHOULD LEARN TO RELAX.
EVERYTHING'S GOING ACCORDING TO PLAN.
YOUR PLAN, YOU IMPUDENT IMP! NOT MINE!
AS SOMEONE WHO APPRECIATES THE POWER OF WORDS, THOSE ARE STRONG ONES.
BUT REMEMBER: BEFORE THIS "IMPUDENT IMP" CAME ALONG, YOU WERE STUCK HERE.
NO HOPE. NO POWERS. NO WAY-OUT.
THAT CAN ALL RETURN...
...IN AN INSTANT!
SNAP
NOW, GET YOUR BOYS OUT TO THE WESTERN PASS...

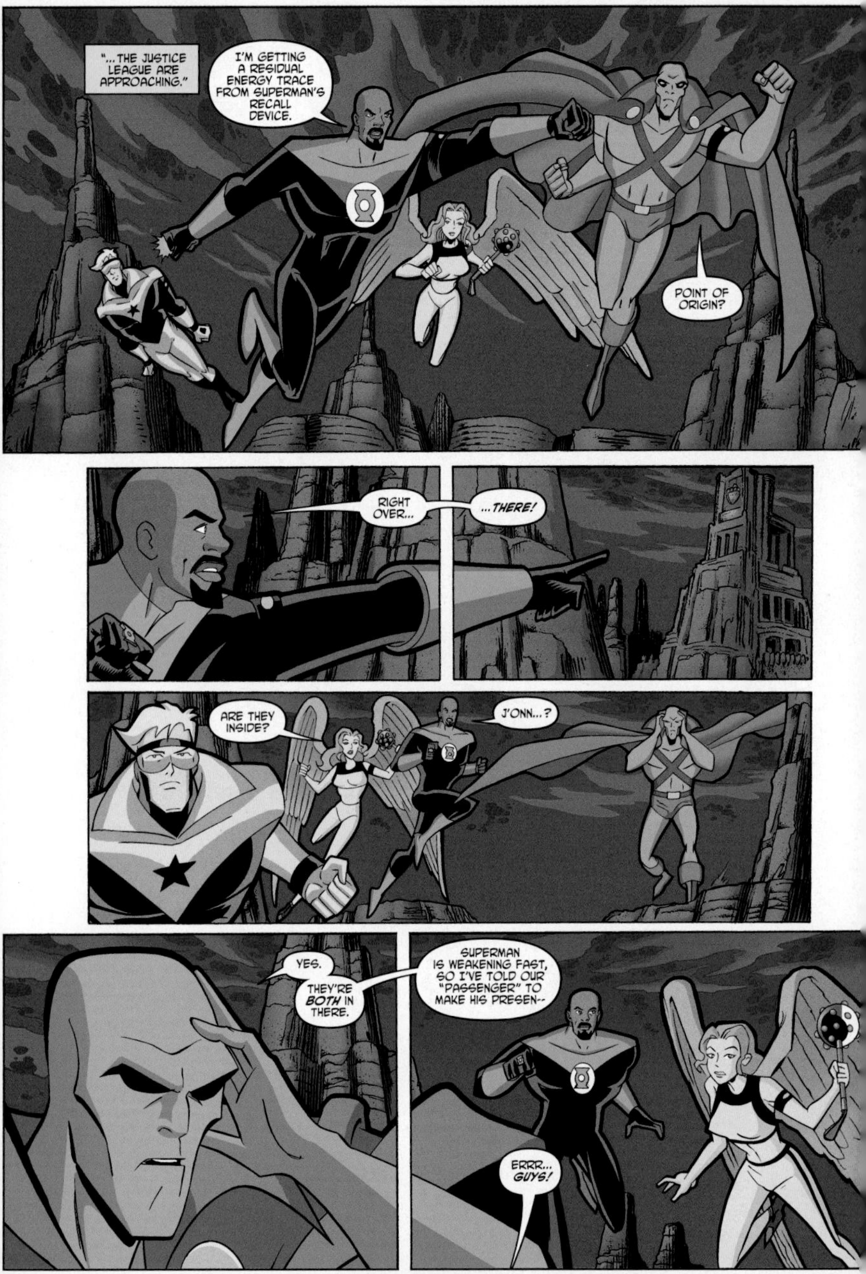
"...THE JUSTICE LEAGUE ARE APPROACHING."
I'M GETTING A RESIDUAL ENERGY TRACE FROM SUPERMAN'S RECALL DEVICE.
POINT OF ORIGIN?
RIGHT OVER...
...THERE!
ARE THEY INSIDE?
J'ONN...?
YES.
THEY'RE BOTH IN THERE.
SUPERMAN IS WEAKENING FAST, SO I'VE TOLD OUR "PASSENGER" TO MAKE HIS PRESEN--
ERRR... GUYS!

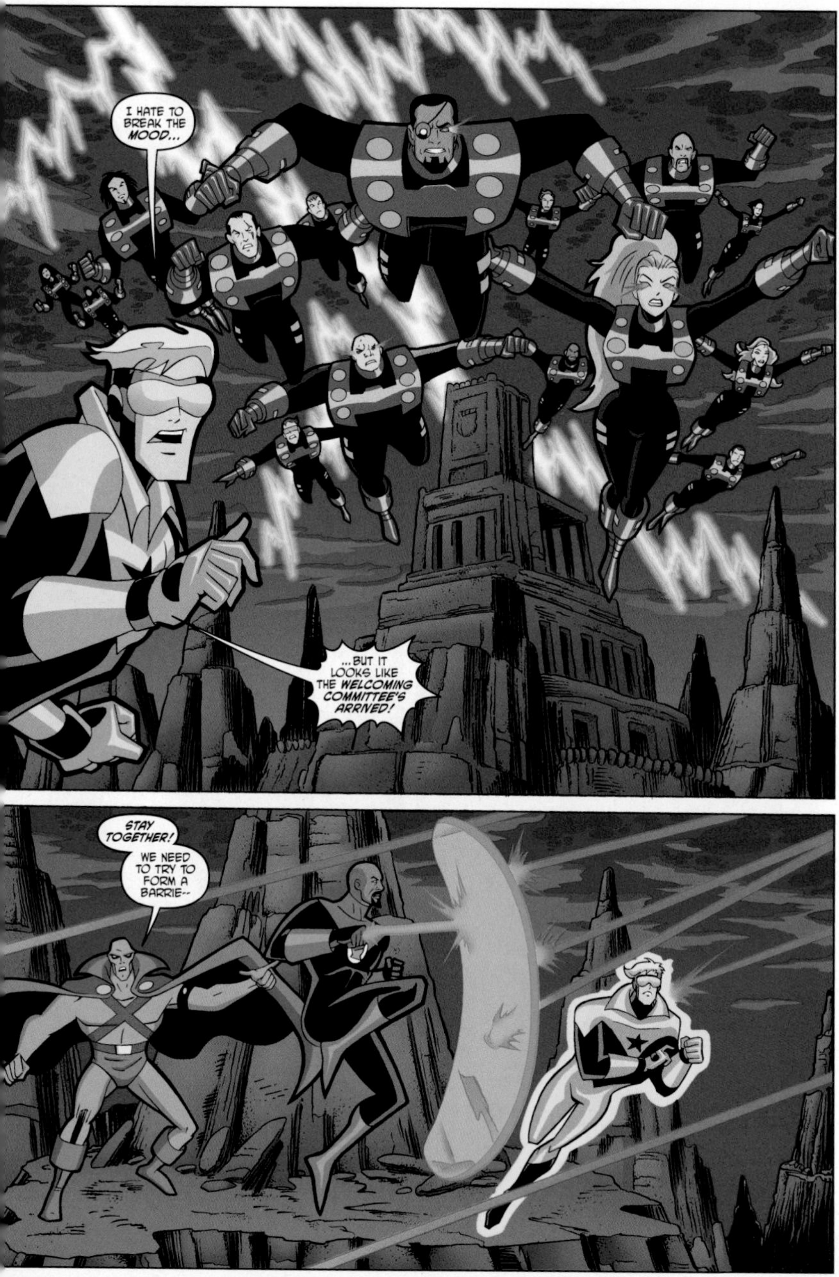
I HATE TO BREAK THE MOOD...
...BUT IT LOOKS LIKE THE WELCOMING COMMITTEE'S ARRIVED!
STAY TOGETHER!
WE NEED TO TRY TO FORM A BARRIE--

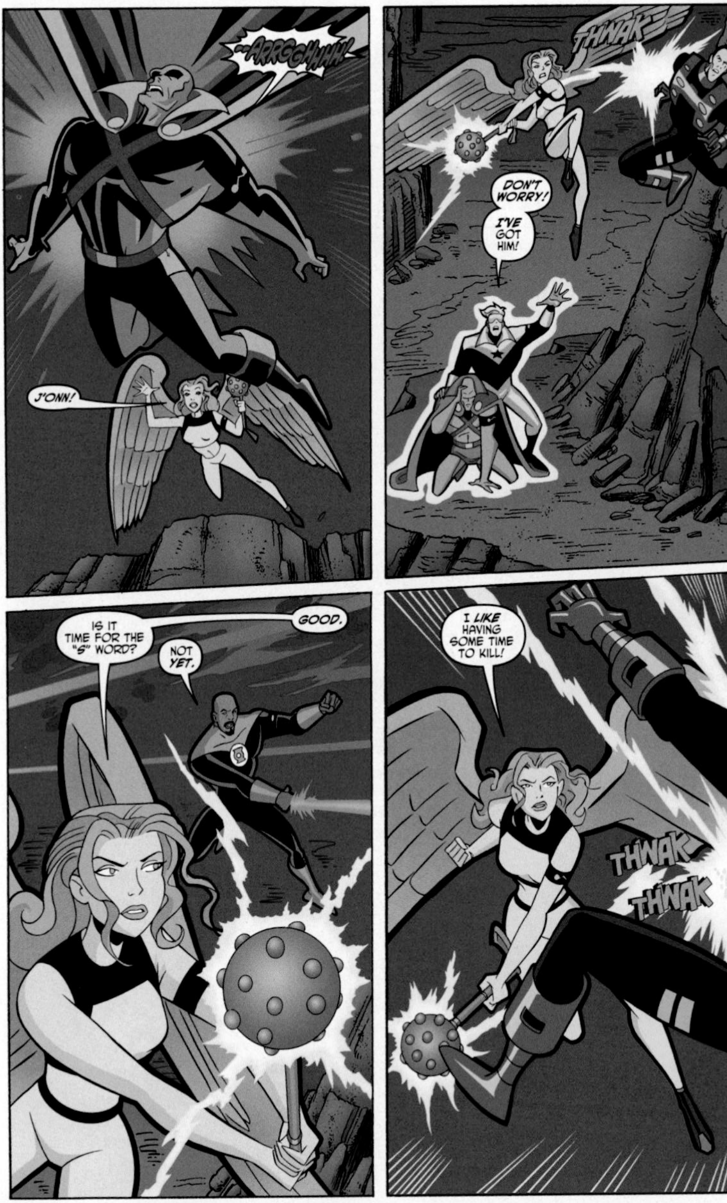
--ARRGGHHHH!
J'ONN!
THWAK
DON'T WORRY!
I'VE GOT HIM!
IS IT TIME FOR THE "S" WORD?
GOOD.
NOT YET.
I LIKE HAVING SOME TIME TO KILL!
THWAK
THWAK

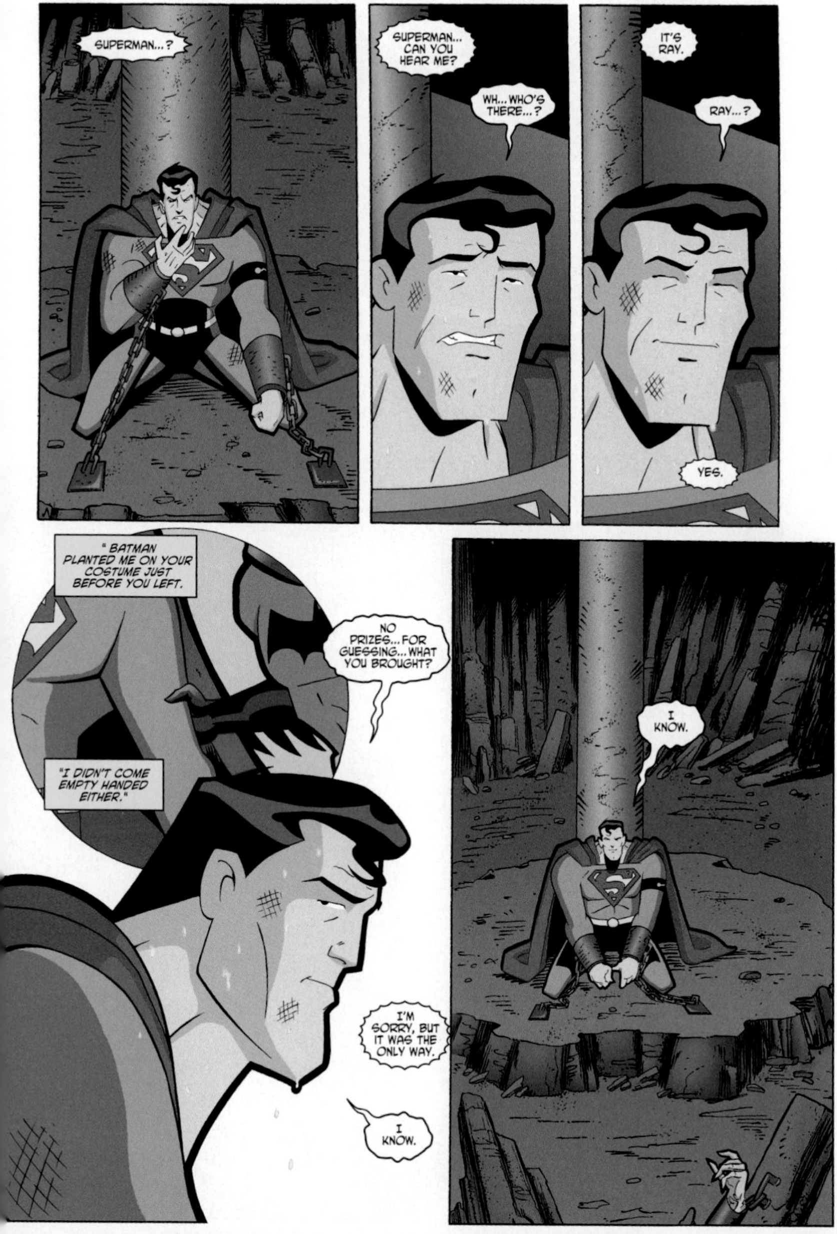
SUPERMAN...?
SUPERMAN... CAN YOU HEAR ME?
WH... WHO'S THERE...?
IT'S RAY.
RAY...?
YES.
" BATMAN PLANTED ME ON YOUR COSTUME JUST BEFORE YOU LEFT.
"I DIDN'T COME EMPTY HANDED EITHER."
NO PRIZES... FOR GUESSING... WHAT YOU BROUGHT?
I KNOW.
I'M SORRY, BUT IT WAS THE ONLY WAY.
I KNOW.

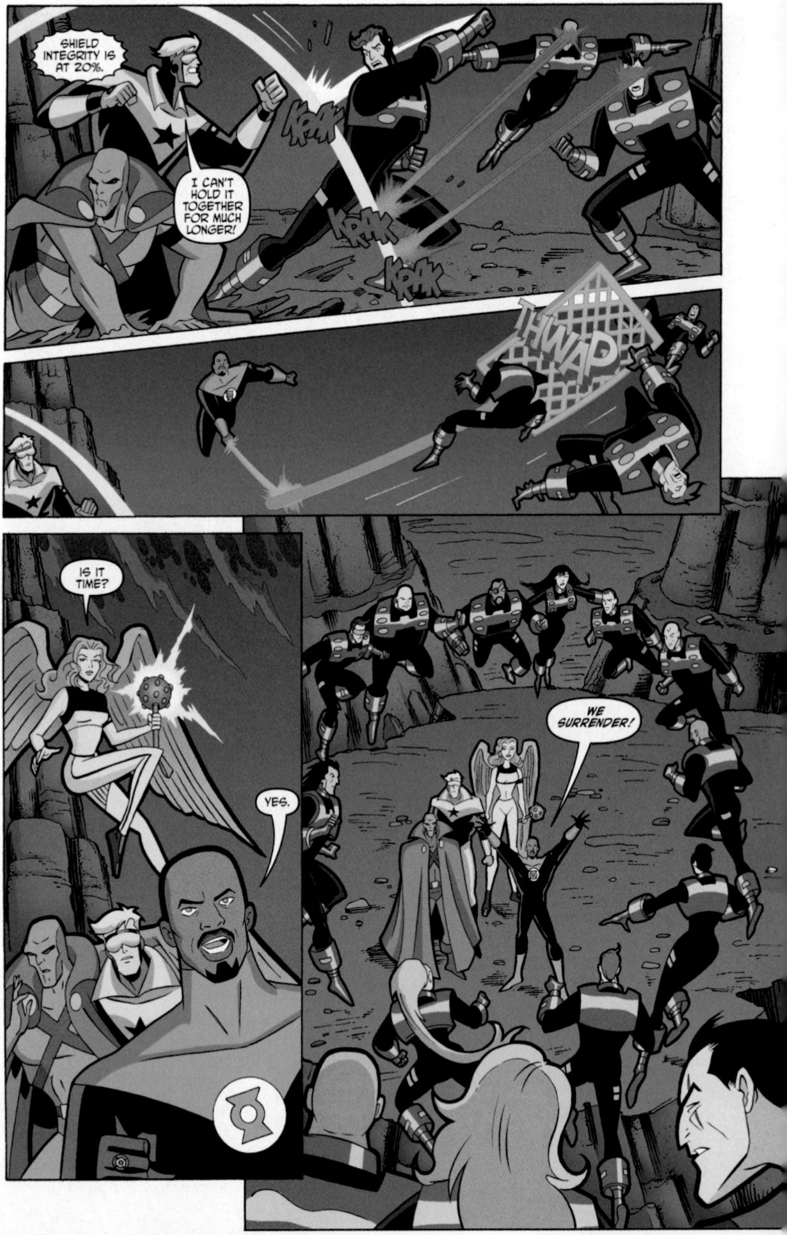
SHIELD INTEGRITY IS AT 20%.
I CAN'T HOLD IT TOGETHER FOR MUCH LONGER!
KRAK
KRAK
KRAK
THWAP
IS IT TIME?
YES.
WE SURRENDER!

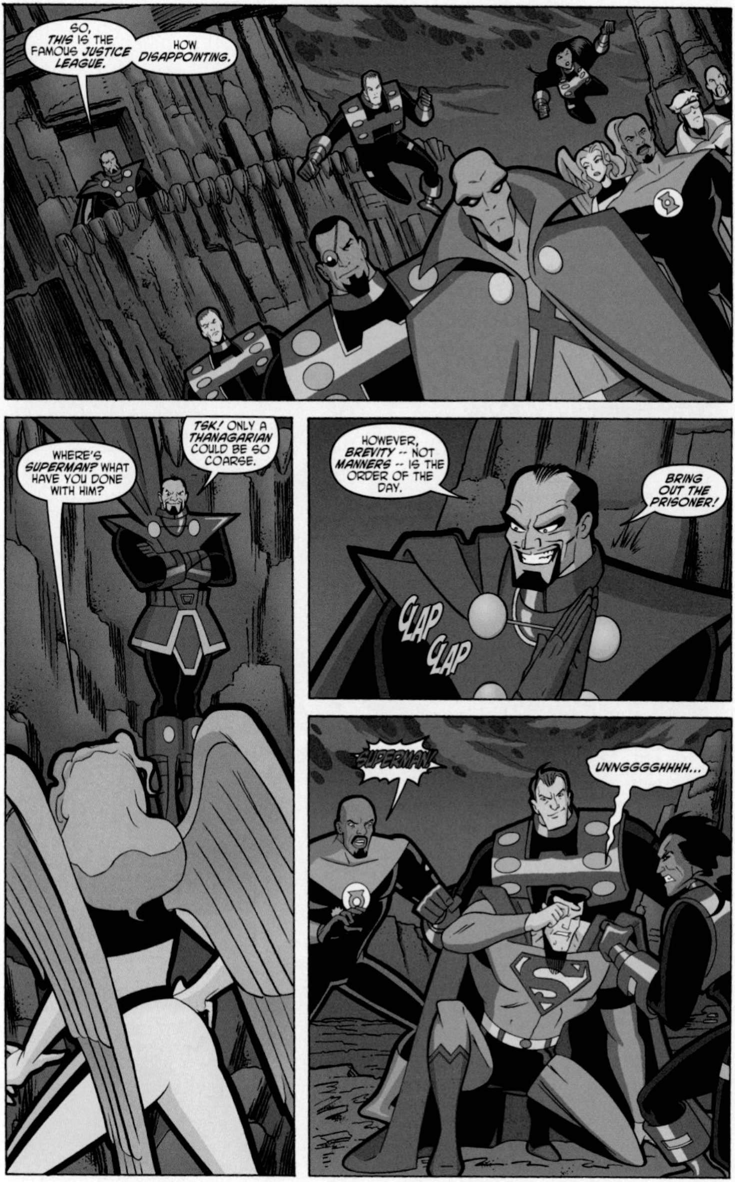
SO, THIS IS THE FAMOUS JUSTICE LEAGUE.
HOW DISAPPOINTING.
WHERE'S SUPERMAN? WHAT HAVE YOU DONE WITH HIM?
TSK! ONLY A THANAGARIAN COULD BE SO COARSE.
HOWEVER, BREVITY -- NOT MANNERS -- IS THE ORDER OF THE DAY.
BRING OUT THE PRISONER!
CLAP CLAP
SUPERMAN!
UNNGGGGHHHH...

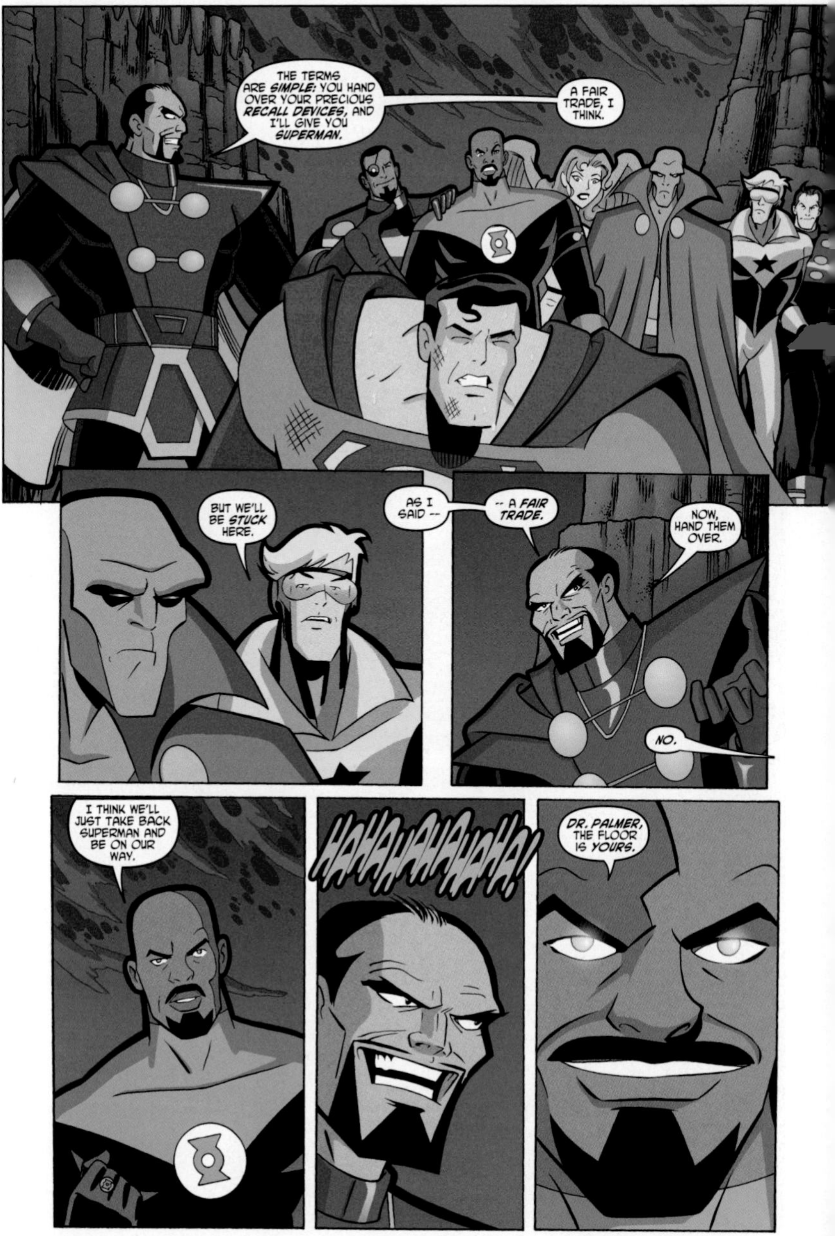
THE TERMS ARE *SIMPLE:* YOU HAND OVER YOUR PRECIOUS *RECALL DEVICES,* AND I'LL GIVE YOU *SUPERMAN.*
A FAIR TRADE, I THINK.
BUT WE'LL BE *STUCK* HERE.
AS I SAID --
-- A *FAIR TRADE.*
NOW, HAND THEM OVER.
*NO.*
I THINK WE'LL JUST TAKE BACK SUPERMAN AND BE ON OUR WAY.
HAHAHAHAHAHAHA!
*DR. PALMER,* THE FLOOR IS *YOURS.*

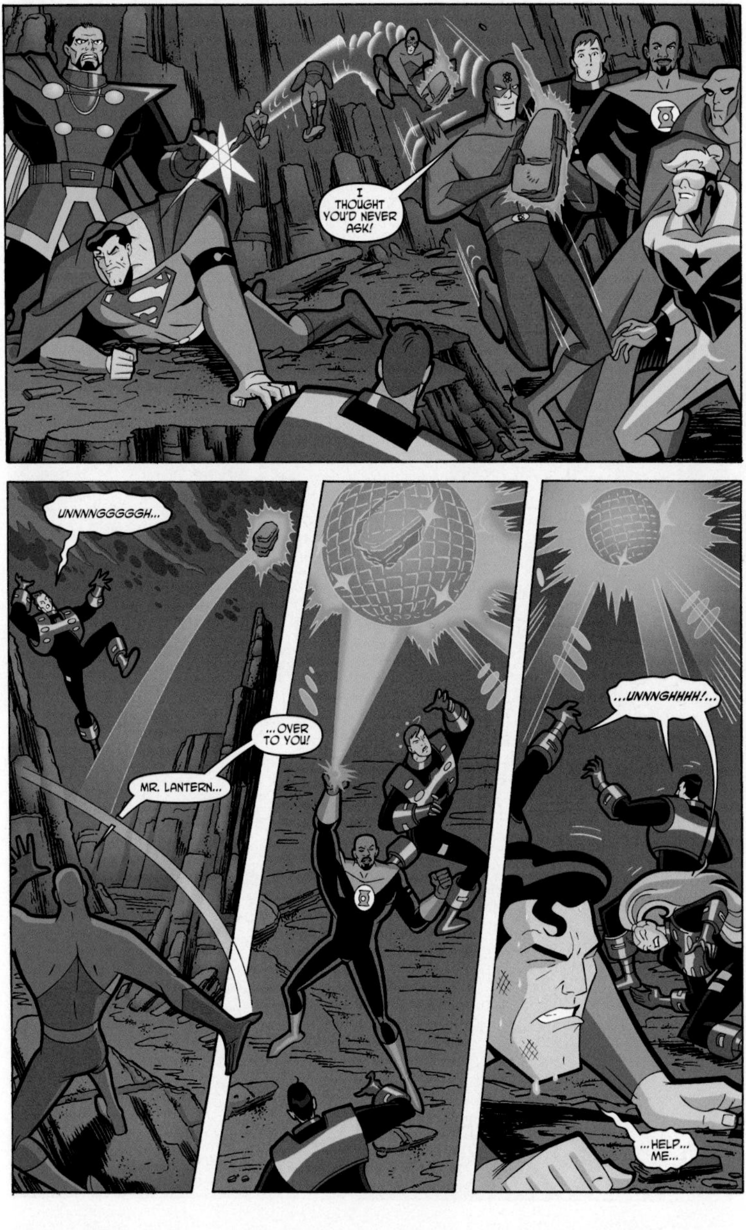
I THOUGHT YOU'D NEVER ASK!
UNNNNGGGGGH...
MR. LANTERN...
...OVER TO YOU!
...UNNNGHHHH!...
...HELP... ME...

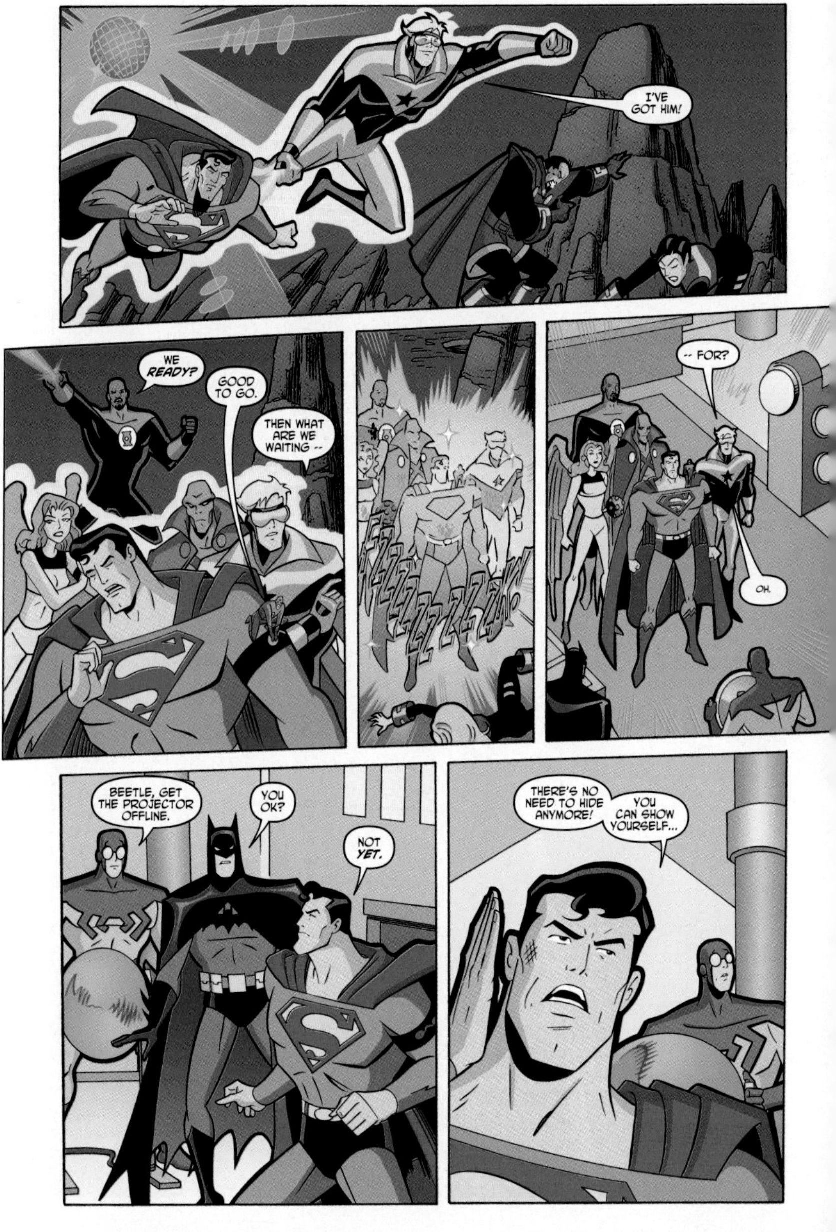
I'VE GOT HIM!
WE READY?
GOOD TO GO.
THEN WHAT ARE WE WAITING --
ZZZZZZZZZAK!
-- FOR?
OH.
BEETLE, GET THE PROJECTOR OFFLINE.
YOU OK?
NOT YET.
THERE'S NO NEED TO HIDE ANYMORE!
YOU CAN SHOW YOURSELF...

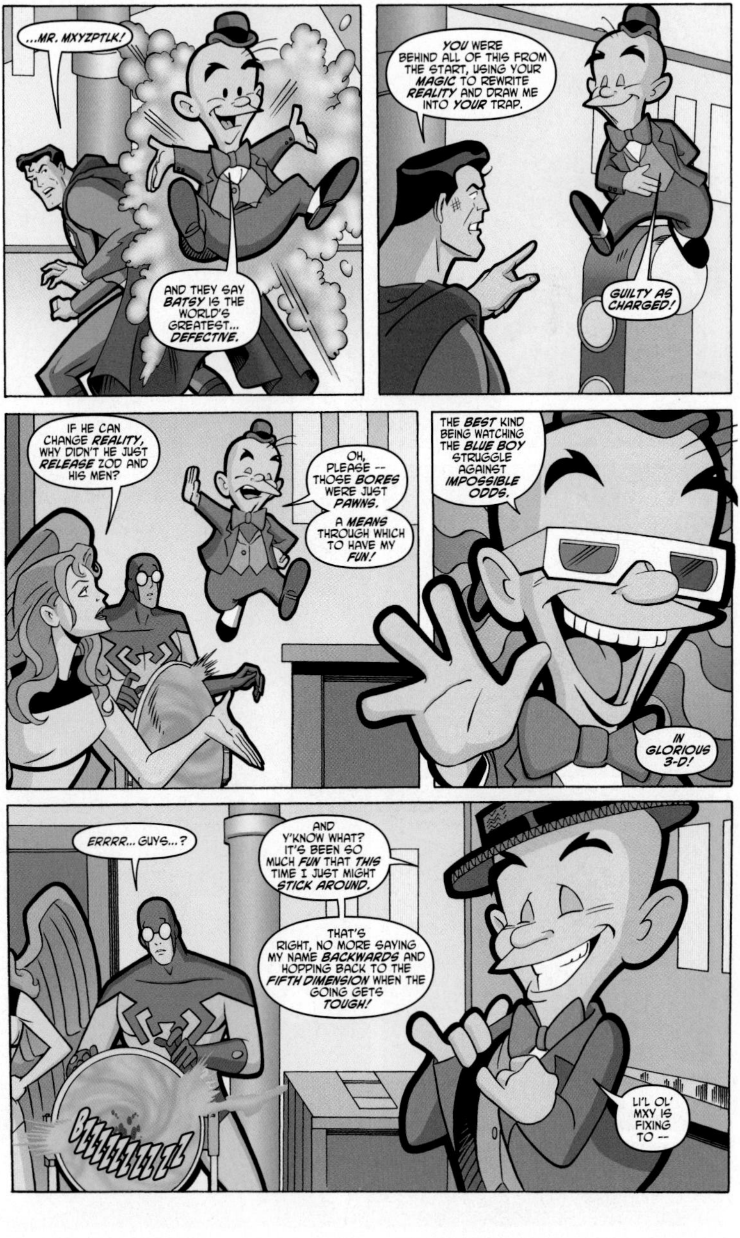

...MR. MXYZPTLK!
AND THEY SAY BATSY IS THE WORLD'S GREATEST... DEFECTIVE.
YOU WERE BEHIND ALL OF THIS FROM THE START, USING YOUR MAGIC TO REWRITE REALITY AND DRAW ME INTO YOUR TRAP.
GUILTY AS CHARGED!
IF HE CAN CHANGE REALITY, WHY DIDN'T HE JUST RELEASE ZOD AND HIS MEN?
OH, PLEASE -- THOSE BORES WERE JUST PAWNS.
A MEANS THROUGH WHICH TO HAVE MY FUN!
THE BEST KIND BEING WATCHING THE BLUE BOY STRUGGLE AGAINST IMPOSSIBLE ODDS.
IN GLORIOUS 3-D!
ERRRR... GUYS...?
AND Y'KNOW WHAT? IT'S BEEN SO MUCH FUN THAT THIS TIME I JUST MIGHT STICK AROUND.
THAT'S RIGHT, NO MORE SAYING MY NAME BACKWARDS AND HOPPING BACK TO THE FIFTH DIMENSION WHEN THE GOING GETS TOUGH!
LI'L OL' MXY IS FIXING TO --
BZZZZZZZZZZZ

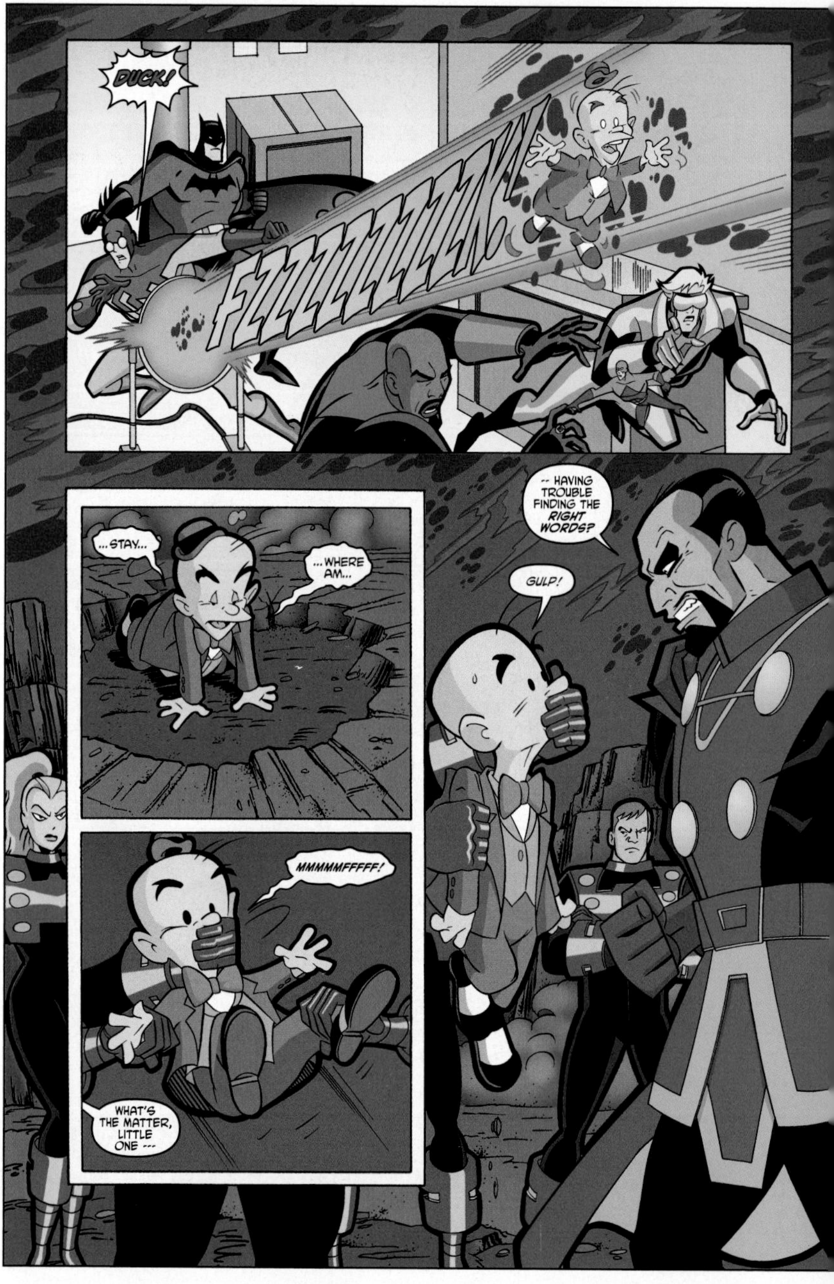
DUCK!
FZZZZZZZZZZZZK!
...STAY...
...WHERE AM...
MMMMMFFFFF!
WHAT'S THE MATTER, LITTLE ONE ---
-- HAVING TROUBLE FINDING THE RIGHT WORDS?
GULP!

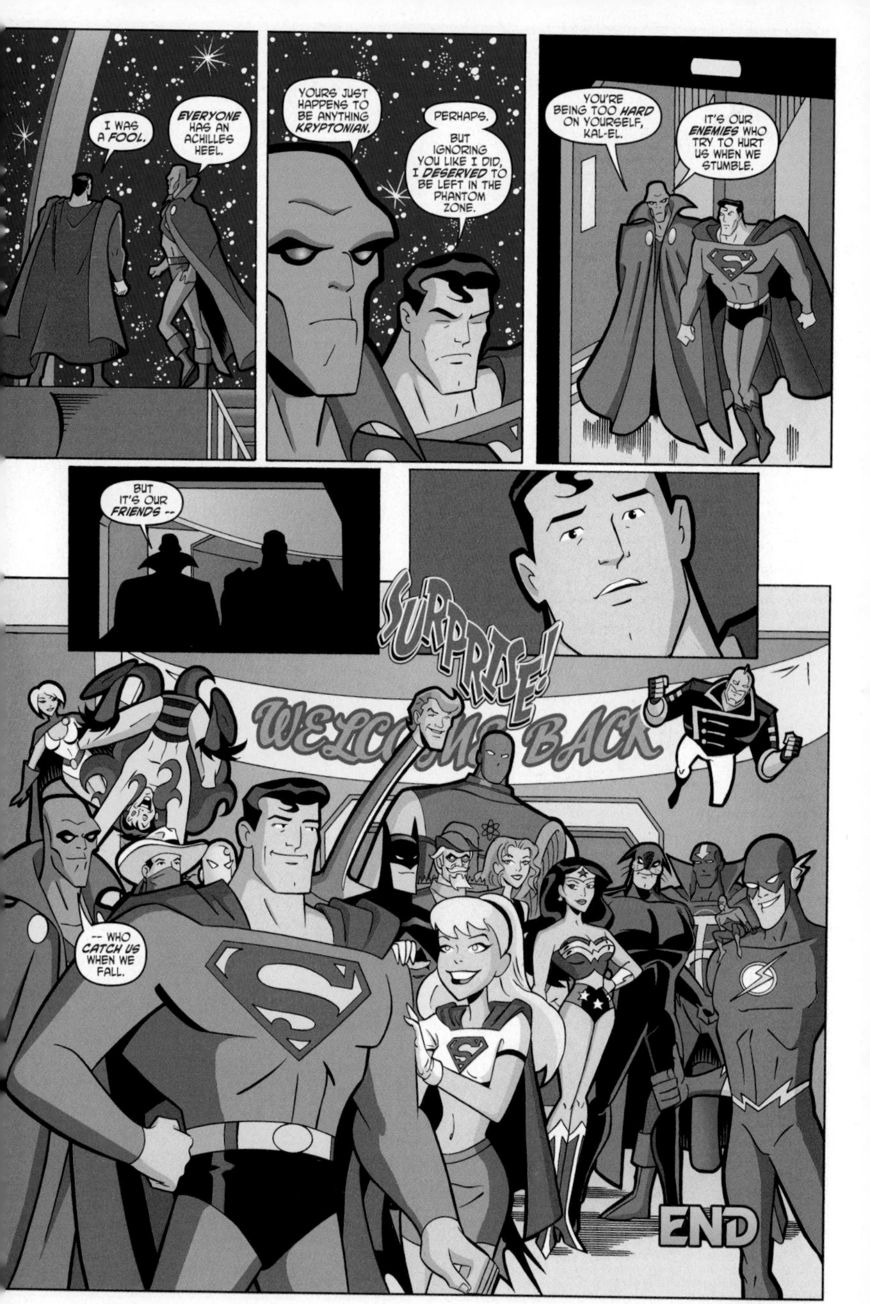
I WAS A *FOOL*.
*EVERYONE* HAS AN ACHILLES HEEL.
YOURS JUST HAPPENS TO BE ANYTHING *KRYPTONIAN*.
PERHAPS.
BUT IGNORING YOU LIKE I DID, I *DESERVED* TO BE LEFT IN THE PHANTOM ZONE.
YOU'RE BEING TOO *HARD* ON YOURSELF, KAL-EL.
IT'S OUR *ENEMIES* WHO TRY TO HURT US WHEN WE STUMBLE.
BUT IT'S OUR *FRIENDS* --
SURPRISE!
-- WHO *CATCH US* WHEN WE FALL.
END

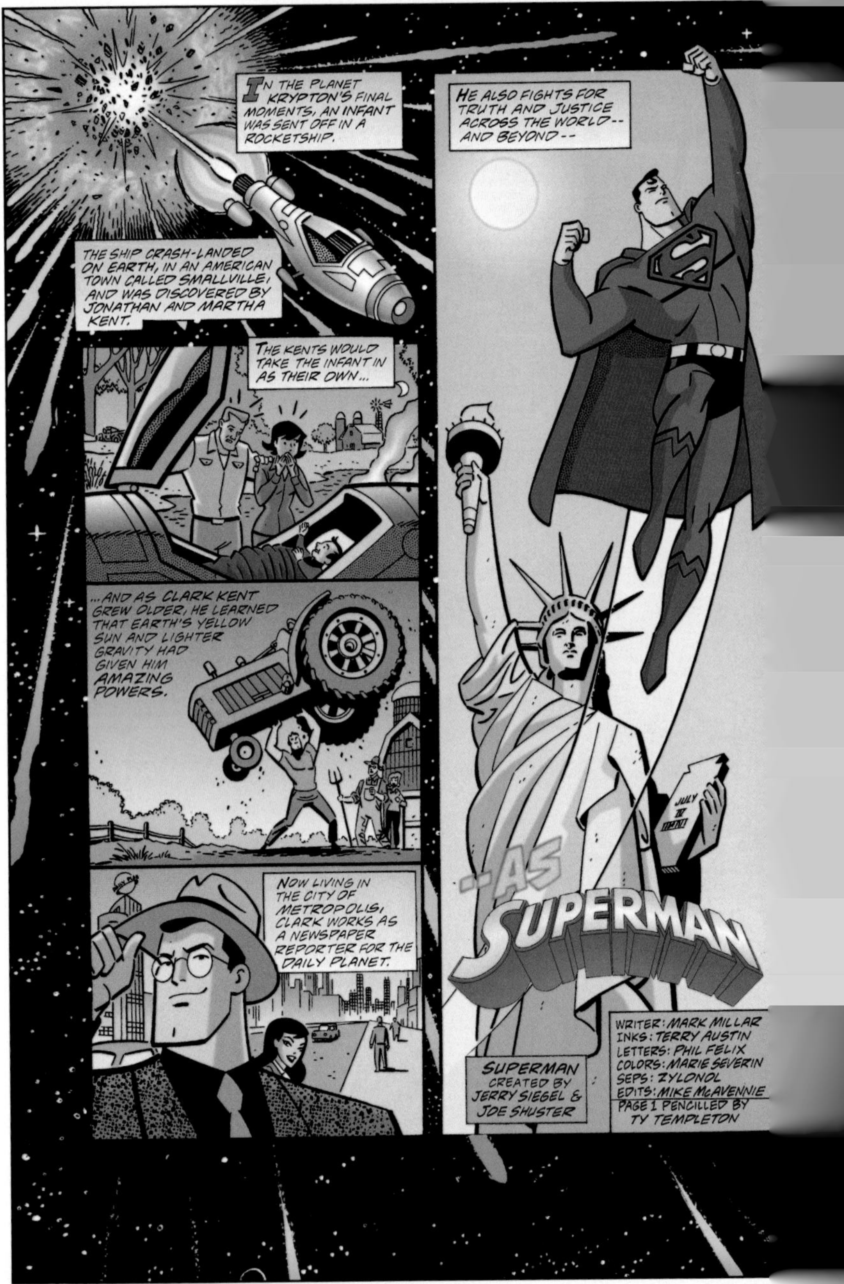
IN THE PLANET KRYPTON'S FINAL MOMENTS, AN INFANT WAS SENT OFF IN A ROCKETSHIP.
THE SHIP CRASH-LANDED ON EARTH, IN AN AMERICAN TOWN CALLED SMALLVILLE, AND WAS DISCOVERED BY JONATHAN AND MARTHA KENT.
THE KENTS WOULD TAKE THE INFANT IN AS THEIR OWN...
...AND AS CLARK KENT GREW OLDER, HE LEARNED THAT EARTH'S YELLOW SUN AND LIGHTER GRAVITY HAD GIVEN HIM AMAZING POWERS.
NOW LIVING IN THE CITY OF METROPOLIS, CLARK WORKS AS A NEWSPAPER REPORTER FOR THE DAILY PLANET.
HE ALSO FIGHTS FOR TRUTH AND JUSTICE ACROSS THE WORLD-- AND BEYOND--
JULY IV MDCCLXXVI
--AS SUPERMAN
SUPERMAN CREATED BY JERRY SIEGEL & JOE SHUSTER
WRITER: MARK MILLAR
INKS: TERRY AUSTIN
LETTERS: PHIL FELIX
COLORS: MARIE SEVERIN
SEPS: ZYLONOL
EDITS: MIKE McAVENNIE
PAGE 1 PENCILLED BY TY TEMPLETON

# "SUPERMAN'S POWER TRIP!"

LOOK OUT! SUPERMAN'S HEAT-VISION HAS GONE BERSERK!

EVERYONE, GET BACK! PLEASE!

GET BACK BEFORE I HURT SOMEONE! I... I DON'T KNOW HOW, BUT MY POWERS HAVE INCREASED BEYOND MY CONTROL!

I CAN SEE AND HEAR EVERYTHING THAT'S HAPPENING IN METROPOLIS! I CAN'T SHUT ANYTHING OUT!

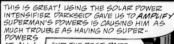

THIS IS GREAT! USING THE SOLAR POWER INTENSIFIER DARKSEID GAVE US TO *AMPLIFY* SUPERMAN'S POWERS IS CAUSING HIM AS MUCH TROUBLE AS HAVING NO SUPER-POWERS AT ALL!

AND THE BEST PART IS HE HASN'T A CLUE INTERGANG'S BEHIND THE WHOLE OPERATION! I LOVE IT!

LET'S SEE IF YOU BOYS ARE SAYING THAT IN TEN-TO-TWENTY!

SUPERMAN?! HOW THE HECK DID YOU *FIND* US?

IF YOU'RE GOING TO MULTIPLY MY SENSES TO THE POINT WHERE I'M AWARE OF EVERY CONVERSATION IN THE CITY, YOU NEED TO LEARN TO KEEP YOUR MOUTH SHUT!

NICE GOIN', CHATTERBOX!

PENCILLER: JOE STATON

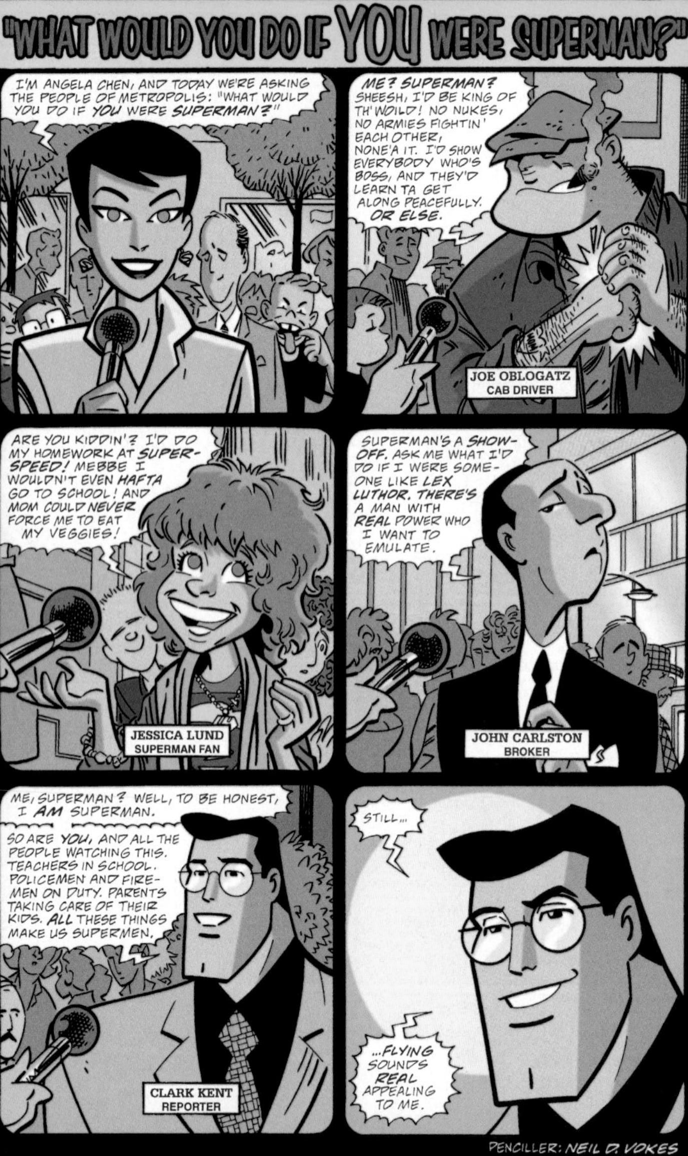
"WHAT WOULD YOU DO IF YOU WERE SUPERMAN?"
I'M ANGELA CHEN, AND TODAY WE'RE ASKING THE PEOPLE OF METROPOLIS: "WHAT WOULD YOU DO IF YOU WERE SUPERMAN?"
ME? SUPERMAN? SHEESH, I'D BE KING OF TH' WOILD! NO NUKES, NO ARMIES FIGHTIN' EACH OTHER, NONE'A IT. I'D SHOW EVERYBODY WHO'S BOSS, AND THEY'D LEARN TA GET ALONG PEACEFULLY. OR ELSE.
JOE OBLOGATZ
CAB DRIVER
ARE YOU KIDDIN'? I'D DO MY HOMEWORK AT SUPER-SPEED! MEBBE I WOULDN'T EVEN HAFTA GO TO SCHOOL! AND MOM COULD NEVER FORCE ME TO EAT MY VEGGIES!
JESSICA LUND
SUPERMAN FAN
SUPERMAN'S A SHOW-OFF. ASK ME WHAT I'D DO IF I WERE SOME-ONE LIKE LEX LUTHOR. THERE'S A MAN WITH REAL POWER WHO I WANT TO EMULATE.
JOHN CARLSTON
BROKER
ME, SUPERMAN? WELL, TO BE HONEST, I AM SUPERMAN.
SO ARE YOU, AND ALL THE PEOPLE WATCHING THIS. TEACHERS IN SCHOOL. POLICEMEN AND FIRE-MEN ON DUTY. PARENTS TAKING CARE OF THEIR KIDS. ALL THESE THINGS MAKE US SUPERMEN.
CLARK KENT
REPORTER
STILL...
...FLYING SOUNDS REAL APPEALING TO ME.
PENCILLER: NEIL D. VOKES

# "A WEEK IN THE LIFE OF LOIS LANE"

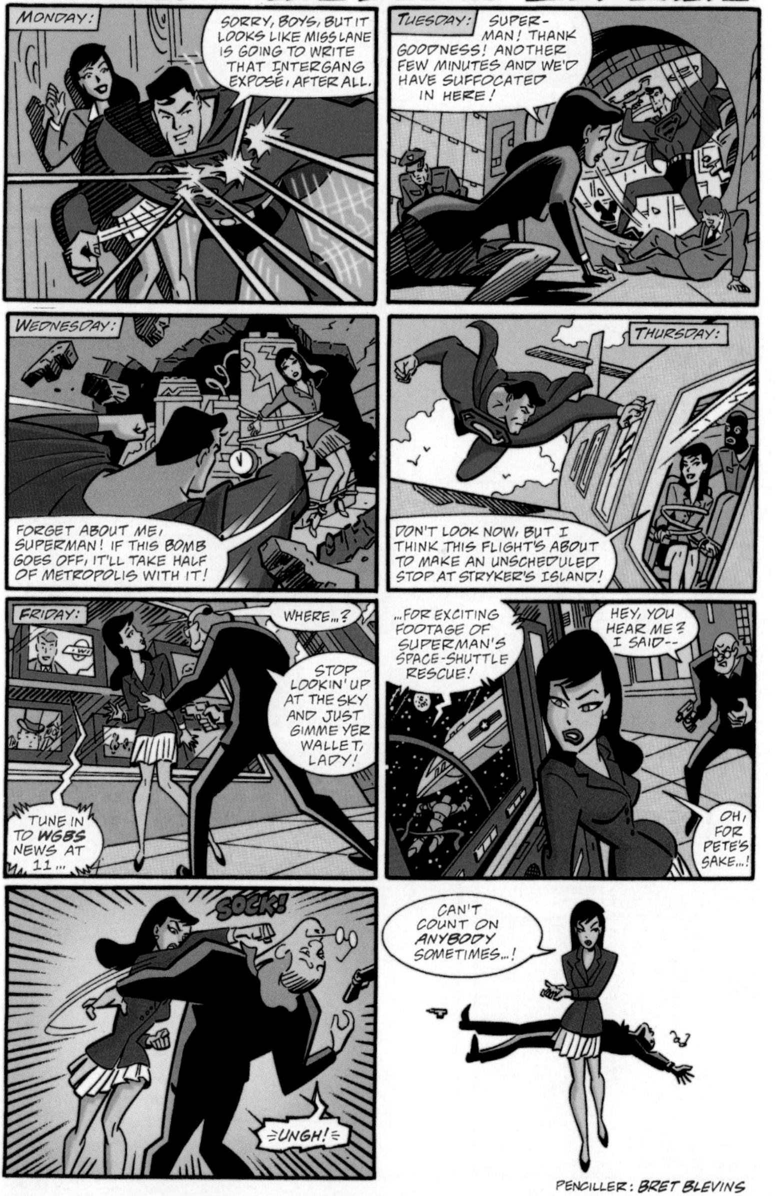
MONDAY:
SORRY, BOYS, BUT IT LOOKS LIKE MISS LANE IS GOING TO WRITE THAT INTERGANG EXPOSÉ, AFTER ALL.
TUESDAY:
SUPERMAN! THANK GOODNESS! ANOTHER FEW MINUTES AND WE'D HAVE SUFFOCATED IN HERE!
WEDNESDAY:
FORGET ABOUT ME, SUPERMAN! IF THIS BOMB GOES OFF, IT'LL TAKE HALF OF METROPOLIS WITH IT!
THURSDAY:
DON'T LOOK NOW, BUT I THINK THIS FLIGHT'S ABOUT TO MAKE AN UNSCHEDULED STOP AT STRYKER'S ISLAND!
FRIDAY:
WHERE...?
STOP LOOKIN' UP AT THE SKY AND JUST GIMME YER WALLET, LADY!
TUNE IN TO WGBS NEWS AT 11...
...FOR EXCITING FOOTAGE OF SUPERMAN'S SPACE-SHUTTLE RESCUE!
HEY, YOU HEAR ME? I SAID--
OH, FOR PETE'S SAKE...!
SOCK!
UNGH!
CAN'T COUNT ON ANYBODY SOMETIMES...!

PENCILLER: BRET BLEVINS

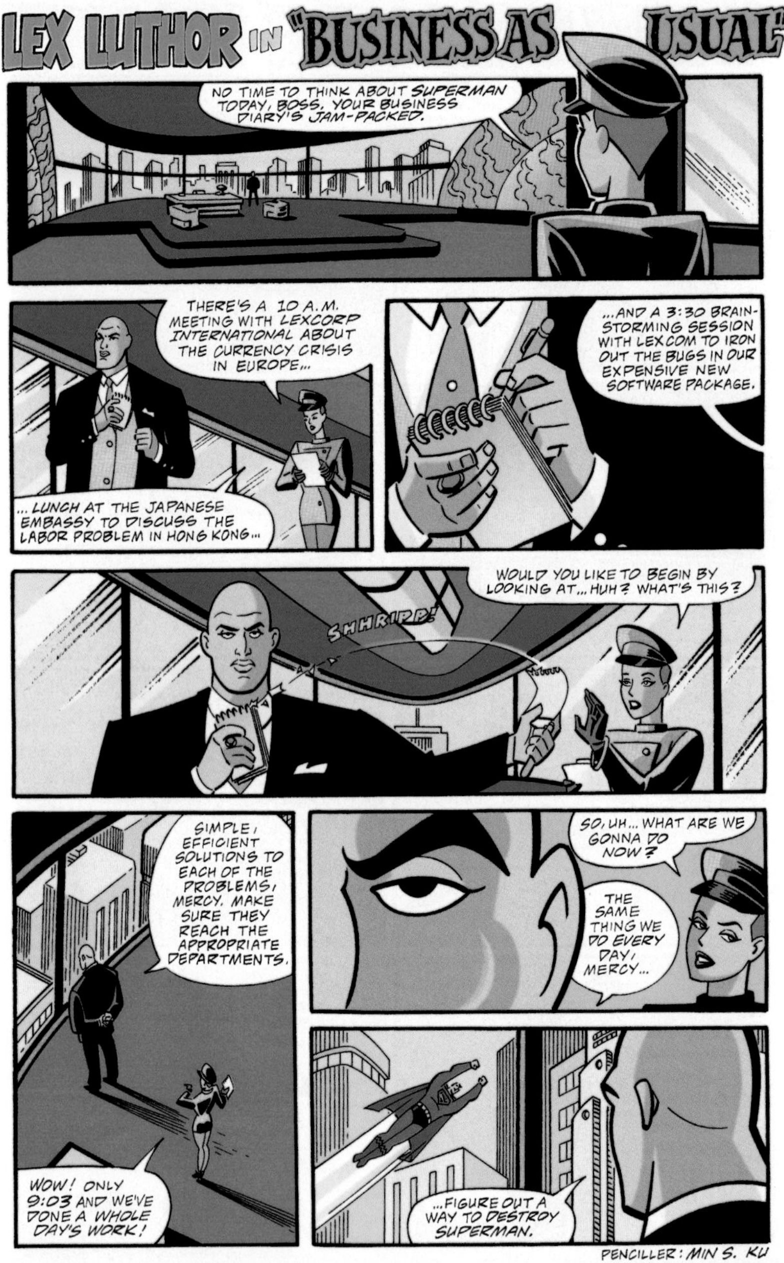
LEX LUTHOR IN "BUSINESS AS USUAL"
NO TIME TO THINK ABOUT SUPERMAN TODAY, BOSS. YOUR BUSINESS DIARY'S JAM-PACKED.
THERE'S A 10 A.M. MEETING WITH LEXCORP INTERNATIONAL ABOUT THE CURRENCY CRISIS IN EUROPE...
...LUNCH AT THE JAPANESE EMBASSY TO DISCUSS THE LABOR PROBLEM IN HONG KONG...
...AND A 3:30 BRAIN-STORMING SESSION WITH LEXCOM TO IRON OUT THE BUGS IN OUR EXPENSIVE NEW SOFTWARE PACKAGE.
WOULD YOU LIKE TO BEGIN BY LOOKING AT... HUH? WHAT'S THIS?
SHHRIPP!
SIMPLE, EFFICIENT SOLUTIONS TO EACH OF THE PROBLEMS, MERCY. MAKE SURE THEY REACH THE APPROPRIATE DEPARTMENTS.
WOW! ONLY 9:03 AND WE'VE DONE A WHOLE DAY'S WORK!
SO, UH... WHAT ARE WE GONNA DO NOW?
THE SAME THING WE DO EVERY DAY, MERCY...
...FIGURE OUT A WAY TO DESTROY SUPERMAN.

PENCILLER: MIN S. KU

# "ALL IN A DAY'S WORK"

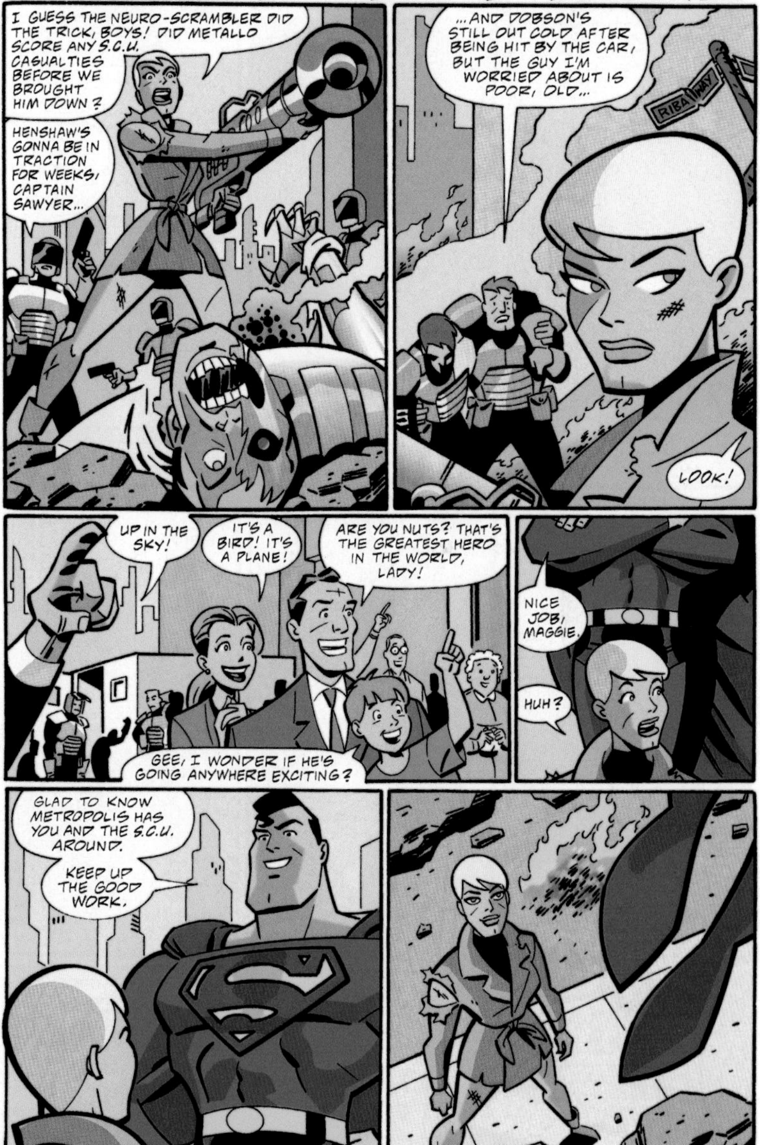
I GUESS THE NEURO-SCRAMBLER DID THE TRICK, BOYS! DID METALLO SCORE ANY S.C.U. CASUALTIES BEFORE WE BROUGHT HIM DOWN?
HENSHAW'S GONNA BE IN TRACTION FOR WEEKS, CAPTAIN SAWYER...
...AND DOBSON'S STILL OUT COLD AFTER BEING HIT BY THE CAR, BUT THE GUY I'M WORRIED ABOUT IS POOR, OLD...
RIBA WAY
LOOK!
UP IN THE SKY!
IT'S A BIRD! IT'S A PLANE!
ARE YOU NUTS? THAT'S THE GREATEST HERO IN THE WORLD, LADY!
GEE, I WONDER IF HE'S GOING ANYWHERE EXCITING?
NICE JOB, MAGGIE.
HUH?
GLAD TO KNOW METROPOLIS HAS YOU AND THE S.C.U. AROUND.
KEEP UP THE GOOD WORK.

PENCILLER: CAMERON STEWART.

# JIMMY OLSEN IN "MR. ACTION"

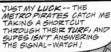

JUST MY *LUCK*-- THE *METRO PIRATES* CATCH ME TAKING A SHORTCUT THROUGH THEIR *TURF*, AND SUPES *ISN'T* ANSWERING THE SIGNAL-WATCH!

ZEE ZEE ZEE

DEAD END, OLSEN! TURN AROUND FOR YER WHUPPIN'!

BACK OFF, DUDES! Y-YOU REALLY DON'T WANNA GET ME *MAD...*!

LISTEN TO SUPER-MAN'S BRAVE LITTLE BUDDY!

ALL *I'M* WORRIED ABOUT--

--IS BRUISIN' MY KNUCKLES ON THIS GEEK'S FRECKLES!

YOU REALLY WANT A PIECE OF *JIMMY OLSEN*, HUH? WELL...

...HERE'S FIVE KNUCKLES AND HIS BEST FIST, CREEPS!

WHAT THE-- UNGH!

WHOOSH

CAN I OPEN MY EYES N-- HUH?

ONE PUNCH AND I DECK THE *METRO PIRATES*?

YOU GUYS AIN'T SO *TOUGH*, AFTER ALL...

...MAYBE I'LL START TAKING THIS SHORT-CUT *EVERY* NIGHT.

PENCILLER: CRAIG ROUSSEAU

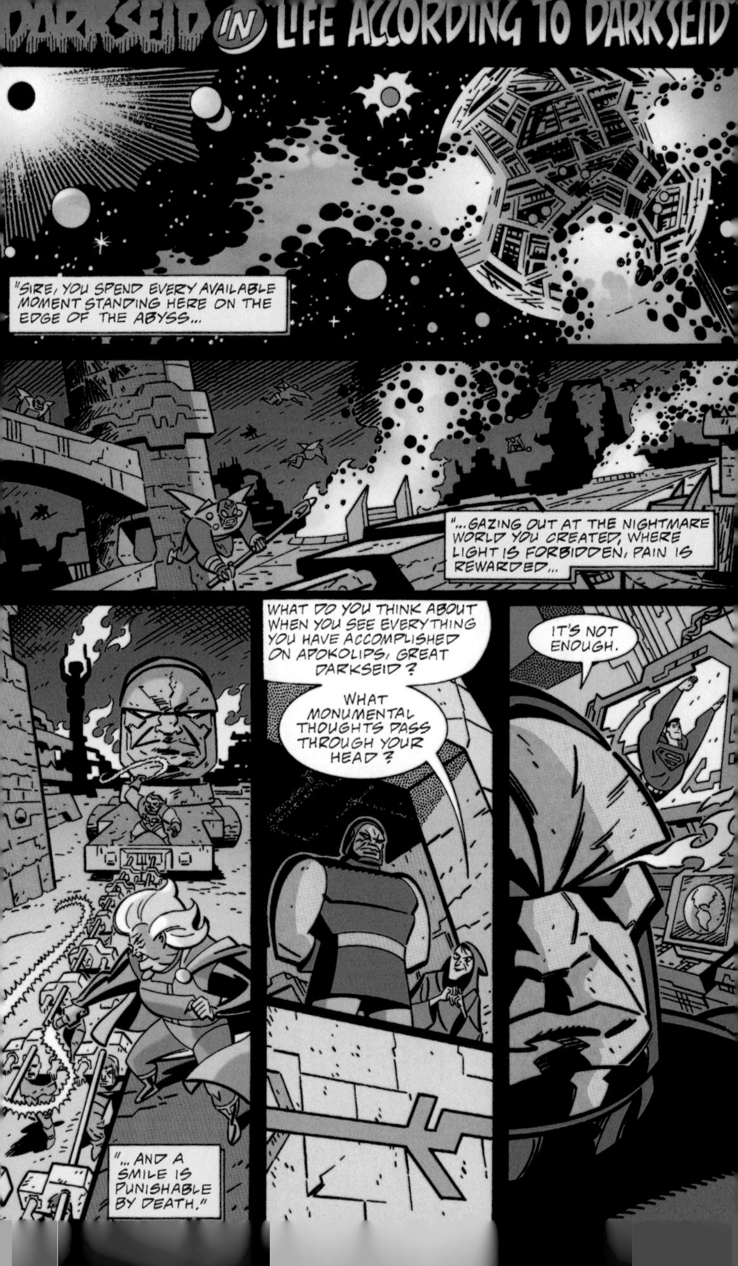
DARKSEID IN LIFE ACCORDING TO DARKSEID
"SIRE, YOU SPEND EVERY AVAILABLE MOMENT STANDING HERE ON THE EDGE OF THE ABYSS...
"...GAZING OUT AT THE NIGHTMARE WORLD YOU CREATED, WHERE LIGHT IS FORBIDDEN, PAIN IS REWARDED...
"...AND A SMILE IS PUNISHABLE BY DEATH."
WHAT DO YOU THINK ABOUT WHEN YOU SEE EVERYTHING YOU HAVE ACCOMPLISHED ON APOKOLIPS, GREAT DARKSEID?
WHAT MONUMENTAL THOUGHTS PASS THROUGH YOUR HEAD?
IT'S NOT ENOUGH.

# "SUPERGIRL'S SECRET EMERGENCY WEAPON"

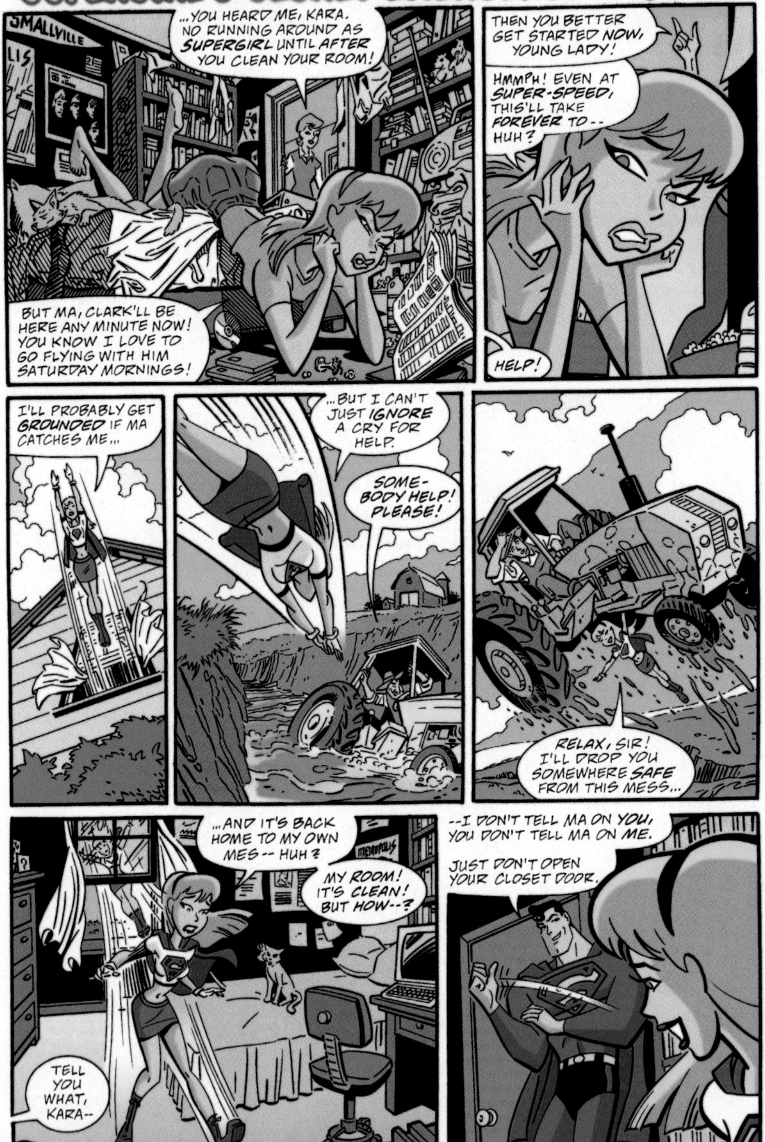
SMALLVILLE
...YOU HEARD ME, KARA. NO RUNNING AROUND AS SUPERGIRL UNTIL AFTER YOU CLEAN YOUR ROOM!
BUT MA, CLARK'LL BE HERE ANY MINUTE NOW! YOU KNOW I LOVE TO GO FLYING WITH HIM SATURDAY MORNINGS!
THEN YOU BETTER GET STARTED NOW, YOUNG LADY!
HMMPH! EVEN AT SUPER-SPEED, THIS'LL TAKE FOREVER TO-- HUH?
HELP!
I'LL PROBABLY GET GROUNDED IF MA CATCHES ME...
...BUT I CAN'T JUST IGNORE A CRY FOR HELP.
SOME-BODY HELP! PLEASE!
RELAX, SIR! I'LL DROP YOU SOMEWHERE SAFE FROM THIS MESS...
...AND IT'S BACK HOME TO MY OWN MES-- HUH?
METROPOLIS
MY ROOM! IT'S CLEAN! BUT HOW--?
TELL YOU WHAT, KARA--
--I DON'T TELL MA ON YOU, YOU DON'T TELL MA ON ME.
JUST DON'T OPEN YOUR CLOSET DOOR.

PENCILLER: BRET BLEVINS

# PROFESSOR HAMILTON IN "WEIRD SCIENCE"

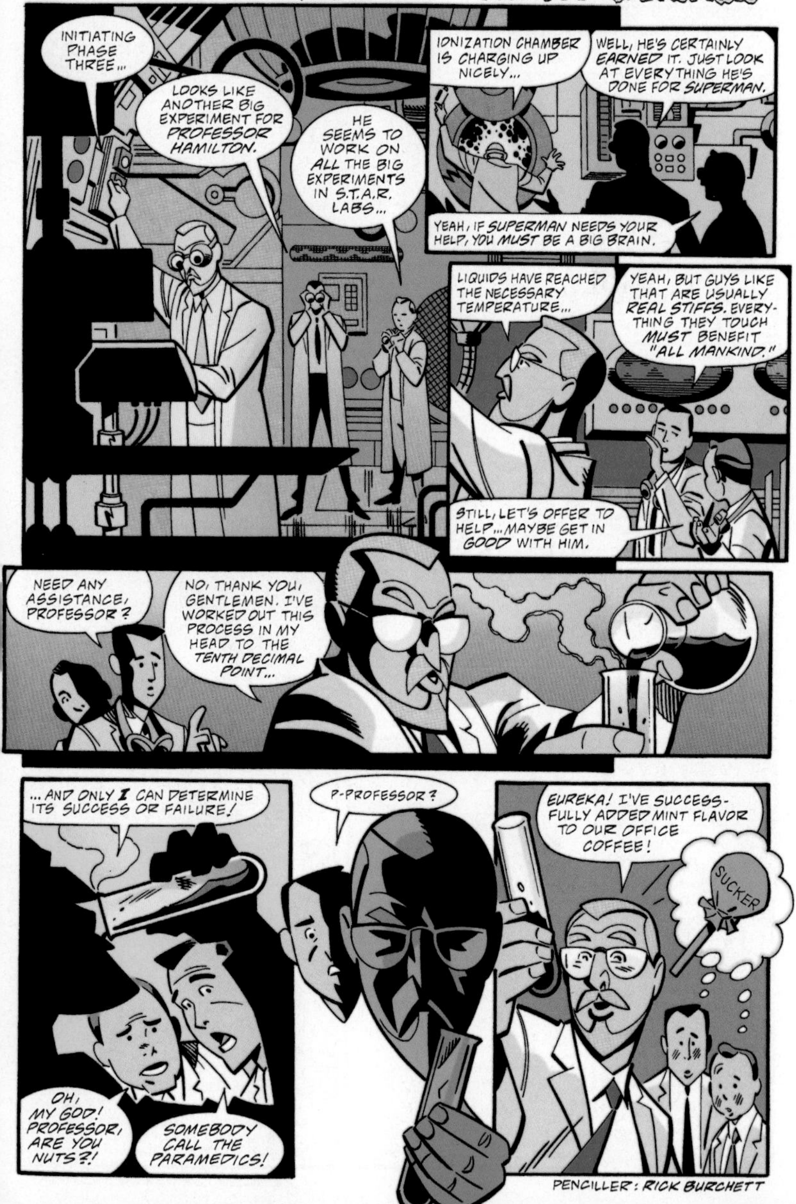
INITIATING PHASE THREE...
LOOKS LIKE ANOTHER BIG EXPERIMENT FOR PROFESSOR HAMILTON.
HE SEEMS TO WORK ON ALL THE BIG EXPERIMENTS IN S.T.A.R. LABS...
IONIZATION CHAMBER IS CHARGING UP NICELY...
WELL, HE'S CERTAINLY EARNED IT. JUST LOOK AT EVERYTHING HE'S DONE FOR SUPERMAN.
YEAH, IF SUPERMAN NEEDS YOUR HELP, YOU MUST BE A BIG BRAIN.
LIQUIDS HAVE REACHED THE NECESSARY TEMPERATURE...
YEAH, BUT GUYS LIKE THAT ARE USUALLY REAL STIFFS. EVERYTHING THEY TOUCH MUST BENEFIT "ALL MANKIND."
STILL, LET'S OFFER TO HELP... MAYBE GET IN GOOD WITH HIM.
NEED ANY ASSISTANCE, PROFESSOR?
NO, THANK YOU, GENTLEMEN. I'VE WORKED OUT THIS PROCESS IN MY HEAD TO THE TENTH DECIMAL POINT...
... AND ONLY I CAN DETERMINE ITS SUCCESS OR FAILURE!
OH, MY GOD! PROFESSOR, ARE YOU NUTS?!
SOMEBODY CALL THE PARAMEDICS!
P-PROFESSOR?
EUREKA! I'VE SUCCESSFULLY ADDED MINT FLAVOR TO OUR OFFICE COFFEE!
SUCKER

PENCILLER: RICK BURCHETT

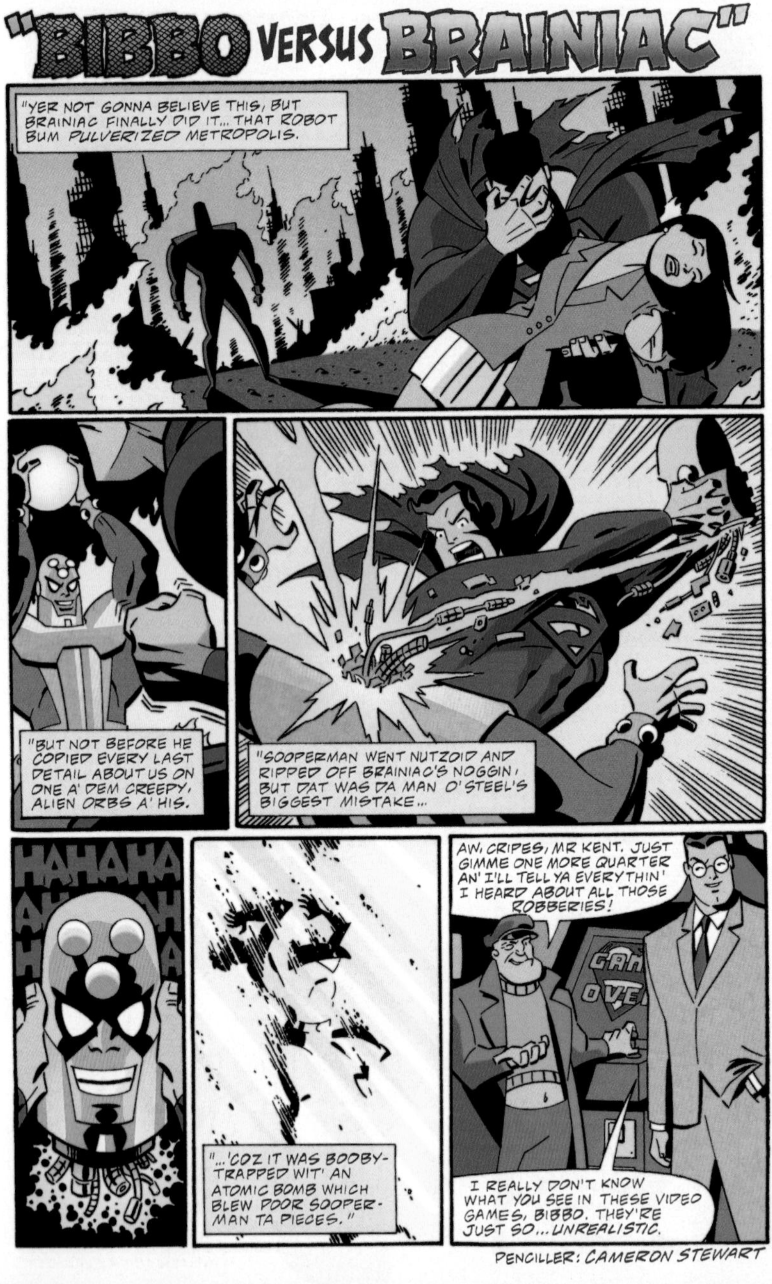
"BIBBO VERSUS BRAINIAC"
"YER NOT GONNA BELIEVE THIS, BUT BRAINIAC FINALLY DID IT... THAT ROBOT BUM PULVERIZED METROPOLIS.
"BUT NOT BEFORE HE COPIED EVERY LAST DETAIL ABOUT US ON ONE A' DEM CREEPY, ALIEN ORBS A' HIS.
"SOOPERMAN WENT NUTZOID AND RIPPED OFF BRAINIAC'S NOGGIN, BUT DAT WAS DA MAN O'STEEL'S BIGGEST MISTAKE...
HAHAHA
"...'COZ IT WAS BOOBY-TRAPPED WIT' AN ATOMIC BOMB WHICH BLEW POOR SOOPER-MAN TA PIECES."
AW, CRIPES, MR KENT. JUST GIMME ONE MORE QUARTER AN' I'LL TELL YA EVERYTHIN' I HEARD ABOUT ALL THOSE ROBBERIES!
I REALLY DON'T KNOW WHAT YOU SEE IN THESE VIDEO GAMES, BIBBO. THEY'RE JUST SO... UNREALISTIC.
PENCILLER: CAMERON STEWART

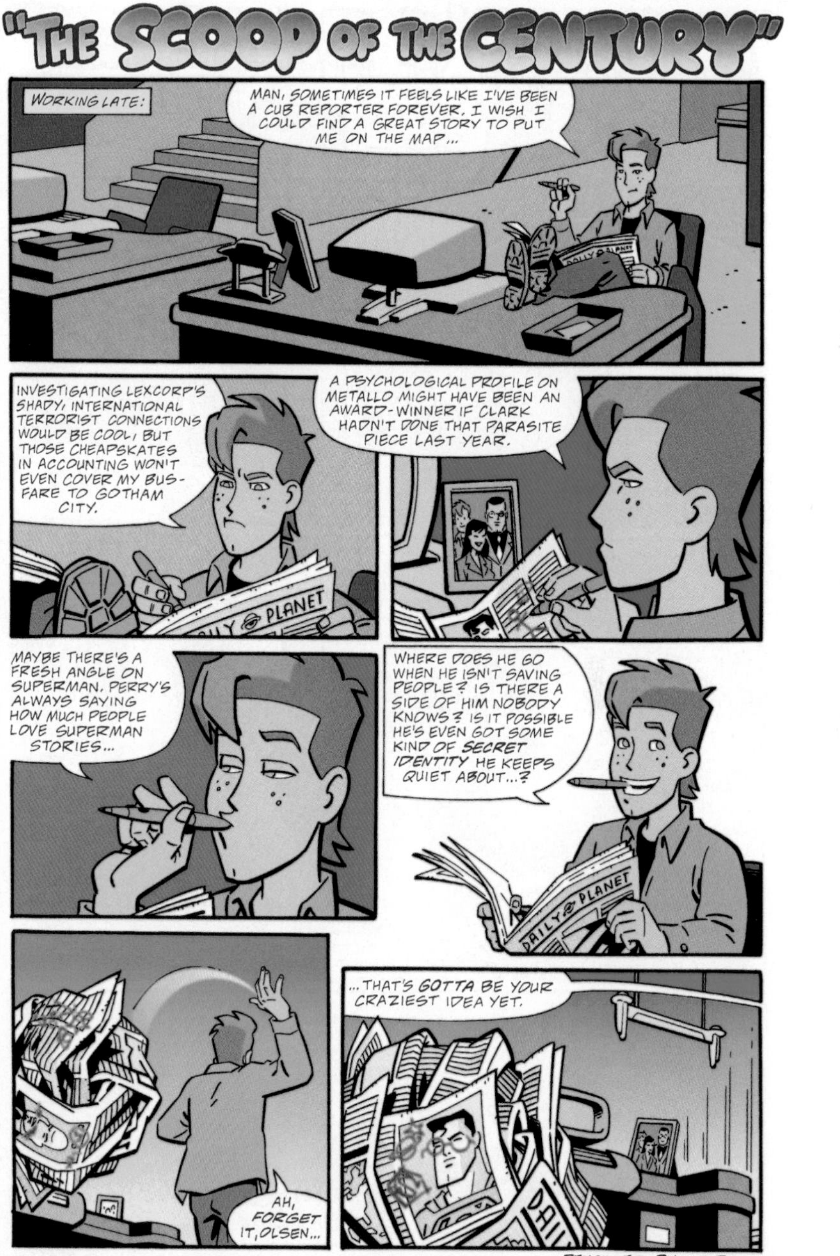

"THE SCOOP OF THE CENTURY"
WORKING LATE:
MAN, SOMETIMES IT FEELS LIKE I'VE BEEN A CUB REPORTER FOREVER. I WISH I COULD FIND A GREAT STORY TO PUT ME ON THE MAP...
DAILY PLANET
INVESTIGATING LEXCORP'S SHADY, INTERNATIONAL TERRORIST CONNECTIONS WOULD BE COOL, BUT THOSE CHEAPSKATES IN ACCOUNTING WON'T EVEN COVER MY BUS-FARE TO GOTHAM CITY.
DAILY PLANET
A PSYCHOLOGICAL PROFILE ON METALLO MIGHT HAVE BEEN AN AWARD-WINNER IF CLARK HADN'T DONE THAT PARASITE PIECE LAST YEAR.
MAYBE THERE'S A FRESH ANGLE ON SUPERMAN. PERRY'S ALWAYS SAYING HOW MUCH PEOPLE LOVE SUPERMAN STORIES...
WHERE DOES HE GO WHEN HE ISN'T SAVING PEOPLE? IS THERE A SIDE OF HIM NOBODY KNOWS? IS IT POSSIBLE HE'S EVEN GOT SOME KIND OF SECRET IDENTITY HE KEEPS QUIET ABOUT...?
DAILY PLANET
AH, FORGET IT, OLSEN...
...THAT'S GOTTA BE YOUR CRAZIEST IDEA YET.


PENCILLER: PHILIP BOND

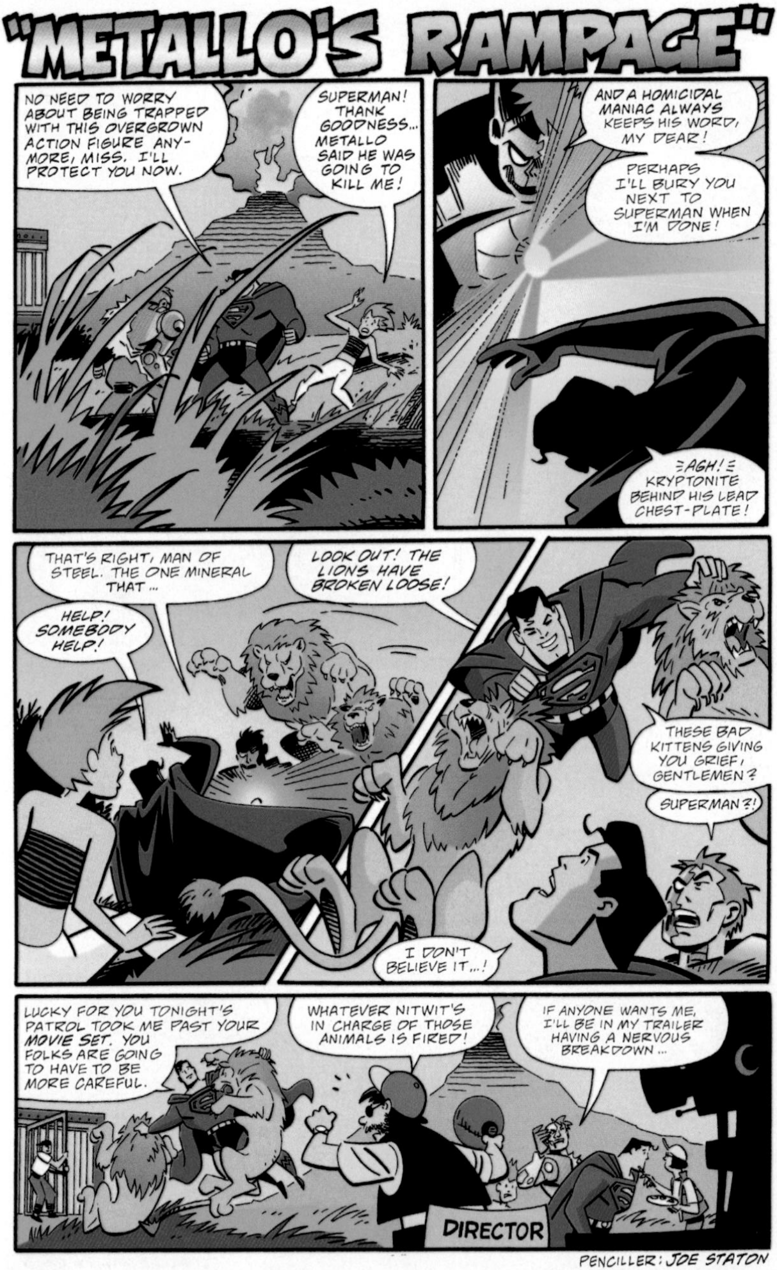

"METALLO'S RAMPAGE"
NO NEED TO WORRY ABOUT BEING TRAPPED WITH THIS OVERGROWN ACTION FIGURE ANY-MORE, MISS. I'LL PROTECT YOU NOW.
SUPERMAN! THANK GOODNESS... METALLO SAID HE WAS GOING TO KILL ME!
AND A HOMICIDAL MANIAC ALWAYS KEEPS HIS WORD, MY DEAR!
PERHAPS I'LL BURY YOU NEXT TO SUPERMAN WHEN I'M DONE!
AGH! KRYPTONITE BEHIND HIS LEAD CHEST-PLATE!
THAT'S RIGHT, MAN OF STEEL. THE ONE MINERAL THAT ...
LOOK OUT! THE LIONS HAVE BROKEN LOOSE!
HELP! SOMEBODY HELP!
THESE BAD KITTENS GIVING YOU GRIEF, GENTLEMEN?
SUPERMAN?!
I DON'T BELIEVE IT...!
LUCKY FOR YOU TONIGHT'S PATROL TOOK ME PAST YOUR MOVIE SET. YOU FOLKS ARE GOING TO HAVE TO BE MORE CAREFUL.
WHATEVER NITWIT'S IN CHARGE OF THOSE ANIMALS IS FIRED!
IF ANYONE WANTS ME, I'LL BE IN MY TRAILER HAVING A NERVOUS BREAKDOWN ...
DIRECTOR


PENCILLER: JOE STATON

# "HERO OF BIZARRO WORLD!"

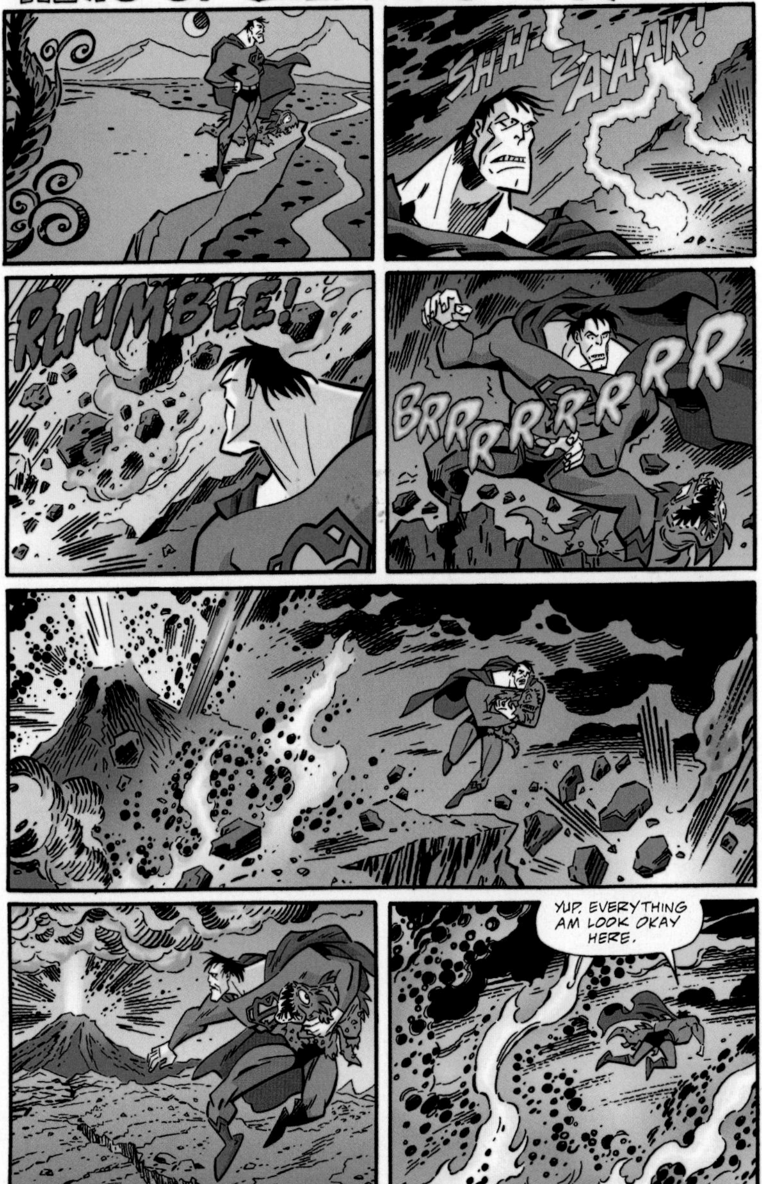
SHH-ZAAAK!
RUUMBLE!
BRRRRRRRRRR
YUP, EVERYTHING AM LOOK OKAY HERE.

PENCILLER: ALUIR AMANCIO

# "WHILE YOU WERE SLEEPING"

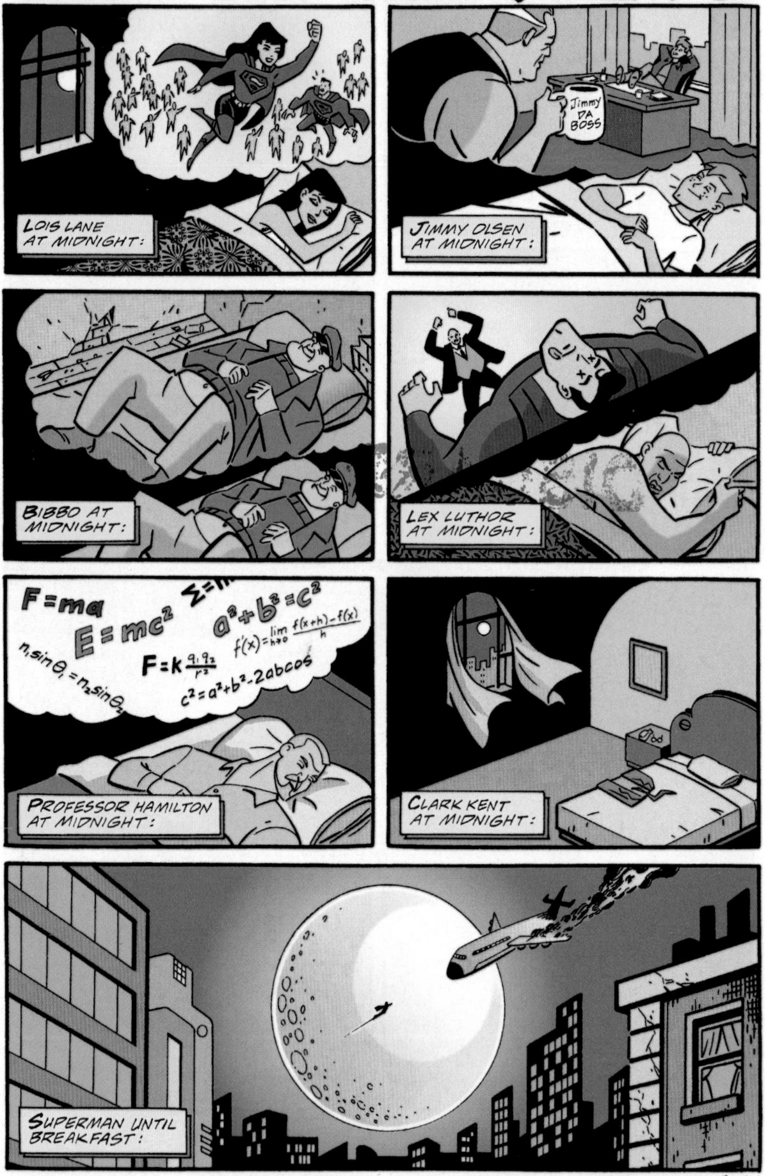
LOIS LANE AT MIDNIGHT:
Jimmy DA BOSS
JIMMY OLSEN AT MIDNIGHT:
BIBBO AT MIDNIGHT:
LEX LUTHOR AT MIDNIGHT:
F=ma
E=mc²
a²+b²=c²
f'(x)=lim h→0 (f(x+h)-f(x))/h
F=k q₁q₂/r²
n₁sinθ₁=n₂sinθ₂
c²=a²+b²-2abcos
PROFESSOR HAMILTON AT MIDNIGHT:
CLARK KENT AT MIDNIGHT:
SUPERMAN UNTIL BREAKFAST:

PENCILLER: MIN S. KU